CHALLENGING UNEVEN DEVELOPMENT

CHALLENGING UNEVEN DEVELOPMENT
An Urban Agenda for the 1990s

edited by Philip W. Nyden
and Wim Wiewel

RUTGERS UNIVERSITY PRESS

New Brunswick, New Jersey

We would like to acknowledge the grants provided by the John D. and Catherine T. MacArthur Foundation and the Joyce Foundation in supporting the project that led to this book.

Library of Congress Cataloging-in-Publication Data

Challenging uneven development: an Urban agenda for the 1990s / edited by
    Philip W. Nyden and Wim Wiewel.
        p.   cm.
    Includes bibliographical references and index.
    ISBN 0-8135-1658-7 (Cloth) — ISBN 0-8135-1659-5 (pbk.)
    1. City planning—United States—Citizen participation.
2. Community development, Urban—United States.   3. Gentrification—
United States.   4. Housing policy—United States.   I. Nyden,
Philip W.   II. Wiewel, Wim.
HT167.U68   1991
307.1'176'0973—dc20   90-45221
                                                                          CIP

British Cataloging-in-Publication information available

CONTENTS

LIST OF TABLES

FOREWORD

The 1980s were grim for cities and city neighborhoods, and the 1990s began the same way. No strong national political leadership had been dealing with problems of urban decay since the 1960s. By the end of the 1960s the war on poverty, the civil rights movement, and urban riots had convinced experts that massive efforts were needed both to upgrade lower-income urban communities and to break down the racial barriers limiting education, housing, and job opportunities. The election of Richard Nixon in 1968, however, brought an end to the expansion of federal intervention. The trends were toward block grants first and then reductions. Subsidized housing commitments were suspended in 1973. The recessions of the 1970s and early 1980s sped the deterioration of central city neighborhoods and the flight of urban employers.

By the 1980s, the problems were much worse than those that had seemed so threatening in the 1960s. But no one seemed to care. The dominant political movement of the 1980s was toward less government and more control by private markets. Urban programs were sharply reduced, particularly in housing and job training, and government actively opposed enforcement of civil rights laws, including those providing affirmative action, school desegregation, and support for integrated neighborhoods. Negative economic trends, negative government, and private markets that continued to move resources and jobs out of central cities combined to create a massive challenge to urban advocacy. The cities, their neighborhoods, and their impoverished minorities were on their own, seeking survival strategies. Many researchers followed the new political agenda; as funding for work on urban policy and poverty dried up, they shifted to studying public-private partnerships, Catholic schools, privatization, drugs, or one of the other topics on the conservative agenda.

Neither national party paid serious attention to the urban crisis in the 1980s. Both were competing for the increasingly dominant suburban vote and both were committed to low taxation and fought only at the margins of each year's budget. There were no major new urban policy proposals; there were large cuts in constant value dollars in existing ones;

and there was very little discussion of any sort about the deepening racial cleavages or the problems of the surging Hispanic communities.

In a period devoid of national leadership, it is extremely important to learn from those who are struggling to help urban neighborhoods and understand urban trends under such circumstances. The urban agenda for the next political cycle will be deeply affected by their experiences.

Chicago is a very good place to examine. It is a vast city with particularly acute social and economic challenges, and it has an unusual concentration of neighborhood activists and urban researchers. Contained in the metropolitan area's more than 1,400 census tracts are some of the nation's poorest and some of its richest. Chicago is the home of the tough-minded school of community organizing developed by Saul Alinsky, the place where urban sociology was born, and the base of the vibrant black political movement that elected a black mayor, Harold Washington, with strong support from community organizations. Chicago is a city with an intense sense of localism, and a city where many important national trends are born.

The 1980s saw a massive boom in Chicago's Loop and the continuing deterioration of many of the city's neighborhoods. Probably no city in the world has so intensively documented a history of its neighborhoods in the twentieth century. The best Chicago leaders and researchers have persisted in their work through all the reversals of the Reagan years and have much to contribute to the development of a contemporary agenda for research and action.

Local insights and research are especially important now because the federal government's role as a source of reliable basic information and research funding was abandoned in the 1980s. HUD studies and even publications of basic statistics were radically curtailed; the annual *HUD Statistical Yearbook* ceased publication after 1980. The government did not collect basic data about tenancy of subsidized housing. The mass media, in general, followed political trends. They dealt much less with urban problems and more with items of interest to upscale suburban readers. They raised few troubling questions about the social and economic despair new suburbanites had left behind. As attention turns back to solving urban problems, we need practical judgments about what is possible now.

The bankruptcy of the conservative model should by now be apparent. Business deregulation brought about the biggest scandal in American financial history—the massive collapse of the savings and loan industry, which had been the backbone of home finance. The dismantling of housing and urban programs at HUD, combined with cynical political manipulation of the small amount of remaining funds for partisan purposes, often provided millions for unjustified and unviable projects recommended by powerful Republicans. The sweeping promises of enterprise zones and industrial development policies produced tax losses and few gains for the many state and local governments who tried them. The market did very little for low-income renters. The number of families trying to carry impossible burdens of rent—two-thirds or more of income for families below the poverty line—soared in the 1980s. As the housing crisis deepened, the trickle-down, "filtering" model of market-oriented economists made little sense. In fact, in gentrifying neighborhoods, housing was moving in exactly the opposite direction, passing from poor and middle-income families to those with high incomes.

The articles herein do not provide all the answers. In fact, many of them arise from a philosophy that is against any simple set of across-the-board answers and insists on input from the grass roots. These articles do, however, suggest the range of issues, the variety of tools available, and the multiple levels of necessary government, community, and private involvement. One of the basic themes—natural after a decade of conservative policy—is the need for mobilization of research and organization to prevent additional damage to threatened urban communities. There is interesting discussion of tactics ranging from intervention in urban land-use practices to organized community and governmental efforts to avoid the disastrous consequences of traditional ghetto expansion by maintaining stable integration. We see exploration of the effects of taxes, development strategies, housing subsidies, zoning, lending policies and practices, and many other forces. Clear evidence in several papers shows that effective communication is beginning to take place between the worlds of research and of community organization. Activists cite research, and researchers search for ways to confront the problems most immediately threatening communities. The interactions between both groups in the Chicago project and in an earlier collaboration on issues of housing discrimination have helped clarify the issues.

Neighborhoods and investigators are most aroused when a clear, dramatic set of changes and overt conflict or crisis occur. The articles in this book tend to focus on the forces related to and the policies for correcting several basic problems—the displacement of families and workplaces from gentrifying neighborhoods, the lack of resources in the declining inner-city communities, and the possibility of preventing a destructive form of ghetto expansion. These papers are useful correctives to the analyses written from aggregate economic data or from the perspective of citywide economic development without serious treatment either of costs to communities or of the possibility that communities can have a positive, powerful role. That is not to say that studies of policies at higher levels of government are not also vitally important.

The articles show that, even when one starts at the community level, it very soon becomes necessary to discuss city, state, and national policy. Community groups fighting disinvestment are critically dependent on data collected by federal agencies under federal law and on regulations allowing them to challenge lenders who want to merge or expand. Better housing policies require federal subsidies; advocates are seeking new state programs and faster release of tax default land from the county; and many groups want new city building codes permitting less expensive maintenance and rehab. Given the complexity and fragmentation of the governmental structure and the need to leverage many forms of private action, a successful neighborhood-based strategy requires layers of research and action.

Anyone who thought that urban policy in the 1990s was simple or that there was one basic solution may well be discouraged by the complexity described here. Anyone, on the other hand, who has been observing the decay and the incoherence of national policy toward cities and their neighborhoods since 1980 would have to be reassured by the intelligent and thoughtful steps toward a new, well-grounded urban agenda represented in these pages. This book, and the project that produced it, shows that in Chicago, and in other cities, there are groups of community leaders and researchers ready to roll up their sleeves and try to clear away the debris of the past decade and develop urban policies that respect the people of urban communities and seek practical answers to fundamental problems. I hope that triggers similar efforts in other cities and helps to reawaken the interests of university researchers.

Gary Orfield
June 1990

Gary Orfield is Professor in the Departments of Political Science and Education, and the College at the University of Chicago. He has published extensively in the areas of school integration and fair housing. In 1985–86 he coordinated a collaborative researcher-practitioner project on "Fair Housing in Metropolitan Chicago: Perspectives after Two Decades" for the Chicago Area Fair Housing Alliance. This research effort, involving seven research projects directly responding to needs of community-based fair housing planners, was used as a model for the process that produced the chapters in this volume.

CHALLENGING UNEVEN DEVELOPMENT

1 INTRODUCTION
Wim Wiewel and Philip W. Nyden

The process of transition from a working-class, manufacturing city to one oriented to white-collar service jobs is not smooth and even. It is full of conflicts over the direction and pace of change. This process of economic restructuring, and its attendant change in urban and neighborhood structure, is occurring in many cities in the world. In each locale it is influenced by different institutions, faced with their city's own unique economic, physical, and social structures. The opportunities that this era of change presents depend on the interaction among local circumstances and institutions and the larger social, economic, and political environments within which we function.

For growth-oriented politicians and urban planners, gentrification, neighborhood revitalization, the new service economy, and white-collar job growth have been the optimistic catchwords of this process of change. Construction of downtown office buildings, the opening of new retail stores, the return of middle-class residents to "hot" neighborhoods undergoing extensive housing rehabilitation, and the conversion of industrial property to new uses are seen as signs of a city's rebirth. However, clearly not all sectors of the urban community are benefiting from this rebirth. Although there is reinvestment in many neighborhoods, one of its side effects has been displacement of residents of communities now invaded by young professionals. While we are seeing a shift to service jobs in cities, the blue-collar workers and communities surrounding the factories that were bustling a decade ago are often in worse shape than ever.

Measuring the quality of life in American cities solely by the amount of new construction, the number of new middle-class residents, or the growth of service jobs ignores the negative consequences of urban restructuring. Implicit in this pro-growth ideology is an acceptance of uneven development—an acceptance that there will be winners and losers, that some people will benefit while others will not. This volume is a challenge to this pro-growth notion—not at a theoretical level, but a challenge at a very practical and programmatic level. Chapters in this volume represent progressive blueprints for policy research and action with a particular focus on two areas: (1) gentrification and displacement in city neighborhoods, and (2) economic restructuring—the decline of the manufacturing sector and the growth of the service economy.

The Growth Machine

Instead of viewing the social and physical structure of the city as a product of "natural" ecological forces, an increasing number of urban scholars and planners have argued that the city has been shaped by a collection of interest groups or a "growth coalition" that views the city as a place that can be used to enhance their personal or institutional well-being. This growth coalition or "growth machine" is a loose network of financial, commercial, and real estate interests that has been the main proponent of real estate development and downtown growth. To them, the city is a growth machine that, if properly manipulated, can improve individual and institutional wealth. In their recent book, *Urban Fortunes,* John Logan and Harvey Molotch state that

> With rare exceptions . . . , one issue consistently generates consensus among local elite groups and separates them from people who use the city principally as a place to live and work: the issue of growth. For those who count, the city is a growth machine, one that can increase aggregate rents and trap related wealth for those in the right position to benefit. The desire for growth creates consensus among a wide range of elite groups, no matter how split they might be on other issues. [Logan and Molotch 1987:50–51]

The "consensus" takes many forms. One of its important elements is an emphasis on a "good business climate" as essential for city survival. The costs of labor and the influence of labor unions are questioned, but the maximization of return on investment and the prerogatives of investors are not questioned. The yardstick used to judge urban reform and urban development is the extent to which the proposed change will improve the business climate—the extent to which the policy will oil the growth machine. From this perspective, schools are defined as in crisis not because they are failing to give inner-city youth the skills needed for self-development, or even advancement in today's society, but because they are failing to give future workers the skills needed by service sector employers. Property taxation policies are not evaluated on the basis of how well they redistribute resources within the metropolitan area but by whether they encourage new housing development and service sector growth. The effectiveness of laws and policies regulating the real estate market is measured by the profitability of the market, not by the extent to which affordable housing is made available or neighborhood racial and ethnic diversity is encouraged.

The growth ideology that dominates most American cities has produced an environment where policies that promote growth (and profit opportunities) have been seen as good. Those who have accepted this mind set criticize as obstructionist or backward any policy proposals that promote more even development, any civic organizations that question unfettered growth, or any community organizations that try to moderate the negative effects of redevelopment. Ironically, critics of the growth ideology are painted as self-serving leaders just trying to protect their political base. In many media accounts, these community activists are seen as the villains, while the thoroughly self-interested character of the growth coalition is ignored (or even celebrated under the banner of "progress") (McCarron 1988).

This book represents an effort to make a case for the alternative side of the urban policy debate and to make it more visible. It is an alternative view consistent with what Pierre Clavel describes as progressive politics. In his study of the new policies adopted in Hartford, Cleveland, Berkeley, Santa Monica, and Burlington during the 1970s and 1980s, Clavel writes that

> The main features of progressive politics as practices in these cities included attacks on the legitimacy of absentee-owned and concentrated private power on the one hand, and on nonrepresentative city councils and city bureaucracies on the other. These attacks led to programs emphasizing public planning as an alternative to private power, and to grass-roots citizen participation as an alternative to council-dominated representation. In most respects, these new programs produced a flood of institutional inventions. [Clavel 1986:1]

The "inventions" can include proposals for more affordable housing (e.g., limited equity cooperative), linked development (the taxing of downtown development to fund development in other neighborhoods),

3

more direct community voice in planning and zoning decisions, and city control of utilities.

This volume contains pieces of an urban policy that include some of these "institutional inventions." This agenda is oriented to those who, unlike the actors in the growth coalition, do not define the city merely as a place to manipulate for personal profit. Rather, it is oriented to people who define the city as a place to *live* and *work*, the people who have the largest stake in improving the quality of life. These people are not merely treating the city as an urban, high-rise stock exchange in which to invest their money with the expectation of generous returns. Instead, these people are putting their families and careers on the line; these people are investing in the viability of their communities.

In fact, these are people who often do not think in the traditional terms of business "investment." A major investment to this larger population is buying a home. Among such homeowners there is usually a deeper, longer-term interest in the community than there is among real estate developers seeking to maximize profits. To still another sector of the urban population, investment is an unfamiliar or hostile term. To many lower-income families and individuals, the present city landscape provides few opportunities or choices; to them survival is a central issue. To them investment is something that takes place in *other* neighborhoods. When it does happen in their neighborhood, it can translate into displacements. This book does not accept the traditional definitions of positive investment or the current arrangements as the best available to us. This book is an agenda for change. It is an agenda for survival and for new choices.

Chicago and Alternative Models of Urban Development

Chicago has always received a disproportionate amount of attention from writers and researchers. From the poetry of Carl Sandberg and the writing of Richard Wright to the novels of Saul Bellow and the oral histories of Studs Terkel, Chicago has been in the literary spotlight. Within the social sciences, the Chicago school of sociology represents a strong tradition of community studies that started in the 1920s and continues today. Chicago has been seen as tough, hardworking city—the "hog butcher of the world" or the "steel capital of America." Less flattering have been descriptions of Chicago as the most segregated city in the nation. Equally sobering is the statistic that ten of the sixteen poorest neighborhoods in the United States are in Chicago (Ziemba 1984). Whatever positive image there was of the city's educational system evaporated a few years ago when U.S. Secretary of Education William Bennett branded Chicago as having the worst public school system in the country. The city and state have since embarked on one of the boldest, most radical school reform programs undertaken in any American city. From the days of the Richard J. Daley machine to the days of Harold Washington's reforms, and now in the days of Mayor Richard M. Daley (the late mayor's son), Chicago has received its share of attention.

More important to the context of this book, in Chicago, the struggle between the growth machine and the neighborhood movement has an unusually long and visible history. Compared to most cities, Chicago has a very rich tradition of strong, community-based organizations. The settlement houses that Jane Addams built in Chicago not only highlighted the social ills of American cities in the late 1800s and early 1900s but also presented a way of dealing with these problems. Decades later, the battles between Saul Alinsky's Industrial Areas Foundation and interests threatening the community—whether they were city hall or large corporations—became legendary in American community politics.

The continued strength of community leaders in Chicago is borne out by the fact that community organizations played an important role in the rise of Harold Washington to formidable political strength. Harold Washington was probably the most progressive of big-city mayors elected in the 1980s. It was no coincidence that such a political leader emerged in Chicago rather than in some other city. Many community leaders had a friend in City Hall. That friend was unusually sensitive to the needs of a broad range of Chicago neighborhoods. Although it did play ball with the powerful growth coalition, the Washington administration also underwrote urban policy plans that represented alternatives to the growth ideology. The voices of progressive urban policy could be heard in the mayor's own cabinet. In some parts of Chicago's city government, the progressive planning process described above by Pierre Clavel did emerge. Because this reform initiative took place in one of the nation's largest cities, a number of researchers have stressed the importance of studying the case of Chicago (e.g., Clavel and Wiewel 1991; Giloth and Betancur 1988; Squires et al. 1987). With Mayor Washington's sudden death came the collapse of the delicate political alliance he had built—but not the end of its constituent elements. Regardless of the twists and turns of Chicago politics or the outcome of future elections, Chicago will continue to be strongly affected by community-based organizations, as this book indicates. It contains urban policy discussions of what may be described as the shadow government in Chicago—the

Linked Development Commission to develop a program that used sur-
charges on major downtown real estate development to finance neighborhood economies. Although the commission's majority report
recommended a system of per-square-foot fees to be used for construction of low-income housing, developers on the commission issued a minority report strongly opposing any mandatory program. The developers
also orchestrated a massive campaign that buried the idea before it was
even introduced in City Council.

However, in a struggle over a plan to retain manufacturing, the pro-
growth coalition that favored a strong move toward service sector employment was not so successful. The issue of retaining industrial jobs was
first raised by the Local Employment and Economic Development Council (LEED Council), a community-oriented, economic development
group on Chicago's Near Northwest side. Manufacturing companies in
this area were increasingly displaced by conversion of factory space to
office, retail, and residential uses. Through a lengthy educational and
lobbying campaign, the LEED Council, assisted by others, was able to
make this a citywide issue and gain passage of a Planned Manufacturing
District ordinance. The most outspoken opposition came from the *Chicago Tribune*, which, in editorial after editorial, berated neighborhood
organizations and the city's Department of Economic Development. The
newspaper's view was that opposition to market forces would ultimately
spell economic doom for the city. Ironically, research on the loss of manufacturing firms had shown that it was not exclusively market forces that
were contributing to the switch from industry to service sector firms.
Active government intervention, in the form of Urban Development Action Grants (strategically granted or denied) and selective building in-
spections, were contributing to the industrial displacement process
(Giloth and Betancur 1988).

All of these issues, from the world's fair and *Make No Little Plans* to
linked development and planned manufacturing districts, increasingly
showed the close interrelationship between changes in the overall urban
economy and the economic and social character of particular neighborhoods. As manufacturing jobs declined, stable blue-collar and minority
neighborhoods experienced economic decline. Residents who were now
unemployed or in lower-paying jobs could no longer maintain their
houses as well, no longer support the neighborhood commercial strip,
and no longer pay rents needed to maintain apartment buildings. Indeed,
the per capita income (adjusted for inflation) in Chicago declined by 6.6
percent from 1979 to 1985, compared to national growth of 3.7 percent
(Wiewel 1990). On the other hand, those who held the well-paying jobs
in the growing service industries bid up the price of housing in the most

desirable areas. As happened elsewhere, the city landscape was increasingly a picture of diverging groups (Harrison and Bluestone 1988).

During the 1980s, broad outlines of this process became clearer to many in the city. However, many specific issues remained obscure. Policy responses were only tentative or, as in the case of the planned manufacturing districts, won only at a tremendous cost in time and energy. The hopes that the newly emerged alliance of progressive community and economic development interests could pressure the city into dealing with these development issues were dashed when Harold Washington died suddenly on November 25, 1987. Little new policy development occurred during the interim mayoralty of Eugene Sawyer, as everyone waited for the elections in early 1989. In this void, the pro-growth coalition redoubled its efforts to fend off the community-based critics. For example, in mid 1988, a *Chicago Tribune* series entitled "Chicago on Hold" attempted to paint the proponents of balanced development either as self-serving community leaders seeking to preserve a dwindling constituency or, at best, as wild-eyed idealists who had no sense of how the economy works (McCarron 1988). The series seemed to be aimed at influencing the agenda for the special 1989 mayoral election. This included discrediting those who had provided many of the ideas for Washington's neighborhood and economic development policies, as well as driving a wedge between the various components of Washington's coalition: community organizations, leaders of grass-roots movements in the African-American community, African-American political leaders, and the progressive white community.

The Research and Action Project

The project that produced the chapters in this book was initiated by the John D. and Catherine T. MacArthur Foundation along with the Joyce Foundation. The foundations were particularly concerned with recent criticisms of the economic development strategies based on balanced growth—strategies used by many of the progressive community-based organizations that they have funded in recent years. The foundations felt that there was a need to look systematically at a number of issues raised in the course of the pro-growth versus balanced growth debate. The foundations were not interested in just more research on various topics but in research that was anchored in the real concerns of community organizations—organizations that are on the front lines every day. On the other hand, there was a realization that the broad view of urban policymakers and academic-based researchers could provide a systematic understanding of specific policy issues.

It was on this basis that we developed a collaborative process involving community leaders and predominantly academic-based researchers. From the beginning, the Project for Chicago Research and Action in the 1990s sought to involve representatives from community-based organizations, civic organizations, government agencies, labor unions, and academic institutions. With the incentive that results of the project would be used in guiding foundation funding decisions in certain areas, we achieved participation at all levels.[1]

The project aim was to identify the urban issues of greatest concern among the groups listed above. Once they were identified, the project would commission briefing papers that would present the state of the art and discuss what was known about the issues—both general knowledge and specific models for social change. This same process would identify gaps in this knowledge and pinpoint areas where no workable models for social change exist.

Areas of Focus

From the beginning the project focused on two broad areas: (1) gentrification and displacement and (2) economic restructuring. We were not looking at these areas through the rosy glasses of a pro-growth ideology—a view that sees only neighborhood revitalization and new white-collar jobs. We were interested in the costs of these changes (both economic and social) and more balanced, even-growth solutions. Each area was described in terms of the questions that needed answering.

We recognized that gentrification often had been viewed only in unquestioning and positive terms. Gentrification has usually been associated with good outcomes, for example, economic development, neighborhood improvement, a better quality of life, improved housing, more opportunities for employment, stabilization of the tax base, rejuvenation of neighborhoods, and revitalization of the city. These phrases do capture one part of the gentrification equation. However, improvement for one family may not be an improvement for another, particularly if it means being forced to move out of a neighborhood and not being invited to share in the benefits of community revitalization. We directed attention to the effect that redevelopment and gentrification has had on those who benefit from the process *as well as* the effect they have had on those who have not benefited and who have been displaced by them. What are the consequences for racial segregation in the city and suburbs? For the availability of low- and moderate-priced housing? Who benefits from the redevelopment and gentrification, and who bears their social and economic costs? What are the prospects for a more even development process in the city and in the metropolitan area, that is, how can all neighborhoods and communities share in the prosperity that has been concentrated in a limited number of communities? What are the prospects for intervention in neighborhoods undergoing reinvestment to assure continued socioeconomic diversity? Since economic development is often a metropolitan area-wide process, what is the relationship between economic development in the city and growth that occurs in the suburbs? What role do and can the suburbs play in facilitating a more even economic development?

The focus on economic restructuring took in the complex changes that many urban areas are facing as the economy (particularly in employment opportunities) shifts away from manufacturing and becomes much more of a service-industry economy. As one of the nation's major manufacturing centers, Chicago has had a particularly wrenching experience as manufacturing employment has declined and service employment has grown.

We asked a number of questions about the nature of economic changes and the influence that they will have on the economy. Is the shift from manufacturing mostly one of relative employment, or does it reflect a real decline in manufacturing production? How much of it is due to a statistical reclassification of workers when a "manufacturing" company eliminates part of its operations and contracts with "service" companies to provide the same services, that is, when the same job once done by a manufacturing sector worker is now done by a service sector worker? What is the linkage between manufacturing and service growth? Has service sector growth (in jobs and revenue) compensated for the loss in manufacturing firms and jobs? How important is it to retain manufacturing activities; and, if it is important, how can this best be done? Will the growth of service employment continue, or is it a temporary phenomenon? How accurate are the stereotypes of the full-time, secure, well-paid manufacturing job versus the low-paid, part-time, insecure service job? What kind of education, training, and retraining is needed to prepare for labor force needs of the future? What are the distributional implications in regard to race, ethnicity, gender, and geographic area? Are there ways in which the gains of some areas or groups can be captured and redistributed to others? What can be done about any of it by local governments, community organizations, educational institutions, unions, civic groups, or business organizations?

Organization of This Book

We do not pretend to answer all of these questions in this book. Moreover, part of the purpose of the chapters included here is to tell us what is known and what needs to be known before adequate answers or solutions can be found. However, by the time the reader finishes this book, he or she will have a sharper understanding of even-growth strategies. The dimensions of a balanced growth agenda should come into clearer focus.

In the second chapter, Mel King, a longtime community activist in Boston, discusses the ideology of community redevelopment. He demonstrates how pervasive and persuasive the growth ideology really is. The growth machine defines the language of the urban development debate. Communities come to be defined as "bad" communities or slums by real estate interests—interests that are constructing a political justification for "developing" the community and making a profit. King warns that urban development and social policy debates are not just made of bricks and mortar and loan packages. They are related to how self-conscious a community is about its strength and how able it is to muster the resources to protect its interests. The following chapter, by Teresa Cordova, more specifically addresses how communities can mobilize resources and play a more active role in the reinvestment process. Cordova provides a road map to the strategies available to communities in gaining control over their future development.

At first glance, the need for preserving racial diversity may seem to be unrelated to the investment and development issues raised in the other chapters. However, as demonstrated in the fourth chapter, housing integration (or lack of it) is intimately linked to community reinvestment issues. Gentrification and displacement most often mean that black residents are being replaced by predominantly white homeowners and renters. The exodus of middle-class homeowners from the city and the erosion of the middle-income tax base is often described as white flight from the city to the suburbs. As Lauber argues, until the issue of racial diversity is dealt with directly, until political and racial divisiveness of blockbusting, racial steering, and racial exclusion is eliminated, communities will be unstable. Stronger, more explicit policies to maintain racial diversity will not only provide more housing options to a broader segment of society but will also eliminate a primary element of destabilization in urban communities.

Historically related to integration is the role of lenders in shaping the urban landscape. The denial of mortgage loans or insurance to homeowners in certain communities—redlining—has been the source of grassroots battles against a key sector in the urban growth coalition—banks and insurance companies. The national anti-redlining campaign of the late 1970s and early 1980s, which resulted in federal legislation, was heavily influenced by Gale Cincotta and the Chicago-based National Training and Information Center. The Woodstock Institute has carried on the tradition of gathering and analyzing information as a means of giving communities control over local investment. Chapter four points out that the changing structure of the residential credit industry—particularly the more prominent role played by mortgage bankers—is providing a new challenge to urban communities wishing to attract investment in housing. The abandonment of communities by the banking community often sets off the downward economic spiral that ultimately makes the community ripe for gentrification and redevelopment. Although this may sound like a neat and clean economic process, it encourages disinvestment in housing and commercial property, displacement of one population (ostensibly through "voluntary" flight from the area), deterioration of once-useful buildings, and, when reinvestment takes place, displacement of yet another population. Although mortgage bankers cannot be blamed for this upheaval, this chapter further underlines the fact that it is the lack of government regulation and the lack of community input into economic decision making that has produced instability in urban communities.

Chapter six represents one of the more detailed urban policy analyses in the book. Tax issues vary from city to city, but as Arthur Lyons shows, taxes shape markets for private homes, rental property, commercial buildings, and industrial sites. For example, he points out that the lower tax rate for condominiums compared to rental properties can result in a rapid rate of condominium conversions—and a displacement of renters —in certain communities. Property tax remains the mainstay of local government finances; thus, it is the keystone of urban policy. In the absence of a correct understanding of how a tax system really works, we run a very high risk of implementing "solutions" that make matters worse because the information on which they are based is wrong.

Clavel, Pierre. 1986. *The Progressive City: Planning and Participation. 1969–1984.* New Brunswick, N.J.: Rutgers University Press.

Clavel, Pierre, and Wim Wiewel, eds. 1991. *Harold Washington and the Neighborhoods: Progressive City Government in Chicago.* New Brunswick, N.J.: Rutgers University Press.

Commercial Club of Chicago. 1984. *Make No Little Plans: Jobs for Metropolitan Chicago.* Chicago: Commercial Club.

Giloth, Robert, and John Betancur. 1988. "Where Downtown Meets Neighborhood: Industrial Displacement in Chicago, 1978–1987." *Journal of the American Planning Association* 54: 279–290.

Harrison, Bennett, and Barry Bluestone. 1988. *The Great U-Turn: Corporate Restructuring and the Polarizing of America.* New York: Basic Books.

Logan, John R., and Harvey L. Molotch. 1987. *Urban Fortunes: The Political Economy of Place.* Berkeley and Los Angeles: University of California Press.

McCarron, John. 1988. "Chicago on Hold." Series of seven articles in the *Chicago Tribune.* 28 August–4 September.

McClory, Robert. 1986. *The Fall of the Fair: Communities Struggle for Fairness.* Chicago: Chicago 1992 Committee.

Molotch, Harvey. 1976. "The City as a Growth Machine: Toward a Political Economy of Place." *American Journal of Sociology* 82 (September): 309–332.

Squires, Gregory, Larry Bennett, Kathleen McCourt, and Philip Nyden. 1987. *Chicago: Race, Class, and the Response to Urban Decline.* Philadelphia: Temple University Press.

Wiewel, Wim. 1990. "Industries, Jobs, and Economic Development Policies in Metropolitan Chicago: An Overview of the Decade." In *Creating Jobs, Creating Workers,* edited by Lawrence B. Joseph. Chicago: Center for Urban Research and Policy Studies, University of Chicago.

Ziemba, Stanley, 1984. "10 of Poorest U.S. Areas in CHA: Study." *Chicago Tribune,* May 23.

Wim Wiewel is director of the Center for Urban Economic Development at the University of Illinois at Chicago. The Center has been closely involved with many city-wide and community-based organizations in economic development, employment development, and urban policy research. Wiewel is co-author of a forthcoming book, *Harold Washington and the Neighborhoods: Progressive City Government in Chicago* (Rutgers University Press).

Phil Nyden is a professor of sociology and chair of the Sociology and Anthropology Department at Loyola University of Chicago. In the past few years he has completed a number of policy reports examining racial diversity in city and suburban communities. Nyden is co-author of *Chicago: Race, Class, and the Response to Urban Decline* (Temple University Press, 1987).

2 A FRAMEWORK FOR ACTION
Mel King

Activists in cities throughout the country learn from each other.[1] If we are able to change and shape the nature of the debate about economic development strategies in Chicago, we will benefit in Boston. People everywhere in the country will benefit. The issues that are addressed here are very, very real, and very much a part of what we deal with in Boston. The issues are what they deal with in Washington, in Detroit, in Los Angeles, and in other cities. There is a challenge in front of us—it is a challenge that economic development strategies be debated both on the terms that leaders understand and on the terms that will make a difference in the lives of the people for whom they serve as advocates. We must become *part* of the economic development process, not mere spectators of it.

Winning Over Minds

I would like to challenge people to think differently about strategies of shaping the future of cities. We are faced with a struggle for land and a struggle for the mind. This is the core of urban community organizing today, and I think it is crucial. It is my contention that, if we win the struggle for the mind, then we will win the struggle for the land. So, we have to think first about where the struggles for the mind exist. Obviously, we have to deal with the issues of race and gender. These are what I call the fallout from the structural issues in this country. This has its basis in our original constitution—a document in which women did not count, in which people of color were three-fifths of a person, and in

17

So, *without a developer's even having put a spade in the ground*, the value of the land went up, and the people who lived in this community found that they were being moved out. Now you talk about gentrification as being part of the problem leading to displacement. We found that the *process* is minimal in comparison to the kinds of actions and activities that come just with the mere *statement* there is going to be development of a major portion of a particular area.

Organizing Community Institutions

Fortunately, some of the folks in these targeted communities have risen up, got organized, and are attempting to change the negative images imposed on their neighborhood by outsiders. They are also working to maintain control over the land. They do have some resources available to them. In addition, they are seeking support from institutions that are no longer actively supportive of the community today but were institutions important to community vitality in the past. They are asking, what about the church? What about the unions? What about the Democratic party? When I look at the city of Boston and at its struggling communities and see little or no involvement by churches, no connection to unions, and no relationship to a strong Democratic party, I ask, "Where are the new institutional relationships where we can learn from each other and help each other? Where can power be organized and harnessed in a way that people can benefit?"

In Boston some traditional institutions have become increasingly aware of the importance of linking themselves to community issues. For example, Local 26 of the Hotel and Restaurant Workers Union have realized that their struggles are community struggles. So when they sit at the bargaining table, they invite people from the community. We sit right behind the union negotiators and face the owners on the other side. There now is awareness on the part of the hotel executives and restaurateurs that they negotiating with a *community*. Large numbers of members of the Hotel and Restaurant Workers Union are women and people of color. They are people who are in some of the lowest-paid jobs. The union has recognized that they have to go beyond the workers themselves and organize the community. The community has recognized that hotel and restaurant workers—union members—are a resource. They bring their wages back to the community. They provide a stable underpinning.

We are talking about people who live right in Roxbury, Jamaica Plains, or the South End.

It is important for the community and union to link together in protecting their common interests. This year in negotiations the union pushed for a housing allowance. They wanted some money—an employer contribution of 1 percent of all wages put aside for building or rehabbing housing. A lot of people come to participate in the negotiations because there are lots of people in that community who needed the housing. This community-union alliance has become an institution. As the union challenges the hotel owners, it is one thing; but as the community-union alliance organizes and helps people to see institutional connections and relationships there, there's power building in that community. They are defining their community as one which *deserves* more resources. But this feeling that they deserve resources comes only as they exercise power.

This reminds me of a statement by Martin Luther King, Jr., in *Where Do We Go From Here: Chaos or Community*. King talks about a people mired in oppression. They realize deliverance only when they accumulate the power to enforce change. We need to talk about *our* programs. Martin Luther King said that "the call to meet [other people's] programs distracts us excessively from our basic and primary task." If we are seeking a home, there's not much value in discussing blueprints if we have no money and are barred from acquiring the land. We are being counseled to put the cart before the horse. We have to put the horse *power* before the cart *program*.

Our task is to discover how to organize our strength into compelling power so that government cannot elude our demands. We must develop constraints in situations in which the government finds it wise and prudent to collaborate with us. It would be the height of ridiculousness to wait passively until the administration had somehow been infused with such blessings of goodwill that it sought us out and supported our program. Community power building is grounded in material realism, not in fantasy.

Programs such as linked development may be more fantasy than reality. In Boston, this program taxes developers of downtown office buildings and uses the money for building affordable housing units throughout the city. Boston has amassed $45 million from this fund. However, that gives you one development; one set of units; maybe 200 to 300 units of housing. Moreover, almost half of this money goes to construction workers who do not necessarily live in the communities we have been discussing.

More appropriate is the approach that we took in the Boston Jobs program. Fifty percent of the jobs went to Bostonians and 25 percent to people of color. This is supposed to apply to existing linked development programs, but it is not. Linked development is good if it gives money to people living in Boston's communities—money that can be used to purchase homes and bolster the vitality of existing neighborhoods.

If this is not done, then linked development is an inappropriate model. It is not an effective redistributive model. We cannot have a policy where the construction of affordable housing depends on whether or not somebody is putting up some buildings downtown. It's like playing the lottery. We cannot have government by chance. We have to have a more direct housing policy that will provide the resource base that people require. How do we bring about these policy changes? I am not sure we can do it without a clearer sense of the politics of social transformation. I keep going back to Vincent Harding's book, *There Is a River*, where he says the we do not want equal opportunity in a *dehumanized* society. We need more than equal opportunity, we need a society responsive to human needs. Without this goal, our work will just represent tinkering within a dehumanized city.

Human Development

Let me move on to another issue. We have been talking about development principally in brick and mortar terms; we need to think about *human* development. As I look at community leaders, the question for us is "are we here because we are more developed as persons than those people who are not here?" I would suspect that there is one characteristic that we share. We have all *personally* experienced human development; but there is a need to facilitate the human development of the people and communities we are supposed to represent. We need to abandon terminologies that refer to these people as "the underclass." If we do not do this, we will just become part of the system that maintains the status quo. We need to see the real potential of our constituencies. We need to see that there is potential for everyday residents to be planners, economic developers, and researchers in the same way that we see ourselves.

We should try to think of a process which will be very inclusive of the people about whom we are talking. They need to be involved in framing the issues and concerns as well as in brainstorming on the ideas for solutions. It is important to remember that we can facilitate development of human resources, but we cannot "develop them." They can only develop themselves. No one "developed" the leadership. Given the opportunity, we developed ourselves. In the process of doing research, we should consider the issue of human development.

We, of course, also need more information about communities. We need to understand "the state of the communities" for all communities. We need a community scoreboard. We need to use existing information, such as census data, and involve community residents in analyzing that information so that they better understand their community. Part of the information that is needed is where their money goes. What decisions are made about where their money goes? Who is making those decisions? Whom is it helping? Whom isn't it helping? This information is the basis for action.

Conclusion

I have talked about the difference between doing research *on* economic development or gentrification versus research that facilitates the *development of human resources* in our communities. If we had been doing more thinking about the second issue—human development—over the past years, we would not be here today! What we all have been working on is redistribution and not transformation. Let us talk about the impediments to meeting individual needs in our communities. Let us talk about how we can collectively mobilize the resources and develop the thinking to overcome those impediments.

We need to empower ourselves as thinkers before we try to empower ourselves as doers. This is an idea that was developed by a trainer at Digital corporation, a Boston-area company. We need to apply this same principle to community activities. We need to become change managers and not just reactors and responders. We need to come to work with less competition and more cooperation—with more negotiation and less confrontations. We need to use new technologies and group processes in this transformation. We need *well-connected* road maps of where we are going, not bits and pieces of solutions, not scraps of theory, not discontinuous plans. The transformation I have been talking about will require a paradigm shift for all concerned. It must be participatory and not administrative. It must be creative leadership and creative followership, as we find that we need different skills, to solve the problems facing us. It requires a philosophy of making the world understandable to all members of the community—a philosophy that clears away the fog of complexity with the clear air of honest simplicity.

NOTE

1. This chapter is based on a speech given before the Project for Chicago Research and Action in the 1990s.

Currently a faculty member in the Department of Urban Studies and Planning at the Massachusetts Institute of Technology, **Mel King** combines a background in community organizing activities, electoral politics, and academic research. He served as the executive director of the Urban League of Boston, spent more than a decade as a representative in the Massachusetts legislature, ran for mayor of Boston, and has been a visible force in the black community of Boston for over thirty years. His recent book, *Chain of Change: Struggles for Black Community Development* (South End Press), shows how black consciousness and power have developed through the struggles around jobs, housing, education, and politics.

8 COMMUNITY INTERVENTION EFFORTS TO OPPOSE GENTRIFICATION
Teresa Cordova

Central cities in the post–World War II era experienced a decline characterized by residential and industrial suburbanization and decentralization
of economic activities. Major urban areas lost population and retail sales
and declined in average household income and tax base (Fainstain et al.
1983).

The preservation of the central business district, however, was critical
to large corporate interests that needed to protect real estate and fixed
capital investments. Further erosion of municipal functions threatened
symbolic dominance through cultural institutions and imperiled the political base of working-class ethnics (Castells 1976).

Coalitions of businessmen and city officials responded almost immediately to urban decline by promoting growth ideology and the redevelopment of downtown areas. The federal urban renewal and
redevelopment programs made this resurgence possible. Improved infrastructure, transportation systems, convention centers, hospitals, and uni-
versities were among the many projects that rejuvenated the municipal
budget.

However, widespread land clearance and displacement of low- and
moderate-income families characterized this redevelopment. Urban
renewal agencies labeled long-standing and stable communities as
"blighted areas" deserving eradication.

Spatial reformation occurred concurrently with an occupational restructuring. By the 1970s the downtown and surrounding area were no

longer the site for extensive manufacturing jobs and blue-collar workers. Rather, a service economy was drawing more white-collar workers into the downtown area to work in finance, communications, insurance, real estate, and associated professions, such as accounting and law. This change in occupational structure gave further impetus to the change in physical structure.

The redeveloped downtown economy necessitated additional office space, much of which was placed in buildings previously used for factories and in neighborhoods heretofore deemed undesirable. Furthermore, the economic and occupational shifts resulted in the rise of housing developments within walking distance of downtown areas. Soon, neighborhoods surrounding the downtown area were targets for residential development for the young urban professional.

This residential development has taken place in inner-city neighborhoods suffering from disinvestment and abandonment. More stable neighborhoods with working-class and moderate-income residents have also been sites for projects that create new housing and renovate old "historic" housing. In the process, however, the move of upper-middle-class professionals into neighborhoods close to their downtown jobs has meant increases in the value of property and the subsequent squeezing out of low- and moderate-income, usually minority, families. This silent, creeping replacement of low- and working-class households by a professional class has become known as gentrification. It has precipitated a new set of academic, policy, and organizing issues.

While academics debated the existence and extent of displacement caused by gentrification, community organizers were establishing a structure and mechanisms to slow this displacement. As the academic literature considered cause and conditions of gentrification, organizing efforts were growing to influence policy and to form community development corporations for neighborhood revitalization and ownership.

Collaboration between academics and practitioners would increase the effectiveness of each. It would enhance intervention to minimize disruption of communities and maximize neighborhood vitality. An examination of community intervention efforts is especially important in light of the paucity of academic literature that addresses the subject and the newspaper images that misconstrue their intents and actions.

This chapter is intended to contribute to the study of gentrification through examining efforts to fight gentrification by community organizations. This chapter represents a preliminary identification of intervention, an assessment of its effectiveness, and a call for further research with policy recommendations.

The necessary information was obtained primarily by direct interviews of community-based practitioners and citywide community development agencies. It was supplemented by studies, reports, and relevant newspaper articles.

Gentrification

Gentrification is inextricably linked to the economic and employment restructuring of the inner city. The systematic replacement of inner-city residents immediately followed urban renewal programs but did not fully emerge as an identifiable process until the mid-1970s. Initially, gentrification was concentrated in a few neighborhoods. Thus many early researchers and policymakers felt that it was not a large-scale problem and therefore not of serious concern. Minimalists argued that census tract information showed that there was not a significant move of white professionals into inner-city neighborhoods (Berry 1985; Nelson 1984). In fact, urban areas were continuing to lose population. A "back to the city" movement did not exist, they said, though movement within the city may have been evident. Thus, some observers saw gentrification as a geographically limited process with little effect on the city (Lipton 1977; Gale 1976, 1977; Berry 1985). However, other researchers found that, by 1976, more than half of U.S. cities of over 50,000 population showed signs of inner-city housing rehabilitation (Urban Land Institute 1976).

THE DEBATE OVER CAUSES

The debate over the causes of gentrification centers around shifts in the urban structure (production) versus shifts in the value preferences of the baby boom generation (consumption). Those emphasizing the demand side of gentrification (Bourne 1977; Clay 1979) cite the demographic characteristics of the young urban professionals who are affluent, highly educated, and have few or no children (Gale 1980; 1985–1986). They are referred to as "trendsetters" (Allen 1984) who value pluralism, community, ethnic diversity, proximity to the workplace, and urban living.

Marxist explanations focus on the political economy of urban growth. They see the process of gentrification as the outcome of a new stage of capital accumulation that is made possible by a "devalorization cycle" that leads to a "rent gap" and thus sets the stage for gentrification (Smith

27

1979; Smith and LeFaivre 1984). This cycle consists of first use, transfer to landlord control, blockbusting, and then redlining. Every neighborhood that experiences gentrification may not go through the entire cycle. For example, a working-class neighborhood may not have experienced blockbusting but may still have been redlined to prevent repairs. Thus, this devalorization process suggests that neighborhoods are "prepared" for gentrification by a "process that is rational by the standards of the capitalist free market" (Smith and LeFaivre 1980:50). A rent gap is the difference between actual capitalized ground rent and the potential rent under a "higher and better" use of the land. Yet another perspective identifies gentrification as the creation of real estate agents, property developers, and banks who control the "who" and "where" of urban property shifts (Hamnett 1976, 1980; Pitt 1977; Power 1973; Williams 1976). This view is not entirely inconsistent with that of Smith and LeFaivre, that the primary actors in gentrification are institutional actors, such as the state, financial institutions, and developers.

Despite ideological cleavages and methodological constraints, it seems most appropriate to view the causes and conditions of gentrification from the political economy perspective, with institutions as key agents of change and yuppies as key consumers. Though consensus may be obtained on these aspects of gentrification, it is probably more difficult to close the political/ideological gap in interpreting the implications of gentrification.

The Consequences of Gentrification

Researchers and policy analysts have hailed gentrification as the new hope for revitalizing central cities and their surrounding neighborhoods (U.S. Department of Housing and Urban Development 1979). The problem is limited, displacement is low, and there are positive benefits, but this does not mean that antidisplacement policy is not warranted. Opponents argue that such reports dramatically and systematically underestimate the negative effects of gentrification (Hartman, Keating, and LeGates 1982; LeGates and Hartman 1981; Schaffer and Smith 1986).

Each position has implications for action. If one believes that gentrification is a panacea for inner-city neighborhoods, then one argues for policies and programs that encourage it, calling it reinvestment, revitalization, or rehabilitation. If, on the other hand, one believes that the uneven consequences of gentrification are unduly negative for low and moderate, usually minority, households and communities, then one would argue that policies and programs should be pursued to curtail gentrification. Neighborhood revitalization should be pursued in the in-

terests of the current residents, although admittedly, defining them becomes difficult in a neighborhood that is already undergoing change, where "current residents" may include new urban professionals that older residents consider intruders. Nonetheless, revitalization insensitive to the potential effect on low- and moderate-income residents runs the risk of revitalizing these residents right out of the neighborhood. The quaint character of the multicultural, multi-income neighborhood that attracts the urban pioneer becomes a victim.

THE LIMITS OF THE LITERATURE

Debates about gentrification, thus, are not purely academic. They are, however, incomplete. While researchers debate the causes and significance of gentrification, the process of urban replacement continues. This mandates a research agenda tied to an in-depth analysis on behalf of those whose communities are unfortunate enough to be in the path of progress.

Thus far, the literature has failed (explicitly and specifically) to identify gentrification in a way that suggests the point at which policy moves are critical in shaping the outcome. More important, analysts have not fully identified and assessed intervention efforts that would maximize community well-being. This paper is an effort to contribute to the study of how gentrification might be controlled in a way that nurtures low- and moderate-income households and the communities that they have built. The starting point for such an analysis is the compilation of strategies currently used—information best obtained from the practitioners themselves.

Community Intervention Efforts

The creeping character of reinvestment displacement is unlike the bulldozers of urban renewal, but the displacement is no less real. Early resistance from community-based organizations includes rallies, boycotts, and lobbying the public sector (Levy 1980). The community organization learns how to present itself, how to be informed on the issues, how to keep the cries of displacement from becoming advertisements for real estate, how to separate organizing slogans from reality, and how to set realistic goals (Levy 1980). Above all, the community organizer attempting to fight gentrification-caused displacement learns that "either you rehabilitate your neighborhood, or someone else will" (Levy 1980:313).

By the late 1970s, community organizations, such as the Queens Village Neighborhood Association in Philadelphia and the Philadelphia Council of Neighborhood Organizations, the Adams Morgan Organization in Washington, D.C., and others in Baltimore and San Francisco had begun to be proactive in defending their neighborhoods.

Rent control, tenants' rights, and technical assistance were some of the strategies. Philip Clay (1979) showed that some of these early efforts were successful in minimizing displacement. In 105 cities where reinvestment was occurring, he classified fifty-seven as gentrifying neighborhoods and forty-eight as "self-help improvement" areas. In forty-five of the fifty-seven gentrifying neighborhoods, he found displacement, whereas he found displacement in only eighteen of the forty-eight self-help neighborhoods. In the late 1970s, HUD was a vital source of funding to the community-based organization attempting to control the future of its neighborhood. Two notable examples of HUD-funded projects were *Gentrification and the Law: Combatting Urban Displacement* (Bryant and McGee, no date) and HUD Innovative Grants for Anti-Displacement (Little, no date).

GENTRIFICATION AND THE LAW

In March 1979, the Los Angeles County Bar Association and its Lawyers for Housing Project (LFH) received a HUD grant to identify legal issues arising from gentrification and to suggest ways to stop its negative effects. The study analyzed gentrification in Los Angeles by examining three distinct neighborhoods, including Venice (near the beach), North University Park (near the University of Southern California and downtown), and Pasadena (a suburban area).

The Lawyers for Housing Project learned about the beginnings of gentrification through their study of Venice. They noted that the increased cost of housing, rising taxes, city, and HUD funding for rehab projects, code enforcement, and city sale of vacant lots to the highest bidder all spurred gentrification.

In the North Park district, the researchers observed potential gentrification through land speculation, preparation for the Olympics, the designation of Historic District, the role of the University, and the increase in the number of urban pioneers. The case of Pasadena was noteworthy for the role that the government played in the displacement process. As a HUD report to Congress declared in February 1979, "Displacement is inextricably tied, both directly and symbolically, to the relationship between government and neighborhoods. The government role (Federal, State, and local) may be direct—through rehabilitation or housing construction—or indirect—through general neighborhood improvements, tax incentives and major infrastructure additions like subway systems." (Bryant and McGee, n.d.:2–12)

On the basis of their study of gentrification in three areas of Los Angeles and their review of legal issues, the Lawyers for Housing describe five areas for potential influence through legal mechanisms: economic and fiscal policy, direct regulation of housing costs, regulations of land use, regulation of the physical condition of housing, and the involvement of the federal government.

Economic and fiscal policy approaches involve taxation and anti-redlining practices. "Upgrading" of a neighborhood is generally followed by raises in property taxes that often mean the displacement of lower-income residents (Bryant and McGee, n.d.:4–1). The extent to which a municipality depends on property taxes for basic services will affect the extent to which a local government will promote the increase of taxes and thus, the negative effect of revitalization. Therefore, the Lawyers for Housing suggest state measures to provide tax relief for lower-income households. They suggest "circuit breakers" to ensure that elderly and lower-income homeowners benefit from state relief from rising property taxes. Income tax credit, cash rebate, or tax offset are some of the kinds of circuit breakers.

Lending practices of banks have for years resulted in what is commonly known as redlining. It has led to disinvestment and its accompanying problems in many inner-city neighborhoods. The Community Reinvestment Act seeks to reverse these trends. However, the LFH warns that several safeguards are necessary so that low-income residents are the beneficiaries—not the young urbanite seeking a good deal in an up-and-coming neighborhood. They suggest, for example, that coordination among the various institutions would help. This might include low down payment requirements on conventional mortgages, FHA/VA insured mortgages, combined loan packages, loans for cooperative ventures, counseling for low- and moderate-income tenants becoming homeowners, refinancing multifamily units to decrease rents, and counseling on rent subsidies.

The rapidly increasing costs of property in the Los Angeles area between 1974 and 1979 suggested a market that was "highly speculative." Under such conditions, the LFH suggests rent stabilization to impede gentrification.

Although there are variations in the provisions of rent control, the most effective are those that ensure a tenant-sustained occupancy without the threat of displacement or rent increases beyond the costs of operating the property. Indeed, the report concludes that "rent control is essential to an anti-gentrification strategy. Without rent control tenants can be priced out of their neighborhoods" (Bryant and McGee, n.d.:6–13). They warn against exemptions, incentives, and the uncontrolled conversion of rental property to condominiums and the consequent effect on the supply of rental housing.

Strategies to restrict conversions, they add, should be accompanied by strategies to increase the supply of rental housing. They suggest ways to increase the availability of multifamily housing. These include more HUD funds for multifamily units targeted to low-vacancy areas, the use of Community Development Block Grant (CDBG) funds for write-downs, local zoning changes, expediting permits for multifamily housing, and a six-month limit on HUD processing.

Rapid speculation and property exchange encourage gentrification. Several places such as Washington, D.C., Davis, California, and Vermont, have passed antispeculation legislation. It redirects profits to serve local needs, such as low-income housing. Legal analysts from the Los Angeles Bar Association suggest that antispeculation should seek to establish "purchaser residency requirements" to slow the turnover of single-family housing and should impose taxes on profit related to the length of ownership so as not to penalize the long-term owner. At the time of this report, the legal authority for such legislation was clear, although the outcome was not.

The lawyers also suggested strategies that involve the municipality's power to affect its built environment. These measures include zoning controls, subdivision restrictions, and inclusionary zoning that elicit benefits from the developer, including a minimum number of low-income units. Other land-use controls include the Transferable Development Rights (TDR), which enable the local planning authority to designate zones and specify the kind of development that may take place.

Housing code enforcement is intended to make housing habitable, but too strict enforcement may, for example, lead to abandonment. It is important, therefore, to balance code enforcement with the housing needs of a community and implement a "dislocation sensitive judicial resolution mechanism" (Bryant and McGee, n.d.:11–13).

Efforts to regulate the physical condition of housing have inspired the movement for historic preservation. However, the renovation and restoration of "landmarks" have been accompanied by the displacement of low- and moderate-income families. One black resident of the Five Points

Area of Denver targeted for historic designation asked, "Whose history is being preserved and at whose expense?" Historic preservation should be accompanied, for example, by housing subsidies such as Section 8, and by a process that fully incorporates community participation.

Finally, an analysis of the legal strategies to deal with gentrification must also review action at the federal level, in particular the role of HUD, which has been criticized for either encouraging or neglecting the effects of displacement. The National Housing Law Project (1978) strongly states that policies by HUD, such as the Community Development Block Grants (CDBG) and Urban Development Action Grants (UDAG), exacerbate the crisis.

HUD INNOVATIVE GRANTS PROGRAM TO STEM DISPLACEMENT

HUD responded to criticisms of the late 1970s and claimed that all its funded projects would be reviewed for potential displacement effect. The federal agency also funded several innovative projects designed to prevent displacement triggered by condominium conversion, gentrification, downtown redevelopment, and speculation. For instance, Baltimore created the Housing Assistance Corporation (HAC), using nearly $1 million of HUD funds. The nonprofit, city-controlled agency had the power to buy, sell, finance, and develop real estate. It emphasized increased low-income housing to combat the negative influence of reinvestment. Its connection to the city made information accessible and allowed for a flexibility that gave it a better chance of competing with private developers. The ability to act quickly, that is, without bureaucratic or financial constraints, enhanced effective action.

On the other hand, the rising cost and scarcity of permanent financing made providing low-cost housing difficult. The many "unanticipated changes in the financing market have been HAC's major problem and have had a significant effect on HAC's operations" (Little, Inc.:12). The cost of financing increased dramatically from the start of the program, making it difficult to implement ideas for recycling funds, developing more rehabilitation projects, and supplying permanent financing.

In Brookline, Massachusetts, an HUD-funded equity assistance transfer program was developed to deal with the problem of conversion of rental property to condominiums. Brookline residents were first granted a six-month eviction stay for displacees and an additional six months for the elderly. This was followed a year later (1979) with a rent control ordinance that banned eviction of tenants in converted structures. In

1980, an elaborate permit process was instituted to require building code standards, 60 percent tenant compliance to either buy or vacate voluntarily, assurance that conversion would not adversely affect the supply of low- and moderate-income housing, and democratic control of the building by the residents and not the developers.

These legal efforts were followed by the development of a financial mechanism to enable potentially displaced households to purchase, rather than be displaced by, the units. Eligibility requirements specified income, assets, and length of residency requirements. The program was generally considered a success in meeting its objectives, although there is a question about its overall effectiveness because of the small number of households affected (35) as compared to the number of units threatened by conversion (5,000).

At the same time, opponents argue that this program can actually have the effect of fueling, rather than stemming, condominium conversion of rental units. Respondents suggest that such a program could be more effective in areas where units "would otherwise go uninhabited" and in any case, would need to be part of a "balanced housing strategy" (Little, Inc.:27).

In Columbia, South Carolina, a Home Loan Conversion Program was established to provide a twenty year no-interest loan to elderly, low- and moderate-income, and handicapped homeowners to rehabilitate or subdivide their property. In exchange, the homeowner agrees to rent units to tenants who qualify for the Section 8 Moderate Rehabilitation program. The Columbia Housing Authority manages and maintains the property, collects the rent, subtracts the costs of maintenance and loan, and returns the balance to the owner. The estimated net gain for the homeowner is $30–$35/month, accounting for increase of taxes and insurance. The amount of time it took to implement the program was longer than expected. Social resistance to the program suggests that it had a limited effect in slowing gentrification, though it did result in creating some rental units.

Denver received a nearly $1 million innovative grant in 1982 and combined this with other resources. It rehabilitated and constructed buildings to be used for potential displacees, converting rental housing to cooperatives, promoting homeownership through subsidized mortgage assistance programs, and supplying a counseling program.

Lessons from the Denver experience, similar to Baltimore's, point to the problems caused by unanticipated factors between design and implementation. Some of these may have been lessened by better planning, but they are more directly connected to the rising costs of property, rehabilitation, and financing. The Denver project "demonstrates that administrative and implementation assumptions should realistically reflect the time and difficulty of operating programs of different character" (Little, Inc.:93). It also suggests the technical expertise essential for the construction phase of the project and the importance of building unforeseen costs into the planning process. A review of other HUD innovative grant recipients points to similarities. In Washington, D.C., efforts to slow displacement caused by condominium conversion led to a "right to first purchase" program that was part of a larger strategy to provide tenant assistance through the provision of seed money, technical assistance, funds for mortgages, gap financing, and rehabilitation assistance. In Seattle, programs were developed to slow the displacement of the elderly and to rehabilitate downtown hotels. In Los Angeles, transitional housing was supplied for skid row residents. In Santa Barbara, a limited equity cooperative was established, a key element of which was a revolving fund.

The experience with these grants showed that increasing costs of financing and the difficulty of obtaining permanent financing were problems across the board, as were the escalating costs of rehabilitation and construction. Technical know-how was critical, and its lack meant delays and extra costs. Coordination among various agencies and management of several financing sources necessitated leadership and expertise. Most significantly, while there was some success in adding to the supply of low- and moderate-income housing units, there are questions about the overall effectiveness of these efforts in stopping gentrification in the neighborhoods. For example, it is possible that many of these efforts did not limit gentrification but simply made it possible for a few low- and moderate-income households to benefit from the process. Of even more concern is that some of these revitalization efforts helped gentrification through increasing the value of property. Follow-up studies are necessary to assess what additional programs were implemented and the current state of these neighborhoods. Finally, while most of these programs involved combining financial sources, the majority of the funds came from federal sources, including the HUD innovative grants, CDBG, and UDAG. These funds all diminished during the Reagan era.

Anti-Gentrification Efforts in the 1980s

The reinvestment process may follow years of behind-the-scenes work, but once it begins in a neighborhood, it is likely to proceed rapidly. The community already organized and ready to defend itself stands a better chance of maintaining control of its resources.

At the same time, the neighborhood that attempts to organize in reaction to a reinvestment process that has already begun must alert itself to certain organizational limitations. For example, research conducted by the University of Illinois at Chicago Nathalie Voorhees Center for Neighborhood and Community Improvement warns that "the conditions inherent in gentrification, especially the change in the social and economic status of the neighborhood, create organizational changes that constrain the evolution of the development role by community groups" (Hannan, Brierre, and Peterman 1988:1). By the time the organization gets going, the gentrifying has begun; as this happens, the organization itself gentrifies. The organization may then work on behalf of current residents, but the characteristics of those residents have changed. Intervention efforts in this context are not effective, as goals and political styles reflect a perspective that either accepts or encourages gentrification. This research suggests not only that community development organizations are themselves vulnerable to gentrification but also that intervention efforts are critical and must occur as early as possible in the gentrification process.

The main goal in the fight against gentrification is to protect communities from increased property values. Most residents in a neighborhood, especially homeowners, would not argue against the benefits of revitalization and increased property values. They are caught between wanting to see their neighborhoods "improved" and fearing that this "improvement" will lead to their displacement, especially because of rising taxes. Even if they manage to hold on, they are faced with the destruction of their community as they know it while they see neighbors depart. Upgrading the neighborhood while maintaining it for the residents who could not afford to stay with higher property taxes, rents, or price tags on houses challenges the community organizer. It is especially challenging, as suggested from previous examples, to prevent the exacerbation of the process through the very efforts that are designed to prevent it.

THE MARKET AS AN ARENA FOR INTERVENTION

Current community efforts to fight gentrification begin with the premise that gentrification is a market-driven phenomenon and should be fought through participation in that market. In other words, changes in control of property occur through obtaining the title to that property. This strategy parallels a philosophy that promotes empowerment through ownership. Strategies have centered on how best to gain control of property on behalf of community residents. At the neighborhood level, community organizations have formed to purchase property as development corporations and to promote ownership by individuals and families. At the citywide level, agencies have served the role of facilitating ownership through research and information dissemination. How well this participation in the market fares will determine the effectiveness of the fight against gentrification.

The ability of a community organization to purchase and renovate property depends on several factors, including the particular stage of gentrification in a given neighborhood. Increases in property values parallel the gentrification process, thus making affordability the primary issue affecting the purchasing strategies of an organization.

The topic of housing affordability is of critical importance even beyond the concerns of gentrification. Indeed, there exists in the state of Illinois a housing crisis of both affordability and availability to the extent that Illinois has the third-largest "affordability gap" in the country (Woodstock Institute 1988). Households that spend more than 30 percent of their income on housing pay more than government standards suggest is reasonable. In the city of Chicago, 36.8 percent of all renters pay "excessive" housing costs, in a city where 19.2 percent of households are below the poverty level. Utilities and additional costs of housing make it increasingly difficult for the low- and moderate-income household to rent, let alone buy, property.

When the costs of operating a two-to-three bedroom apartment are compared with the income of three categories of family income, the affordability gap is illustrated. Voice of the People, a long-standing organization in Chicago's Uptown, estimates that the average operating costs of a two-to-three bedroom apartment are $475/month, including taxes, insurance, utilities, maintenance, purchasing, renovating, and development. For a clerical worker who makes $15,000 per year, the wage earner who makes $5.00 per hour, and the mother of three who receives AFDC payments of $386 per month, the affordability gaps are $100, $211, and $359 per month, respectively. (These figures do not reflect variation among neighborhoods and may, in fact, be on the low side, particularly for areas that are especially targeted for gentrification.) These facts highlight the housing crisis that makes it even more difficult for the community organization to purchase and renovate property and still be able to rent it as "affordable housing."

A 1988 report from the Joint Center for Housing Studies of Harvard University confirms the housing crisis at the national level. It concludes that, despite the gains in the housing industry and the decline in mortgage interest rates, an increasing number of households are being shut out of

homeownership and reasonable rental costs. The costs of homeownership are up, while the rates of homeownership are down. Gross rents are
at an all-time high, while the supply of low-cost rental housing has
shrunk. The percentage of income spent on rent has skyrocketed, and the
numbers of homeless have risen dramatically. The fight to stop gentrification occurs in the context of increasing "housing haves and have-nots."

The high costs of development adversely affect the not-for-profit organization, which is at a distinct disadvantage in comparison to the private developer. As one practitioner from People's Housing in Chicago
said, "if we have to compete against private development for private
housing, we'll lose, both economically and politically." This is especially
true during and after an era of Reaganomics—which this same practitioner described as an era when "Reagan gave a big party for developers." The policies of the 1980s provided accelerated depreciation,
more advantageous capital gains, and tax credits for landmark districts.
The last especially benefits the developer, and some community practitioners earmark it as a clear sign that gentrification has appeared in the
neighborhood.

It is no surprise, therefore, that community practitioners worry most
about how to cut the costs of acquisition and renovation in order for the
property to serve as low- and moderate-income housing. Antigentrifica-
tion strategies, therefore, require extensive searches for local, state, and
federal programs and funds to subsidize development expenses. Similarly, ways are sought to join with the private sector, to cut costs, and to
finance projects. Community intervention to control reinvestment in Chicago includes the range of approaches.

LOCAL PROGRAMS

Before or at the early stages of gentrification, community-based organizations can take advantage of the local tax reactivation program. In June
1983, the Cook County Board established the Multifamily Tax Reactivation Program. Under this program, Cook County obtains tax delinquent
properties at the Scavenger Sale, clears all liens, and then transfers the
property to "qualified" not-for-profit development organizations.
Through this program, community organizers have a mechanism by
which they can acquire property at a negligible cost and at least minimize
one of the cost factors in the overall development process.

An assessment of this program by the Woodstock Institute concluded
that the program was "extremely successful in generating savings totaling over $4 million to developers attempting to provide quality afford-

able housing for low- and moderate-income people" (Woodstock Institute 1988: iii). The county benefited by having the properties returned to the tax rolls and by generating surplus dollars. The analysts deemed the program a success in spite of minor administrative problems.

The extent to which additional local assistance is available will depend a great deal on the political climate whereby a given municipality may or may not wish to commit resources to develop low- and moderate-income housing. In a more favorable environment, resources may include funds, tax relief, legal mechanisms, and the assistance of planning and economic development offices. On the other hand, as is often the case, a city may favor the developer with the philosophy that a developer-defined business climate is "better" for the health of the city.

In order to promote neighborhoods that maintain their low- and moderate-income families, community developers in Chicago have used the Chicago Equity Fund, to whom they sell tax credits and in return receive an additional layer of financing used to purchase property. These syndicated relationships make property acquisition possible but at the potential expense of control. This partnership is onerous because ownership is tied into the Equity Fund whose affiliates include foundations, corporations, and banks. Analysts have studied syndication strategies so that more effective means can be developed to obtain the financing but with fewer deed restrictions and more control.

The Neighborhood Institute (TNI) in Chicago is a nonprofit affiliate of Shorebank Corporation and has effectively used the Chicago Equity Fund Partnership in conjunction with other sources to develop several units of low- and moderate-income housing. The additional sources include bank loans (Harris Bank, Bank One of Columbus, Ohio, and First National Bank of Chicago), tax-exempt bonds floated by the Chicago Metropolitan Housing Development Corporation and by Rescorp Mortgage, the City of Chicago Department of Housing, Local Initiative Support Corporation (LISC), Community Investment Corporation, the Chicago Housing Authority, and the Illinois Development Finance Authority. Many of the TNI projects also utilized Section 8 Rental Assistance and the Tax Reactivation Program.

The above list of sources used for fifteen different projects totaling 597 units illustrates the necessity to combine several sources of funding in order to put together low- and moderate-income housing. It is also important to note that these projects were developed in a neighborhood that might have one day been ripe for gentrification but was tackled at the end of the "devalorization cycle," that is, at the point of disinvestment. This scenario depicts a neighborhood that may have been saved from both deterioration and rampant revitalization.

Given the decline of federal funding, the high cost of acquisition and development, and the necessity for rental subsidies, the fine art of financing packaging is perhaps the most crucial component of the current strategy to fight gentrification through ownership. Its importance, therefore, calls for a more complete description and analysis—one beyond the scope of this effort. Some community developers have a sophisticated understanding of the complexities of layered financing, while others are struggling to find dollars to build a few units. The nonprofit agency is especially at a disadvantage, because, without cash flow and equity, it has a harder time influencing a given neighborhood. Layered financing, syndication, and community trusts are only a few of the financial mechanisms that should be assessed. It would also be helpful to examine the strategies employed by these agencies.

STATEWIDE INITIATIVES

At the state level, the Statewide Housing Action Coalition—which includes representatives from the governor's office, the Illinois Housing Development Authority (IDHA), Local Initiatives Support Corporation (LISC), Woodstock Institute, the Chicago Equity Fund, and the Leadership Council for Metropolitan Open Communities—promoted the idea of establishing a housing trust fund. In light of the Illinois crisis in housing, and based on examples from twenty-six other states, the coalition recommended the creation of an affordable housing program that would include an affordable housing trust fund. The program is "to provide and leverage: financial aid for programs designed for development and rehabilitation of affordable housing (Woodstock 1988:13).

The revenue for such a trust fund has, in other states, come from "development fees or taxes, real estate taxes and escrow accounts, and revenues or interest earnings from other programs such as bond reserves or Urban Development Action Grant repayments. Three additional states have established Housing Trust Funds with state appropriations" (Woodstock Institute 1988:10). In Illinois, the coalition recommended that the trust fund combine several sources, including CDBG, CSBG, UDAG, Illinois Development Action Grant (IDAG), and IDHA. These funds are then available to individuals and families who meet federal Section 8 guidelines. Community organizations advise residents of the availability of these funds and the mechanisms by which to apply.

FEDERAL PROGRAMS

As stated, federal funds have been drastically reduced or eliminated. Many practitioners, nonetheless, point to the importance of federal subsidies as critical for community development organizations to ensure the mixture of affordable housing into any development plan. Section 8 housing is the most coveted because it is based on income; yet it too has suffered serious cutbacks during the Reagan years.

These years have also threatened HUD low-income housing, but practitioners are applying their professional expertise to legal ways to prevent the units from being lost as low-income units.

Community intervention approaches also include strategies to encourage homeownership by individuals and families. The community development organization facilitates the packaging of loans and directs individuals to government programs for home improvement. The Community Reinvestment Act (CRA) and the Home Mortgage Disclosure Act are particularly instrumental in providing a procedure by which banks can be pressured into halting their redlining policies and to reinvest in neighborhoods. Pressure on financial institutions makes agreements possible between Community Development Corporations (CDCs) and banks whereby an X number of dollars becomes available for mortgage loans to qualified individuals whose income is below a cutoff point. A neighborhood council ensures the funds are directed to the intended recipients.

The CRA is especially noteworthy for a number of reasons. First, it effectively makes millions of dollars available. Second, it demonstrates successful lobbying at the national level, even in the face of well-financed and well-organized opposition. Third, the effort to establish the CRA demonstrates the workability of a coalition that crosses regional and racial boundaries. Fourth, the information required to prove redlining reveals the significance of race in demarcating disinvested and reinvested neighborhoods. Finally, the Community Reinvestment Act provides a means to direct reinvestment toward neighborhood ownership and stability. The CRA needs public pressure and careful monitoring if its enforcement is to be ensured. The value of the act is only as good as its watchdogs. Even more important, for every dollar financed by private means, two dollars are needed from public funds for housing projects to serve families with incomes under $14,000 (Lenz 1988). Consequently, in many cases committed CRA funds have gone unused—again pointing to the importance of advocacy efforts to obtain more public money for low-income housing.

NEIGHBORHOOD ORGANIZING

In conjunction with property acquisition and renovation, community intervention practitioners promote the organization of the neighborhood

41

Conclusion

Gentrification disrupts communities and displaces residents. Communities must act swiftly despite the creeping and encompassing effect of gentrification and despite the economic and political forces shaping the process of neighborhood turnover. Neighborhood change is not automatic, even given the strong institutional impetus, but is the outcome of a process of conflict—an outcome not predetermined. Community intervention can influence how neighborhoods are shaped but must do so with consciousness of the process, resources for mobilization, and effective strategies.

Policy Implications

Communities that are already ready for action have a better chance of success than the community that has to learn the what and the how of development. A timely response can be aided by an early warning system. Early warning signals have been identified but need to be refined and more widely dispersed.

The importance of an early and proactive response is expressed well in the notion that "either you rehabilitate your neighborhood or someone else will." However, this is more than a matter of rehabilitation. The future of the community is at stake. Local residents need to be educated about gentrification and its implications and encouraged to retain their properties and stay in the neighborhood.

Communities need to have a plan, a vision for their future. A community is less likely to be acted on if it has a vision for itself and a process to achieve that vision. Despite the conflicts that would emerge in such a process, community organizers can help facilitate a process for full community participation.

Clearly, to help communities do this we need to know more about gentrification in different neighborhoods. Gentrification occurs in neighborhoods that range from severely disinvested to vital and stable. Replacement in each type of neighborhood should be identified in order to develop strategies most effective under particular conditions. More research is needed on gentrification, the communities it affects, and the efforts required to intervene. Existing case studies should be compiled and patterns clearly demarcated; a nationwide assessment should be made of community intervention efforts; and consideration should be given to the establishment of a data bank to disseminate the scope of intervention efforts.

Attacking the problem of gentrification requires resources from all levels of government. Development occurs through the coalescence of real estate development and finance interests with the aid of municipal officials, state sanctions, and federal funds. Strategies for even development should similarly consider all levels of government. The federal government should be particularly targeted in light of its cutbacks in spending for housing and in the absence of a comprehensive housing policy. The continuation and increase of Section 8 allowances are especially critical. Without them, the construction of affordable housing for low-income households is next to impossible.

Notions of ownership should be expanded beyond property control to include ownership of the neighborhood itself, including its symbols, culture, and modes of interaction. The ideas of community ownership have been limited to property deeds. However, a community that owns itself not only deters intruders but provides incentive for neighborhood protection. Avenues to promote this should be explored.

Related to this proactive approach, popular images of the practitioners as anti- any development need to be dispelled. Efforts should be made to actively promote an image that is more closely connected to the truth. It is especially important to do this as early as possible. There are many committed individuals working to fight reinvestment through the promotion of homeownership and tenant assistance via market mechanisms. While these efforts may not always stop gentrification or the housing crisis, they do warrant continuation. Layered financing is an especially critical component of this effort, although the levels of expertise on how to put together these packages vary. More systematic information should be made available on financial packaging for moderate- and especially low-income housing.

Implementation of all the above-mentioned strategies is aided by collective action that pressures public and private institutions and gives impetus to community concern and involvement. Community organizers often find themselves involved in territorial and personality disputes, but there is a need for leadership to help transcend these obstacles so that advocacy can play an integral role in shaping communities. It is all the more important that communities have a sophisticated understanding of gentrification and an ability to assess the implications of a given strategy.

The urgency of the situation cannot be overestimated. Uncontrolled reinvestment continues in neighborhoods that cannot withstand the shift in property values. Those who utilize community intervention approaches are committed, experienced, and knowledgeable. They must increase and sharpen their tools if there is to be any chance of winning against irresponsible replacement of one class by another and the subsequent destruction and disruption of communities.

REFERENCE LIST

Allen, I. 1984. "The Ideology of Dense Neighborhood Redevelopment." In *Gentrification, Displacement, and Neighborhood Revitalization*, edited by J. Palen and B. Lined. Albany: State University of New York Press.

Berry, B.J.L. 1985. "Islands of Renewal in Seas of Decay." In *The New Urban Reality*, edited by P. Peterson. Washington, D.C.: Brookings Institution.

Bourne, L. S. 1977. *Perspectives on the Inner City: Its Changing Character, Reasons for Decline and Revival*. Toronto: Centre for Urban and Community Studies. Research Paper 94.

Bryant, Don, and Henry McGee, Jr. No Date. *Gentrification and the Law: Combatting Urban Displacement*. Los Angeles: Lawyers for Housing.

Castells, M. 1976. "The Wild City." *Kapital State* 4 (5): 2–30.

Clay, P. 1979. *Neighborhood Renewal: Middle-Class Resettlement and Incumbent Upgradings in American Neighborhoods*. Lexington, Mass.: Lexington Books.

———. 1978. "Neighborhood Revitalization and Community Development." *Center for Community Economic Development Newsletter* (August/October), Massachusetts Institute of Technology.

Fainstain, S., N. Fainstain, R. Child Hill, D. Judd, and M. P. Smith. 1983. *Restructuring the City: The Political Economy of Urban Redevelopment*. New York: Longman.

Gale, Dennis E. 1976. *The Back to the City Movement . . . Or Is It?* St. Louis: Washington University.

———. 1977. "The back-to-the city movement revisited." Occasional Paper, Dept. of Urban and Regional Planning. St. Louis: Washington University.

———. 1980. "Neighborhood Resettlement: Washington, D.C." In *Back to the City*, edited by S. Laska and D. Spain. New York: Pergamon.

———. 1985–1986. "Demographic Research on Gentrification and Displacement." *Journal of Planning Literature* 1 (1) (Winter): 14–29.

Grier, G., and E. Grier. 1978. "Urban Displacement: A Reconnaissance." Prepared for the Office of the Secretary, U.S. Department of Housing and Urban Development.

Hamnett, C. 1976. "Social Change in London: A Study of Gentrification." *Urban Studies* 13:261–271.

———. 1980. "Social Change and Social Segregation in Inner London, 1961–1971." *Urban Affairs Quarterly* 15:469–487.

Hannan, S., K. Brierre, and W. Peterman. 1988. "Growing into a Development Role: A Case Study in a Gentrifying Neighborhood." Paper presented at the eighteenth annual meeting of the Urban Affairs Association, St. Louis.

Hartman, C., D. Keating, and R. LeGates. 1982. *Displacement: How to Fight It.* Berkeley: National Housing Law Project.

Henig, J. R. 1982. "Neighborhood Response to Gentrification: Conditions of Mobilization." *Urban Affairs Quarterly* 17(3): 343–358.

Joint Center for Housing Studies of Harvard University. 1988. "The State of the Nation's Housing."

LeGates, R., and C. Hartman. 1981. "Gentrification-Related Displacement." *Clearinghouse Review* 15(3):207–249.

Lenz, T. 1988. "Neighborhood Development: Issues and Models." *Social Policy* 18(4):24–30.

Levy, P. 1980. "Neighborhoods in a Race with Time: Local Strategies for Countering Displacement." In *Back to the City*, edited by S. Laska and D. Spain. New York: Pergamon.

Lipton, S. G. 1977. "Evidence of Central City Revival." *Journal of the American Institute of Planners* 43:136–147.

Little, Arthur D., Inc. No date. *Housing Displacement Demonstration Projects: Volume 1 and 2.* Cambridge, Mass.: Arthur D. Little.

"National Housing Law Project." 1978. *Housing Law Bulletin* 8(5).

Nelson, K. 1984. "Urban Economic and Demographic Change: Recent Shifts and Future Prospects." In *The Changing Economic and Fiscal Structure*, edited by R. Edel. Vol. 4, *Research in Urban Economics.* Greenwich, Conn.: JAI Press.

Pitt, J. 1977. *Gentrification in Islington.* London: Barnsbury People's Forum.

Power, A. 1973. *David and Goliath: Barnsbury 1973.* Holloway Neighborhood Law Centre, Islington, London.

Schaffer, R., and N. Smith. 1986. "The Gentrification of Harlem." *Annals of the Association of American Geographers* 76(3):347–365.

Smith, N., and M. Le Faivre. 1984. "A Class Analysis of Gentrification." In *Gentrification, Displacement, and Neighborhood Revitalization*, edited by J. Palen and B. Lined. Albany: State University of New York Press.

Smith, Neil. 1979. "Toward a Theory of Gentrification: A Back to the City Movement by Capital not People." *Journal of American Planning Association* 45 (October):538–548.

Urban Land Institute. 1976. *New Opportunities for Residential Development in Central Cities.* Report 25. Washington, D.C.

U.S. Department of Housing and Urban Development, Office of Policy Development and Research. 1979. *The Conversion of Rental Housing to Condominiums and Cooperatives*. Washington:USGPO.

Williams, P. 1976. "The Role of Institutions in the Inner London Housing Market: The Case of Islington." *Transactions of the Institute of British Geographers* 1:72–82.

Woodstock Institute. 1988. *The Illinois Affordable Housing Trust Fund: A Working Proposal of the Statewide Housing Action Coalition*. Chicago: Woodstock.

Currently Assistant Professor of Planning in the Department of Community and Regional Planning in the School of Architecture at the University of New Mexico, **Teresa Cordova** was an assistant professor of Latin American Studies at the University of Illinois at Chicago from 1986 to 1991. She has long been involved in community action research. Cordova is currently involved in a national research project on "Latinos in a Changing U.S. Economy," sponsored by the Inter-University Program for Latino Research. As an activist she has worked with neighborhood groups such as Pilsen-Aztlan Neighborhood Coalition, a group representing prominent Latino neighborhoods south of Chicago's downtown. These Latino communities have been particularly sensitive to the potential negative impact of uncontrolled gentrification.

4 RACIALLY DIVERSE COMMUNITIES: A NATIONAL NECESSITY   Daniel Lauber

Elected officials and civil rights leaders are reluctant to address the issue these days. However, continuing racial segregation in housing and in education are intimately intertwined with nearly every aspect of our everyday lives and are a basic cause of so many of our nation's domestic difficulties, including uneven development.

Racial segregation has produced more than a growing and increasingly permanent underclass among the nation's African-American population. It has also contributed greatly to crime and drugs in our inner cities. Resegregation from all-white to all-black brings with it the disinvestment and misinvestment that rob integrating neighborhoods of the financial lifeline they need to retain their economic viability. It has resulted in white flight and the increasingly long commutes suburban whites must take to reach their jobs in the central city and African-Americans must take to reach jobs in the burgeoning suburbs while discriminatory practices in housing exclude them from living there. Housing segregation results in increased air pollution and inflation from the higher fuel prices it causes. It causes higher housing costs, as whites pay a premium for housing away from the central city and African-Americans forced to remain in there or in predominantly black suburbs pay a "black tax" in terms of higher insurance rates, lower levels of municipal service, and lower rates of housing appreciation. It prevents America's black population from fully participating in the American Dream solely, and perpetually, on the basis of color. *As long as housing and education remain racially segregated, the United States will never be able to solve most of its domestic ills.*

Segregation is the product of a complex and interrelated set of discriminatory practices that institutionalize racial prejudice. According to a

660 F.Supp. 668, 670 [E.D.N.Y. 1987]), while refusing to sue to end segregation in housing projects that exclude African-Americans.

State and Local Government   State government actions and omissions can affect the stability of diverse neighborhoods and the strength of the dual housing market. For example, the Illinois State Real Estate Licensing Department, which can suspend or terminate the licenses of agents who engage in discriminatory practices like racial steering, has suspended only one agent's license for steering white prospects away from integrated communities (South Suburban Housing Center April 1988:2). Similarly, the state's Civil Rights Commission has been all but silent on racial discrimination in housing.

With the great control it has over awarding funds to developers, the Illinois Housing Development Authority could require genuine affirmative marketing of the developments it finances and site them to assist racially diverse communities. Instead, it continues to finance single-racial developments throughout the state. This is similar to what happens in most other states.

Over the years, local government practices have had a profound influence over residential location by race. These have varied from the now clearly illegal laws that required segregation in housing and the public schools to policies that promoted resegregation such as failing to alter school boundaries, reducing public services to integrating neighborhoods, placement of public and subsidized housing, and exclusionary zoning (Rabin 1987).

A Comprehensive Program to Preserve Racially Diverse Communities

Few big-city neighborhoods that have experienced black in-migration have been able to counteract the forces of resegregation. Consequently, the general public has come to think that complete racial transition is the "natural" and inevitable outcome of residential integration, the natural way of things. Successful efforts to preserve diversity have to eliminate the myth that segregation is natural. There is a substantial demand for housing in integrated communities by both black and white homeowners. Programs to preserve racial diversity not only meet this demand but go a long way toward eliminating the high costs of housing segregation. All efforts to preserve racial diversity really focus on replacing the dual market with a unitary market in which all Americans participate. And to achieve that end, *it is essential to continue to attract whites to integrated neighborhoods and municipalities and blacks to all-white neighborhoods and municipalities.*

The effort to preserve racial diversity requires a broad-based, comprehensive attack on the many factors that promote resegregation. Communities must initiate a two-pronged strategy that focuses primarily on policies, practices, and programs internal to the community and secondarily on those external to the community at the regional, state, and national levels.

Although there are some universal truths and common themes in efforts to achieve and preserve racial diversity, there is no simple checklist of what steps a community should take (deMarco 1989:3). Although each activity that follows contributes to success, not every one is necessarily appropriate for every integrating community but will vary with each community's unique characteristics. In the absence of effective state and federal support, the local level is where pro-integrative initiatives must be taken. Local laws on fair housing, for example, can supplement state and federal laws (Obermanns and Quereau 1989:3–4).

Pro-integration initiatives have been more successful in suburbs, in part because of the smaller size and the stronger voice of any one particular neighborhood relative to the whole suburb. Also, in a smaller community the negative effect of resegregation is likely to affect more quickly the whole suburb than is a similar change likely to affect an entire city. This is not to say that it is impossible to preserve racial diversity in larger cities. If a neighborhood within a large central city is to achieve and preserve such diversity, the municipal government must adopt a policy promoting it and provide the funding and staff necessary to implement the strategies and techniques that are essential to preserving it.

Strategies and Tools for Achieving and Preserving Racial Diversity

Passage of a Fair Housing Ordinance

Perhaps the most basic way a municipality can promote racial diversity is enacting, publicizing, and implementing a fair housing ordinance.

While such laws generally follow the language of the Fair Housing Act of 1968 as subsequently amended, a local ordinance enables a community to respond quickly to suspected violations through a local mechanism for initiating, investigating, and prosecuting complaints. A local fair housing ordinance is vital during periods—particularly such as the late 1980s and early 1990s—when the state and federal governments rarely prosecute violators. Many local government officials believe that a local fair housing ordinance functions as an effective deterrent to segregation (Engstrom 1983:7).[6]

Fair housing ordinances may include a number of provisions and may be accompanied by other ordinances that promote diversity and bolster residents' confidence in their community. Legal provisions include anti-solicitation clauses, ban of for-sale signs, requirement of filing of intent to sell, requirement of social effect statements for new developments, strict housing code enforcement, and insurance programs guaranteeing house sale value. Each provision is briefly discussed below.

Solicitation   By regulating solicitation by real estate agents, a municipality can discourage illegal panic peddling and blockbusting or make their detection much easier so they can be stopped. (Obermanns and Quereau 1989:6). Since the most important aspect of real estate brokering is listings, a real estate agent frequently writes to homeowners to make them aware of the broker's name so when they decide to sell, they will list their house with that broker. At the same time, such practices—typically used by blockbusters and panic peddlers—can increase anxieties among residents fearing total neighborhood transition.

Anti-solicitation provisions in a local fair housing ordinance cannot completely ban realtor-homeowner contact, but they can be used to prevent blockbusting and panic peddling.[7] Some municipalities require any broker or agent who wishes to solicit homeowners for the purpose of selling their homes to register in person. Other communities allow residents to sign a statement that they do not wish to be solicited. The village then compiles a list of all residents who sign the non-solicitation statement and distributes it periodically to all real estate firms active in the village. To reach more residents, a community could annually send a non-solicitation statement, with an explanation of it, to each household with, say, its water bill.

"For Sale" Sign Bans and Regulations   Several integrated communities have banned or regulated residential for sale signs because their proliferation is often seen as a sign of a neighborhood undergoing transition.

The appearance of signs can contribute to homeowner fears. Blockbusting real estate agents often use the presence of many "for sale" signs to panic residents into selling.

Intent to Sell Ordinance   Such an ordinance requires those who put their homes on the market to notify the city of their intent to sell. The homeowner gives the city his or her address, the name of the listing real estate broker and company, and sometimes how the home will be advertised. The information this ordinance provides allows the city to monitor real estate activity in general. It also alerts the city to notice areas where there are suspiciously high levels of activity and to schedule a housing inspection if it requires one upon a change in occupancy.

Inspection/Occupancy Permit Ordinance   These are fairly common outside the Midwest. They require an occupancy permit on a change of occupancy in ownership and rental dwellings, which gives a municipality the opportunity to inspect the unit for code violations. Such ordinances typically require that the unit be brought up to code before an occupancy permit can be issued. This is an effective way of guaranteeing that *all* property in a municipality is well maintained. Failure to do so—particularly in integrated neighborhoods—can allow the decline in the quality of housing and contribute to neighborhood transition.[8]

Social/Racial Diversity Effect Statement   Virtually any action or policy decision of a municipality can affect its ability to remain racially diverse (deMarco 1989:1). A city would be wise to establish a policy to review all municipal spending and capital improvements for their "social effect." A community can amend its zoning ordinances to require a social effect statement for parcel and major rezonings, zoning and subdivision text amendments, planned unit developments, subdivisions, major developments, school and other public facility construction, and special use permits. Social connotes such concerns as housing, education, physical and mental health, dislocation, recreation, personal safety, sense of community, personal mobility, population density, sociability, equity, economic needs, and income and job opportunities (Lauber 1976).

A number of communities in the United States and Canada have informally and formally employed social effect analysis in reviews of zoning and development proposals. These include the Social Planning Department in Vancouver, British Columbia (Lauber March/April 1975a); the housing statement required by Lakewood, Colorado; socially informed comprehensive planning conducted by Cleveland, Ohio, during the 1970s; and the two-tiered review of social effects used in Richfield, Minnesota (Lauber 1976).

Equity Assurance Program   One of the most common, albeit false, fears that whites have about integration is that their property values will fall substantially. To allay that fear, Oak Park, Illinois, established the nation's first Home Equity Assurance Program in 1977. Financed by bond funds, this program insures owners of single family houses against depreciation in the market values of their homes. Under this voluntary program, homeowners pay for an appraisal of their homes (cost about $110) and register them with the village. There is an initial five-year waiting period, during which the house must be owner occupied, before a house is eligible for coverage.

Once the owner notifies the Equity Assurance Commission's staff that he or she has put the house on the market, a 120-day cycle begins. During the first ninety days, no claim can be made. During the next thirty days, if the highest offer is less than the appraised value, the homeowner forwards the offer to the commission, which can approve the offer and pay 80 percent of the difference between the offer and the five-year-old appraised value, or buy the house itself at the offered price and pay 80 percent of the difference, or order that the house be kept on the market until the 120 days end. After 120 days, the commission buys the house at the highest price plus the 80 percent difference.[9]

Unless accompanied by a set of other ordinances and local government services, equity assurance alone will have little or no effect on the ability of a community to peacefully and successfully become and remain racially diverse. As Sherlyn Reid, the Oak Park (Illinois) Community Relations Director, explains:

> By itself, equity assurance is nothing. To have any value, it's got to be accompanied by an array of other things. The mindset of people is what's most important. Living in a racially integrated community is an Oak Park attitude. [Reid 1988]

RACIAL DIVERSITY POLICY STATEMENT

A racial diversity statement fills the gaps left by traditional fair housing ordinances by effectively addressing racial steering and other practices that generate pressures for resegregation. These statements, whether issued separately or incorporated into a fair housing ordinance, declare that promoting a stable, integrated living environment is a basis for policy and decision making by the local government. They discuss the social, economic, and professional benefits of integration over segregation and the importance of replacing the dual housing market with a unitary market (Engstrom 1983:10). The major value of such a declaration is that it forcefully states the commitment of the community's elected leadership to preserve racial diversity. Such public pronouncements help build confidence among community residents.[10]

Public Relations Communication and Education

Perceptions guide so many actors in the housing market: it is vital that these perceptions be accurate. People often assume that past patterns will always hold true and that, because white to black transition has occurred so often in the past, it will inevitably happen in their community too. Local governments must develop and use public relations skills to explode this myth and the concomitant myths about declining property values, schools, and services in integrated neighborhoods (Onderdonk et al. 1977:35).

Local government first must demonstrate its commitment early in the integration process. For example, as a vote of confidence, Oak Park, Illinois, built a $4 million village hall in the eastern section of the village—an area where residents were anxious about initial signs of racial transition. This investment also stimulated economic growth in the surrounding commercial district (Raymond 1982:88).

Second, the local government must persuade prospective home buyers and renters, real estate brokers and landlords, lenders, appraisers, and developers that integration is going to work in its community, that the local government fully supports integration, and that the best interests are served by integration. Realtors and lenders, for example, usually do not engage in racial steering or redlining out of malice. They usually act in ignorance of the actual conditions that exist in an integrated setting. Local governments and their nonprofit allies should give formal training programs for each of these groups within their jurisdiction to educate on racial diversity issues, fair housing law, and affirmative marketing. See the sections that follow on housing service centers and affirmative marketing for more details.

Public Schools

The racial diversity of a neighborhood or municipality and its public schools are intertwined (see Obermanns and Oliver 1988). Schools, whole school systems, tend to resegregate before housing markets do (deMarco 1989:4). Without intervention to insure citywide integration, white households with children will perceive certain neighborhoods as having undesirable schools and will not move into those areas or will leave them if they currently live there. This concern over schools is so vital that Juliet Saltman (1990:395) labels the absence of systemwide school desegregation one of two "killer variables" that can doom a community to resegregation.[11]

It is vital that municipal government, local agencies, and the schools work together to preserve racial diversity. For example, both the city and school board finance and govern the Shaker Heights (Ohio) Community Services Department that manages the community's housing services and other pro-integrative efforts. The municipal governments and school boards of Cleveland Heights, Shaker Heights, and University Heights jointly sponsor the East Suburban Council for Open Communities (ESCOC), which promotes nontraditional moves by, for example, blacks to the predominantly white Hillcrest suburbs (Obermanns and Quereau 1989:10).

In addition, local governments should carefully monitor school racial composition figures, because changes in public school composition can foreshadow changes in the racial composition of housing (Engstrom 1983:18). They should widely disseminate a joint public policy statement prepared with local school officials that recognizes the links between school and housing segregation and the mutual responsibility of the schools and local government to alleviate it. They must use their influence with public and private schools to assist prospective minority home seekers with children and make them address issues of racial diversity and equity. Some school districts in the Cleveland area started doing so on their own. The schools should invite school officials to serve on all municipal boards/commissions that deal with issues affecting housing integration, and request municipal representation on any school committees whose agenda affects balanced school enrollments. They should discuss the potential for regional and metropolitan-wide solutions to patterns of segregation in housing and schools with municipal and school officials through the subregion or metropolitan area.

A systemwide program for achieving and maintaining racially balanced public schools removes the racial composition of the integrated neighborhood's schools from the factors whites consider when choosing where to live since all the schools in the municipality or school district have roughly the same proportion of white students. There is less reason for whites with children to move out of the integrated neighborhood because wherever they might move in the municipality or surrounding area, all of the public schools are likely to be integrated (Saltman 1989:627). Equally important, systemwide integration makes the possibility that an individual school would resegregate much more remote. In addition, since blacks and whites are equally distributed throughout the whole school system, the integrated neighborhood is no longer identified as "the one with black schools," a characterization that discourages white housing demand. Successfully integrated municipalities and neighborhoods tend to replace neighborhood schools with grade centers or magnet schools that draw pupils from throughout the school district or subregion (Lauber 1974:15).[12]

AFFIRMATIVE MARKETING

Getting both whites and blacks to consider nontraditional moves, within and without an integrated community, is essential to creating the unitary housing market every racially diverse community ultimately needs to remain integrated. Affirmative marketing is a positive race-conscious approach to housing that attempts to expand the housing choices of both black and white home seekers. To achieve maximum success, affirmative marketing requires the cooperation of local governments with realtors, rental agents, and landlords within and without racially diverse municipalities (Engstrom 1983:10–11). Affirmative marketing is completely different from racial quotas. Affirmative marketing makes home seekers aware of a wider array of housing choices available to them. The choice of where to look for housing and what housing to buy or rent remains with the home seeker.[13]

Affirmative marketing can also be built into zoning standards. Zoning and subdivision regulations protect the health, safety, and general welfare of a community. Most municipalities set forth the goals and objectives they choose to promote health, safety, and the general welfare in their comprehensive plan. Many expand on the plan's goals in a racial diversity policy statement. Such a goal can be incorporated into a city's comprehensive plan. When a municipality has set racial diversity as a goal, its zoning and subdivision ordinances, which are intended to implement and comply with its comprehensive plan, certainly can require a developer to prepare and implement an affirmative marketing plan that meets the city's standards in order to receive approval for a residential development. The author is unaware of any municipality that has adopted this sort of zoning or subdivision provision.

HOUSING SERVICE CENTERS

Some racially diverse municipalities and nonprofit organizations have established housing service centers to assist in the affirmative marketing of their communities and develop a unitary housing market. Some centers are fully funded by municipal monies. Other privately operated centers receive an average of one-half of their funding from government sources, including Community Development Block Grants and federal Fair Housing Assistance Plan (FHAP II) funds.

Among the basic services such centers provide is counseling to introduce prospective tenants and home buyers to the wider range of housing choices. For example, the Homeseekers Service operated by the South Suburban Housing Center counsels prospects to consider all options available to them in Chicago's southern and southwest suburbs and not limit their choices on the basis of race. The service recently inaugurated a Corporate Relocation Service to work with businesses to introduce the southern suburbs to employees moving to the Chicago area. In the Cleveland area, the East Suburban Council for Open Communities operates a similar housing service to encourage both whites and blacks to explore all their housing choices. Oak Park's counseling focuses largely on encouraging integrative moves to apartment buildings (Fischer 1986:84).

Other housing service center functions include: receiving, investigating, and pursuing complaints of violations of fair housing laws; building morale to discourage racial turnover, using public relations efforts to promote a positive image of the racially diverse community or communities; auditing and testing; litigating; affirmative marketing; educating through training workshops for real estate agents and rental managers and landlords, such as those conducted by the South Suburban Housing Center; and escorting clients who may be reluctant to view a home by themselves in a nontraditional area (Fischer 1986).

Fully developed housing service centers, like those in Shaker Heights and Cleveland Heights, Ohio, also conduct tours of the community and schools and refer home buyers to real estate agents who have demonstrated a commitment to racial diversity and affirmative marketing by promoting areas where the buyer's race is underrepresented (Obermanns and Quereau 1989:7). Publicly recognizing and rewarding the efforts of real estate agents who promote integrated housing patterns through their sales practices is also effective (Engstrom 1983:11).[14]

ADVOCACY

Local governments can influence all branches of the state and federal governments through lobbying, separately or collectively. Local governments can seek state and federal policies and programs that further the goals of integration and elimination of the dual housing market. Given the present political climate and the failure of so many black leaders and organizations who are invested in segregation to support racial diversity efforts, it is unlikely that widespread support can be found to better enforce state and federal fair housing laws or change state and federal policies and regulatory practices to help preserve diverse communities and open all-white communities. However, incremental victories are possible, as in Ohio where pro-integration groups banded together twice to persuade the Ohio Housing Finance Agency to designate millions of dollars for below-market-rate mortgage loans to first-time home buyers who bought in neighborhoods where their race was underrepresented.

Mixed communities should also do their best to persuade public housing authorities to agree not to build additional public housing in racially mixed communities. Juliet Saltman, who has studied attempts to preserve racial diversity, describes the introduction of new public housing into a racially diverse neighborhood a "killer variable" that has toppled otherwise effective efforts.

Professional and religious organizations can also be added to the lobbying coalition. Efforts by representatives of the East Suburban Coalition for Open Communities and the Cuyahoga Plan led the National Presbytery to adopt a strong resolution in 1988 on the Presbyterian church's responsibility for achieving fair housing (East Suburban Council for Open Communities 1989:7). Winning support for pro-integrative national policies from the leading national associations involved in government, such as the National League of Cities, National Association of Housing and Redevelopment Officials, American Planning Association, American Society for Public Administration, and International City Management Association can create an effective lobbying coalition at the national level. Most of these organizations maintain sophisticated lobbying operations in the District of Columbia.

COLLECTING AND ANALYZING DATA

By maintaining accurate information on housing questions, a local government can quickly respond to rumors and half-truths that inevitably are spread about a community's integrated housing (Onderdonk et al. 1977:37). Equally important, no municipality can determine what strategies it should employ unless it has an up-to-date racial profile of all neighborhoods and blocks so it can identify emerging trends that may reflect illegal activities and threaten the delicate balances integration maintenance requires to succeed. Data that show rapid racial change can alert a village to possible illegal real estate practices (Perry 1983:1).[15]

Data on real estate transactions can provide information on (1) the race of new and departing residents; (2) which real estate firms are active in the community; (3) any evidence of real estate agent steering; and (4) the characteristics of the community that attract new residents—characteristics that should be stressed in marketing the community (Engstrom 1983:16). These techniques give the local government a better picture of future racial composition than does the current occupancy. Data-gathering techniques include the following:

Entrance survey.—Forms distributed by a public utility such as the water department typically ask for the resident's race or ethnic classification, place of employment, previous place of residence, and the factors that influenced his or her move to the community. Several questions that specifically relate to the real estate transaction and how the real estate agent marketed the community also provide crucial information (Perry 1983:1).

Exit interview.—Distributed in a similar fashion to the entrance survey, the exit survey allows the local government to learn whether people are moving within the village or elsewhere, why they are moving, and the racial composition of those who move (Perry 1983:1).

Seller's register.—Local governments can use the multiple listing service to identify home sellers and then ask them to voluntarily record information about the prospects who see their home. Information requested includes the date of showing, name of the real estate company and agent, and race of the prospect (Engstrom 1983:16–17). This information enabled the village to monitor compliance with its fair housing ordinance and ascertain ownership housing traffic patterns (Perry 1983:1).[16]

Real estate audits.—Some of the most valuable data that identify discriminatory practices come from real estate audits, or testing, conducted largely by the municipal and regional housing service centers. These data can alert a municipality to illegal real estate and rental practices that threaten racial diversity. An audit is a study used to determine whether the clients of a real estate firm or rental property manager receive any differences in the quantity, quality, and type of information and service that could result only from a difference in the clients' race. Under a coordinator's supervision, trained pairs of home seekers, one white and one black, attempt to obtain identical housing at different controlled times and sequences from a specific real estate or rental agency (Peterman and Hunt 1986:447; Saltman 1978:92). Each testing pair is matched in terms of income, family size, housing needs, and other characteristics relevant to housing choice. The only difference is that one individual/couple tester is black and the other individual/couple is white. They visit the real estate office at different times, request the same type of housing, and give the same basic information to the agent. Immediately afterward, the tester records her experience on a standardized form. By comparing the treatment each pair of the testers receive, or by comparing the treatment black testers as a group and white testers as a group receive, the level of racial discrimination, if any, can be measured (South Suburban Housing Center August 1988:1).

Audits have generally been conducted after discrimination complaints have been made. Audits typically do not find blatant discrimination, such as an outright refusal to deal with a black tester. However, the evidence uncovered by audits frequently shows that black home seekers or renters have been treated differently than whites. Black testers were usually shown fewer houses than white ones. Often they were told "nothing was available," while similarly qualified white testers were shown houses (Peterman and Hunt 1986:447, 481–482, 485–486).

Audits frequently uncover racial steering. Black testers are frequently told only about homes in areas with significant African-American populations, while white testers are told only about homes in areas with few or no black residents (Peterman and Hunt 1986:486–587). Testers and housing service centers have standing to sue for damages and an injunction under the Fair Housing Act—and they have used it to win substantial penalties and settlements. Suits based on testing data have been used to impose affirmative marketing programs on recalcitrant real estate firms and agents.

As long as their results are well publicized to the real estate community in particular, audits also serve as a deterrent. The more recent the audit, the less steering after its results have been released. When audits have not been conducted recently, the level of discrimination has increased. "Clearly, the more auditing done, and the more feedback and follow-up in the community, the greater the likelihood that discrimination will decrease" (Saltman 1978:107–108).

PLAN FOR RACIAL DIVERSITY

To assure the most effective coordinated efforts, municipalities should develop comprehensive policy plans to guide their endeavors to preserve racial diversity. Subregional and metropolitan-wide policy plans developed with input from all involved parties would also more effectively focus and coordinate each municipality and community organization's efforts within the larger regional framework where the dual housing market must be replaced by a unitary market.[17]

ATTACK THE DUAL HOUSING MARKET ON LOCAL AND
REGIONAL LEVELS

Anything a local government can do to expand the housing choices of minorities will add to the stability of the municipality's housing market and enhance the city's prospects for preserving its racial diversity by easing the focus of black demand on the municipality. Actions that get white home seekers to consider integrated neighborhoods in their housing search will help maintain the biracial demand so crucial to preserving diversity.

To be effective, this effort to expand housing choices must be undertaken at both the local and regional level. Municipal and regional housing centers should be established to provide the housing counseling necessary to convince both black and white home seekers to consider nontraditional locations.

Financial incentives can be given to real estate brokers and landlords for making pro-integrative sales and implementing pro-integrative rental policies. Cleveland Heights, Ohio, and Hazel Crest, Illinois, both operate a preferred real estate agents program where agents who successfully complete municipally sponsored training seminars are certified to participate in the city's home sales referral program and are included in ongoing promotional literature (Engstrom 1983:19, 97). Cleveland Heights built on this program to establish its cooperative Preferred Realty Office program, which certifies real estate agents and apartment building managers to participate in affirmative marketing activities. "Through a variety of promotional services, these companies will be recommended to prospective homeseekers and to residents who wish to sell their homes" (Cleveland Heights City Council Resolution 26, 1976, as amended December 3, 1979).

Some communities and private organizations have offered financial incentives to help build white demand in integrated neighborhoods and black demand in virtually all-white communities. Examples of such programs are (Obermanns and Quereau 1989:7):

- The Fund for the Future of Shaker Heights, sponsored by the Shaker Heights Community Services Department. With more than $300,000 provided by local foundations and private donations, the program offers 6 percent deferred payment loans of up to $4000 for downpayments or to buy down mortgage interest rates, and loans of up to $4,800 to be applied to monthly mortgage payments. Repayment of these loans is deferred for five years (Husock 1989:11).

71

- The East Suburban Housing Fund, run by the East Suburban Housing Service of the East Suburban Council for Open Communities and established by three cities and two school districts in the Cleveland area in 1983, offers five-year, deferred payment loans of up to $3000 to black households who purchase a home in the nearby predominantly white community.
- Cleveland Heights and University Heights joined ranks to establish the Heights Fund in 1987 for encouraging pro-integrative moves by blacks and whites throughout these two cities and the Hillcrest suburban region. Low-interest loans to be used for closing costs, points, and/or a portion of the downpayment are made available.[18]

A variety of other mortgage-based incentive programs exist elsewhere (Ohio Housing Finance Agency 1988; Keating 1985:5; Husock 1989:13).

LEGAL ACTION

When real estate brokers and rental agents continue to steer or lenders still insist on redlining despite all the education, public relations, regulatory, and lobbying actions a community undertakes, then legal action may be the last resort. While all the lawsuits under the Fair Housing Act have failed to make much of a dent in housing discrimination (Sanders 1988:882), lawsuits can be effective on a "micro" scale.

DELIVERY OF PUBLIC SERVICES

It is vital that a municipality maintain or increase the level of services it provides integrated neighborhoods. Otherwise, white demand will almost surely falter as residents and housing prospects see one of the assumed results of black in-migration—deteriorating city services or property maintenance—appear. With their greater choices, whites can simply move. With their more restricted choices, blacks cannot.

Not all residents of the community will find a reduction in services disturbing. As was learned when South Shore was resegregating, even after the levels of city services and building maintenance were reduced in the integrating neighborhood, new black residents considered them to be higher than the levels they received in the ghetto (Molotch 1972:103–104). Hence, while reduced services and property maintenance discourage whites from the integrated neighborhood's housing market, it may not have the same effect on blacks who are leaving the ghetto.

Conclusions: Essential Strategies

Preserving racial diversity requires a two-pronged strategy to (1) immediately maintain a sufficient level of white demand to keep the community stably integrated, while at the same time (2) pursuing the long-term effort to replace the dual housing market with a single, unitary market process. No single tactic will implement these strategies. Not every implementation strategy or tool described above is necessarily effective or even appropriate for every racially diverse community.

There are, however, a number of techniques that a quarter of a century of experience has shown are absolutely essential to short- and long-term success:

Whatever is done, it must start early before any neighborhood becomes racially identifiable.

Integrate the public schools systemwide well before any schools are racially identifiable.

Both municipal government and public school officials must offer strong, vocal support for diversity at an early stage.

An aggressive community organization that adopts the goal of racial diversity before any neighborhood becomes racially identifiable is essential.

Develop and implement a coordinated and comprehensive plan for achieving and preserving diversity.

Educate, persuade, cajole, and, if necessary, threaten local real estate brokers and rental agents to market affirmatively. Make them aware that they can make a fine living this way.

Establish both a local and subregional housing service center.

Plan and implement a public relations program to build the community's image.

Maintain a high level of services to all neighborhoods within the jurisdictions.

Implement an aggressive housing and building code enforcement program with financial assistance for repair or rehabilitation, particularly in communities with an old housing stock.

Collect racial data from real estate and rental agents to spot trends and identify violations of local ordinances and the Fair Housing Act.

Do not allow any new public housing to be built in or close to the racially diverse neighborhood.

Foster economic development.

Coordinate racial diversity efforts with other racially diverse communities to attack the dual housing market at the subregional and metropolitan levels.

New Directions in Research, Strategy, and Policy

While researchers know that these techniques are vital to preserving diversity, and why so many neighborhoods resegregate, more information is needed to gauge the actual extent of discrimination and devise more effective local, regional, and national strategies to alleviate the unnatural pressures on racially diverse communities that force them to take extraordinary measures to preserve their diversity. Steps that need to be taken include:

1. *Conducting a systematic, multidisciplinary study of racially-diverse communities.* This chapter has only been able to touch the surface of all the efforts a growing number of communities have taken to achieve and preserve diversity. Some of these communities have remained stably integrated for over twenty years. A thorough, systematic, and multidisciplinary study of stable, racially diverse communities that compares them to analogous communities that resegregated would enable researchers to determine why certain techniques have worked for some communities but not for others.

2. *Developing research and action models for altering institutional and governmental impediments to racial diversity.* Institutional and governmental practices and policies that cause or hamper efforts to preserve racially diverse communities must be changed. For example, the predominant practices of real estate institutions are major factors that cause resegregation. There is a crying need to reduce the intense segregation in real estate brokering. Programs should be implemented not only to promote greater African-American participation in real estate brokering but also to encourage white-owned real estate firms to hire black agents and black-owned firms to hire white brokers. Incentives should be offered to

brokers who promote pro-integrative moves. More effective enforcement of laws that prohibit steering and blockbusting is essential. It is vital that all Americans have equal access to housing market information. If the real estate industry won't do it, an institutional structure must be developed to disseminate housing market information in a nondiscriminatory manner. Fair housing councils can play this role.

3. *Developing a plan to rebuild a political constituency for racial diversity.* Government support for racial diversity will not come by merely appealing to the public's rectitude. A politically astute strategy must be developed to bring the issue to the forefront of public policy debate and rebuild a political constituency for racial diversity in housing, education, and employment. *Such a strategy includes effectively quantifying the costs of housing and school segregation.* In addition, it is essential to develop a public relations blitz to debunk the long-standing myths about housing and school integration that lead to the self-fulfilling prophecies that result in resegregation and its attendant problems.

All this research, though, will be for naught if there is no vehicle available to utilize it. A regional agency is needed to coordinate local and subregional fair housing service centers and adequate funding for all three levels is essential to preserving racial diversity in the long run. Lacking a major national constituency for the fair housing movement, resources for promoting racial diversity continue to be scarce. They must be used "more efficiently by significantly increasing the level of systematic monitoring of market practices, sharing of information, and targeting enforcement and other resources on the most important problems at any give period" (Orfield 1986:32).

An ongoing, staffed agency is needed to coordinate these efforts and others on the metropolitan level.

While such an agency would not supplant existing local fair housing organizations, it would coordinate their efforts in such arenas as auditing. It should also serve as the main public relations vehicle for the fair housing movement. Education and training are vital for many of the players in the housing market. This regional agency should develop training in fair housing and racial diversity for newspaper, magazine, television, and radio reporters and editors. The regional agency should build upon the existing affirmative marketing training for real estate brokers, rental agents, and lenders already conducted by municipal and subregional open housing agencies. It should facilitate communication between the subregions.

There is also a need to identify new funding sources for fair housing centers. Existing funding and staffing are clearly inadequate. There is a need for new housing service centers in the outer ring suburbs where most new jobs and the most desirable new housing are being created (Orfield 1986:33). In addition to using existing funding sources, both the proposed regional agency and existing fair housing agencies need to tap the business community for funding. In many cities, when the business community discovered how the low quality of the public education was leaving them with a shrinking qualified work force, businesses started pouring hundreds of thousands of dollars into public school reform. Similarly, if the business community can discover how much continuing American "apartheid" is costing business, its coffers could be tapped on behalf of open housing and racial diversity efforts.

For over twenty years, Oak Park and Park Forest, Illinois, and Shaker Heights, University Heights, and Cleveland Heights, Ohio, have proved that black in-migration into a previously all-white community does not inevitably lead to any of the myths associated with integrated communities. These municipalities and others in a growing number of cities are demonstrating that racial diversity can be achieved and preserved as long as the community and local government view integration as an opportunity, not a problem, and they take the steps necessary to overcome the pressures to resegregate generated by the dual housing market and all the institutional, cultural, governmental, and individual factors that continue to prop it up. Until this dual market is replaced with a single, unitary housing market in which all Americans participate, communities that have the opportunity to integrate will have to take extraordinary steps to overcome these extraordinary forces.

Until America builds an unitary housing market, the debilitating and costly cycle of the ghetto will continue, the black underclass will continue to grow and become more permanent, and the nation's limited resources will continue to be fruitlessly drained to deal with a problem that would not continue were it not for the deeply ingrained racial prejudice that has shaped local, state, and national housing policy in the twentieth century.

NOTES

1. The emphasis in this chapter will be on *preserving* racial diversity rather than on *desegregation*. Recent controversies, such as the events surrounding housing

desegregation battles in Yonkers, New York, in the past few years, will not be discussed directly. This is not to say that desegregation efforts are not important; they are critical to the development of diversity. However, given the limited space available in this book and the limited amount of information on how to maintain diversity in communities where some degree of integration already exists, I will not provide a detailed analysis of the dynamics of desegregation.

This chapter does not examine the situation where wealthier whites move into a poor, virtually all-black neighborhood and eventually displace the black residents through the process known as gentrification. Although significant, this type of resegregation is based largely on economics and not race. The discussion of gentrification elsewhere in this book addresses some of the problems produced by it.

2. For example, despite its best efforts, Chicago's South Shore community was unable to preserve its diversity in the 1960s even though it never experienced any white flight or panic selling. It underwent nearly complete racial change simply through a process of stable property turnover in which virtually all home buyers and new renters were black. As long as housing demand is nearly exclusively black and discriminatory practices in the sale and rental of housing continue, resegregation seems inevitable even in stable neighborhoods like South Shore (Molotch 1972:171–173, 205).

3. For a quarter of a century, Article 34 of the Code of Ethics of the National Association of Real Estate Boards (NAREB) provided: "A realtor should never be instrumental in introducing into a neighborhood a character of property or occupancy, members of any race or nationality, or any individual whose presence will clearly be detrimental to property values in the neighborhood."

4. The courses and institutes sponsored by the Society of Real Estate Appraisers and the American Institute of Real Estate Appraisers that shape the decision-making process appraisers use called for them to downgrade property in racially integrated communities even as late as the 1970s (Onderdonk et al. 1977:44–45; Saltman 1978:28–29).

5. Withdrawing credit for mortgages or home improvement loans for racial or socioeconomic reasons that have nothing to do with the bona fide qualifications of borrowers is known as redlining and is illegal under both federal and state fair housing laws (Obermanns 1989:1).

6. Complaints are generally filed with the city's community relations director, who administers the law and monitors real estate activities. If conciliation fails, a formal hearing under due process standards is conducted, usually by the local human relations commission or fair housing review board. The fair housing ordinance can empower this hearing body to require remedial measures and impose fines (Engstrom 1983:9). Racially integrated municipalities in the Chicago area that have adopted a fair housing ordinance include Calumet Park, Chicago, Evanston, Glenwood, Hazel Crest, Homewood, Matteson, Oak Park, Park Forest, and University Park. Both the Oak Park and Park Forest ordinances were adopted before Congress enacted the federal Fair Housing Act of 1968 (Engstrom 1983:97). In Ohio, racially diverse Shaker Heights, Cleveland Heights, and University heights have enacted and implemented fair housing ordinances.

7. In 1989, U. S. District Court Judge Harry Leinenweber found the anti-solicitation ordinances of the Illinois municipalities of Country Club Hills, Glenwood, Hazel Crest, Matteson, and Park Forest unconstitutional as applied to some realtors' mailings as violations of constitutionally protected free speech and due process, but not a violation of the Fair Housing Act. By effectively banning all mailings from realtors, the ordinances went too far. Judge Leinenweber found that the municipalities' interests in preventing blockbusting and panic peddling "clearly could be met by a much less restrictive ordinance: the banning of solicitations actually seeking to induce the sale, rental or listing of a dwelling. . ." (*South Suburban Housing Center v. Board of Realtors*, 713 F.Supp. 1068, 1095 [1989]).

8. Some cities have provided money to pay part of the cost of rehabilitating apartment buildings. In return, a portion of the units must be reserved for low- and moderate-income households for three years (Village of Oak Park 1979:12). Such rehabilitation programs often increase rents beyond the reach of the of low- or moderate-income households who lived in the units before rehabilitation. This problem can be mitigated by converting rehabilitated apartments to limited-equity cooperatives or placing their ownership in the hands of a mutual housing association. In Oak Park, where a local government agency has bought and rehabilitated a great number of apartment buildings, conversion to limited-equity cooperatives could be achieved quite easily.

9. In its first twelve years, only 156 homeowners have even registered for the Equity Assurance Program. Most of the owners who have registered live in the village's overwhelmingly white northwest quadrant. Very few who lived in the southeast section where blacks were most heavily concentrated chose to participate. "By the time we adopted the ordinance, few people needed it as a security blanket," explains Community Relations Director Sherlynn Reid. "We had openly discussed equity assurance for four years first. During that time realtors learned they could make money selling to both blacks and whites and residents had already developed a sense of confidence about Oak Park." No claim has ever been made (Reid 1988).

10. Municipalities in the Chicago area that have adopted a racial diversity statement include Calumet Park, Glenwood, Hazel Crest, Matteson, Oak Park, Park Forest, Richton Park, and University Park. University Heights, Cleveland Heights, and Shaker Heights have adopted racial diversity statements. Over thirty-one Cleveland-area municipalities have adopted fair housing resolutions or proclamations, but few have publicized them. Without touting them, they can do little to promote racial diversity (Obermanns and Quereau 1989:5).

11. Leaders in Oak Park, Illinois, where the elementary school district and village share the same boundaries, have long recognized the role its public schools play in maintaining racial diversity. The village's Racial Diversity Task Force has noted, "As long as a dual housing market exists, District 97 will continue to bear a major responsibility for maintenance of racial diversity in this village" (Task-Force on Racial Diversity 1984:8). Even during the early days of integration, Oak Park leaders recognized that its schools had to adjust to accommodate racial and socioeconomic changes. In 1974, elementary school teachers began intensive

training at the National College of Education to prepare them to teach an economically and racially mixed student population. According to the district's hiring manual, teachers are also required to take training in human relations and appreciation of cultural differences (Lauber 1974:15). Patterns of racially unbalanced enrollment emerged in the early 1970s as larger proportions of African-Americans moved into the village's heavily rental east end. In 1976, the school district reorganized the schools to create two junior highs in central locations and adjusted elementary school boundaries to achieve racial diversity in every school. Before reorganization, the percentage of minority students ranged from 6.1 to 33.6 percent. Reorganization reduced the spread to 11.7 to 22.8 in 1981 (Raymond 1982:89). As the proportion of black children grew, the district readjusted boundaries again to preserve systemwide racial diversity. At the beginning of 1988, when the racial composition of the village was 80 percent white and 16 percent black, Oak Park's elementary student body was 66 percent white and 26.5 percent black. Schools ranged from 20.4 percent to 44.7 percent black, with most around 35 percent. Community relations director Sherlynn Reid notes that there has been no movement of white children to private schools. Only 276 of the 1882 students in the village's three private schools live in Oak Park (Reid 1988). Although school districts serving Oak Park and Park Forest have reorganized to facilitate racial diversity, no Illinois school district has become as closely involved with local governments in preserving racial diversity as in the Cleveland area.

12. Realtors in Montclair, N.J., report that the elimination of neighborhood schools resulted in opening up the entire town, and city staff report that neighborhoods have been reintegrated (Obermanns and Oliver 1988:125). Replacing neighborhood schools with grade centers having district-wide attendance is a more productive alternative to establishing magnet schools and retaining neighborhood schools. Not only does the latter fail to solve the problems caused by neighborhood schools, but far too many magnet schools skim off the best students and leave the neighborhood schools resegregated socioeconomically. Systemwide school integration gets much of the credit for the successful stability of racially diverse neighborhoods in Indianapolis, Milwaukee, Denver, Nashville, Rochester, and the West Mt. Airy neighborhood in Philadelphia (Saltman 1978:626). In the Chicago and Cleveland areas, suburbs like Oak Park, Park Forest, and Shaker Heights, have desegregated their schools systems as part of their comprehensive racial diversity strategies.

13. In Illinois, Hazel Crest and Matteson have adopted ordinances to require developers to affirmatively market their new construction ownership and rental housing. A building permit cannot be issued until the village approves the developer's affirmative marketing plan (Engstrom 1983:11, 97). Affirmative marketing practices were upheld in *South Suburban Housing Center v. Board of Realtors*, 713 F.Supp. 1069, 1086.

14. Chicago-area housing centers include local centers in Bellwood and Oak Park. Regional and subregional centers include the South Suburban Housing Center (which serves Calumet Park, Chicago, Country Club Hills, Glenwood, Hazel Crest, Matteson, and University Park, among others), HOPE (serving

DuPage County), Minority Economic Resource Corporation (northwest suburbs), Northwest Indiana Fair Housing Center, SER/Lake County (Illinois), North Suburban Housing Center, Near West Suburban Housing Center (in Westchester, serving western Cook County suburbs), and the Leadership Council for Metropolitan Open Communities (Fischer 1986). Housing centers in the Cleveland area include those in Shaker Heights, Cleveland Heights, and University Heights, and the more regional and subregional Cuyahoga Plan's Housing Information Service and East Suburban Council for Open Communities (Obermanns and Quereau 1989:3).

15. For example, both Matteson and Glenwood require real estate brokers to submit a monthly report that identifies the race of home seekers and the addresses of the properties they were shown, the addresses of homes prospects offered to purchase, and the address of the home if ultimately bought. The realtors are required to keep a record of the name, address, and phone number of each prospect that is available to the village on request (*South Suburban Housing Center v. Board of Realtors*, 713 F.Supp. 1068, 1096–1097 [1989]). The ordinances require strict confidentiality in the use of the data, precisely define and limit access to the information, and impose substantial penalties for any violation (*ibid.* at 1098). These practices were upheld in Judge Harry Leinenweber's decision, cited earlier.

16. Chicago suburbs that have used seller's registers include Glenwood, Hazel Crest, Matteson, Richton Park, and University Park (Engstrom 1983:98). Some communities have used selling experience interviews as an alternative to seller's registers, which are difficult to administer. This tool has been used mostly in neighborhoods with the greatest potential for rapid change. Municipal fair housing staff work closely with homeowners' groups to generate resident interest and participation. Longer than the seller's register form, selling experience interviews ask more specific questions about the how long a home has been on the market, whether the sales agent mentioned there would be any difficulties selling the home, and what types of financing were suggested. Residents have generally been cooperative (Engstrom 1983:17).

17. In 1977, Park Forest produced a very comprehensive plan, Integration in Housing: A Plan for Racial Diversity (Onderdonk et al. 1977), that analyzed the causes of residential resegregation and established a set of goals, objectives, and policies to remedy them. Other jurisdictions have adopted less thorough plans for racial diversity. In 1973, Oak Park's Community Relations Commission established "The Fourteen Points" (Lauber 1974:15), and Cleveland Heights formally adopted "The Nine-Point Plan" in 1976, to guide their respective diversity efforts.

18. Loan applicants must (1) be racially underrepresented in the census tract where the property is located; (2) qualify for a mortgage loan with a mortgage financing institution; (3) have at least 5 percent of unborrowed money for the down payment; and (4) occupy the house as his/her principal place of residence.

REFERENCE LIST

Alexander, Robert C., and Mary K. Nenno. 1974. *A Local Housing Assistance Plan: A NAHRO Guidebook.* Washington, D.C.: National Association of Housing and Redevelopment Officials.

American Institute of Real Estate Appraisers. 1977. *Affirmative Action Program.* Chicago: American Institute of Real Estate Appraisers.

———. 1973. *The Appraisal of Real Estate.* Chicago: American Institute of Real Estate Appraisers.

Bier, Thomas, and Ivan Maric. 1985. *High-Risk Mortgage Lending in Cuyahoga County, Ohio, 1983.* Cleveland: Cleveland State University. September.

Brune, Tom. 1979. "Realtors Challenge Suburban Integration Maintenance Laws; Nation Debates Housing Policy Goal; Black Groups Split." *The Chicago Reporter* 8(5):1,4–6.

Comarow, Avery. 1973. "It Pays to Stay When Blacks Move In." *Money,* November.

Day, Ralph. 1982. *Housing Price Appreciation and Race in Cuyahoga County.* Cleveland: Cuyahoga Plan of Ohio.

de Marco, Donald. 1982. "Promoting and Preserving Racial Residential Diversity: The Park Forest Case." *Housing: Chicago Style—A Consultation.* Chicago: Illinois Advisory Committee to the U.S. Commission on Civil Rights.

———. 1989. *"Pro-Integrative Policy and Program."* Testimony presented to Cleveland Community Relations Board.

de Vise, Pierre. 1973. *"Integration in the Suburbs—Who Needs It? From a Fair Share to a Fair Shake in Open Housing Plans for the Suburbs of Chicago."* Working Paper II.17, Chicago Regional Hospital Study.

East Suburban Council for Open Communities. 1989. *Annual Report 1988.* Lyndhurst, Ohio: East Suburban Council for Open Communities.

Engstrom, James. 1983. *"Municipal Fair Housing Notebook: A Description of Local Ordinances, Tools, and Strategies for Promoting a Unitary Housing Market."* Park Forest, Ill.: Fair Housing Legal Action Committee.

Fischer, Paul. 1986. "Twenty Years Later: An Organization Assessment of Fair Housing in Metropolitan Chicago," in *Fair Housing in Metropolitan Chicago: Perspectives after Two Decades,* edited by Gary Orfield. Chicago: Chicago Area Fair Housing Alliance.

Galster, George. 1990. "Racial Steering in Urban Housing Markets: A Review of the Audit Evidence." *Review of Black Political Economy* 18:105–129.

Grayson, George W., and Cindy L. Wedel. 1968. "Open Housing: How to Get around the Law." *New Republic,* June 22.

Hartmann, David. 1986. "Race Ethnic Composition of the Chicago SMSA: Post-Census Estimates Using Annual Birth and Death Data," in *Fair Housing in Metropolitan Chicago: Perspectives After Two Decades,* edited by Gary Orfield. Chicago: Chicago Area Fair Housing Alliance.

81

Heights Fund. 1987. *The Heights Fund: An Incentive Mortgage Program Designed to Maintain Integration in the Cities of Cleveland Heights and University Heights, Ohio.* Cleveland Heights, Ohio: Heights Fund.

Hellman, Peter. 1988. "A Dilemma Grows in Brooklyn: Starrett City Fights to Keep Its Quotas and Its Racial Mix." *New York*, October 17.

Helper, Rose. 1969. *Racial Policies and Practices of Real Estate Brokers.* Minneapolis: University of Minnesota.

Henderson, Harold. 1987. "Color Coordination: The Southern Suburbs' Fair-Housing Quagmire." *Chicago Reader* 16(38):1, 24–26, 30–34.

Hirsch, Arnold R. 1983. *Making the Second Ghetto: Race and Housing in Chicago, 1940–1960.* New York: Cambridge University Press.

Husock, Howard. 1989. *"Integration Initiatives" in Suburban Cleveland.* Cambridge, Mass.: Kennedy School of Government Case Program.

Keating, W. Dennis. 1989. *"Open Housing in Metropolitan Cleveland: Twenty Years after the Kerner Commission and the Fair Housing Act."* Baltimore: Urban Affairs Association Conference.

Lauber, Daniel. 1974. "Integration Takes More Than a Racial Quota." *Planning*, April–May, pp. 14–17.

———. 1975a. "Social Planning, Vancouver," in *Planning.* March/April.

———. 1975b. "The housing act & discrimination," in *Planning.* February.

———. 1976. "Socially Informed Planning and Decision Making: Some Preliminary Ideas." *Intergovernmental Planning, Approaches to the "No Growth" vs. "Growth is Good" Dilemma.* Urbana, Ill.: Bureau of Urban and Regional Planning Research.

———. 1977. "HCD: An Evaluation of the First Three Years." Iowa State University.

Lauber, Diana, and G. Alfred Hess. 1985. *Dropouts from the Chicago Public Schools: An Analysis of the Classes of 1982–1983–1984.* 2d ed. Chicago: Chicago Panel on Public School Policy and Finance.

Laurenti, Luigi M. 1972. *Property Values and Race.* Berkeley: University of California Press.

McCourt, Kathleen, and Philip Nyden. 1986. "Finding Housing in Non-Traditional Communities: The Client's Perspective," in *Fair Housing in Metropolitan Chicago: Perspectives After Two Decades,* edited by Gary Orfield. Chicago: Chicago Area Fair Housing Alliance.

Molotch, Harvey. 1972. *Managed Integration: Dilemmas of Doing Good in the City.* Berkeley: University of California Press.

Moore, Barbara. 1989. Telephone interview with Barbara Moore, Director of Community Relations, Village of Park Forest, Illinois, August.

Murphy, Margaret. 1977. *"A Study of Concentrated FHA Activity in Cuyahoga County and Its Impact on Racial Segregation."* Cleveland: Housing Advocates.

Myers, Linnet. 1989. "It's a Crime: Town Al Capone Adopted Tries to Overcome an Image." *Chicago Tribune*, August 12.

National Committee against Discrimination in Housing. 1970. *Jobs and*

Housing: A Study of Employment and Housing Opportunities for Racial Minorities in Suburban Areas of the New York Metropolitan Region. Interim Report. New York: National Committee against Discrimination in Housing.

National Institute of Health. 1986. *Project Concern.* Washington, D.C.: National Institute of Health.

Nelson, Kathryn P. 1979. *Recent Suburbanization of Blacks: How Much, Who, and Where?* Washington, D.C.: HUD Office of Policy Development and Research.

Nelson, Phyllis I. 1985. *Marketing Your Housing Complex in 1985.* Homewood, Ill.: South Suburban Housing Center.

North, William D. 1978. *Statement of William D. North on Behalf of the National Association of Realtors concerning H.R. 3504 Fair Housing Amendments Act of 1977 before the Housing Judiciary Committee Subcommittee on Civil and Constitutional Rights.* Washington, D.C.: National Association of Realtors.

Obermanns, Richard. 1989. *Race and Mortgage Lending in Cleveland, 1985.* Cleveland: Cuyahoga Plan of Ohio.

Obermanns, Richard, and Louisa Oliver. 1988. *New Dimensions in School and Housing Desegregation Policy for Ohio.* Cleveland: Cuyahoga Plan of Ohio.

Obermanns, Richard, and Gay Quereau. 1989. *Municipal Approaches to Fair Housing in Greater Cleveland.* Cleveland: Cuyahoga Plan.

Ohio Housing Finance Agency. 1988. *Policy Statement on Fair Housing Policy and Integrated Communities.*

Onderdonk, Dudley, Donald DeMarco, and Kathy Cardona. 1977. *Integration in Housing: A Plan for Racial Diversity.* Park Forest, Ill.: Planning Division.

Orfield, Gary, editor. 1986. *Fair Housing in Metropolitan Chicago: Perspectives after Two Decades.* Chicago: Chicago Area Fair Housing Alliance.

Perry, John. 1983. Memorandum to President and Board of Trustees. Subject: Data Collection. September 8.

Peterman, William, and Kim Hunt. 1986. "Fair Housing Audit Inventory for Metropolitan Chicago." In Orfield, 1986.

Rabin, Yale. 1987. "The Roots of Segregation in the Eighties: The Role of Local Government Actions," in *Divided Neighborhoods,* edited by Gary Tobin. Beverly Hills: Sage.

Raymond, Roberta. 1982. "Racial Diversity: A Model for American Communities," in *Housing: Chicago Style—a Consultation.* Chicago: Illinois Advisory Committee to the U.S. Commission on Civil Rights.

Reid, Sherlynn. 1988. Interview conducted June 27.

Richie, Winston H. 1989. "Ohio Should Push Housing Integration." *The Plain Dealer,* January 18.

Roosevelt Center for American Policy Studies. 1989. *Old Doctrines vs. New Threats: Citizens Look at Defense Spending and National Security.* Washington, D.C.: Roosevelt Center for American Policy Studies.

Saltman, Juliet. 1978. *Open Housing: Dynamics of a Social Movement.* New York: Praeger Publishers.

———. 1990. *A Fragile Management: The Struggle for Neighborhood Stabilization*. New York: Greenwood Press.

Saunders, Richard H. 1988. "Individual Rights and Demographic Realities: The Problem of Fair Housing." *Northwestern University Law Review* 82(3), 874–939.

Shlay, Anne B. 1986."Credit on Color-Segregation, Racial Transition, and Housing Credit Flows," in Orfield, 1986.

Slayton, Robert A. 1986. "An Accepted Member of the Community," in Orfield, 1986.

South Suburban Housing Center. 1988. *An Audit of the Real Estate Sales and Rental Markets of Selected Southern Suburbs*. Homewood, Ill.: South Suburban Housing Center.

Staton, Spenser, and Arthur Lyons. "Trends in Prices of Houses in Metropolitan Chicago Areas," in Orfield, 1986.

Task Force on Racial Diversity. 1984. *Report to the Board of Trustees, Village of Oak Park by the Racial Diversity Task Force*. Oak Park, Ill.: Task Force on Racial Diversity.

Tauber, K. E., and A. E. Tauber. 1965. *Negroes in Cities*. Chicago: Aldine.

U.S. Commission on Civil Rights. 1973. *Understanding Fair Housing*. Washington.

U.S. Commission on Civil Rights. 1979. *The Federal Fair Housing Enforcement Effort*. Washington: U.S. Commission on Civil Rights.

U.S. Department of Housing and Urban Development. 1979. *The Role of the Real Estate Sector in Neighborhood Change*. Washington: HUD Office of Policy Development and Research. 1979.

Village of Oak Park. *Comprehensive Plan 1979*. 1979. Oak Park, Ill.: Planning Department.

Williams, Kale, and Donald DeMarco. 1979. *"Affirmative Action in Housing: An Emerging Public Issue."* Unpublished draft. Chicago Leadership Council for Open Metropolitan Communities.

Daniel Lauber is an attorney, urban planning consultant, and publisher. In the past he has been a columnist for the *Chicago Sun-Times*, completed research for the Lawyers Committee for Better Housing (Chicago), and worked as a planner for the Village of Oak Park (Illinois) and the State of Illinois. He was the principal author of the award-winning Oak Park *Comprehensive Plan 1979* which dealt with preserving racial diversity in the village nationally known for its successful integration efforts. Much of his legal work has centered around housing issues, particularly advocacy for group homes for the developmentally disabled.

5 THE INVISIBLE LENDERS: THE ROLE OF RESIDENTIAL CREDIT IN COMMUNITY ECONOMIES   Jean Pogge and David Flax-Hatch

The practice of "redlining" was first identified and named in the late 1960s on the West Side of Chicago in the Austin neighborhood. Community residents struggling with school issues discovered that savings and loan associations, at the time the primary source of residential mortgages, had labeled Austin a declining neighborhood and actually drawn a red line around Austin and other neighborhoods on a city map. The lenders had decided the redlined areas were vulnerable to racial change and, therefore, not a good credit risk. The resulting limitations on the availability of residential credit became a self-fulfilling prophecy, residents could not easily sell or buy homes at normal market prices, prices fell, home improvement loans were not available, homes deteriorated, and finally, many residents sold their houses at a loss and moved out.

In response, Austin residents organized to fight for their neighborhood. In 1969, the Organization for a Better Austin (OBA), led by Gale Cincotta, joined with other West Side organizations to fight redlining. The West Side Coalition fought and won victories with local lenders to open access to residential credit. But the victories with individual lenders in Chicago were not enough to stop redlining because there was no information to monitor individual lender performance or to determine which other lenders might be redlining.

At the same time as Chicago residents were fighting redlining, residents of urban neighborhoods in other cities found that it was also a problem in their communities. In 1972, the First National Housing Conference was held to generate national attention and action on the housing problems in urban neighborhoods. From that conference, Cincotta, with organizer Shel Trapp, formed two national organizations: the National Training and Information Center (NTIC), to provide information and coordinate organizing efforts; and the National People's Action on Housing (NPA), to act as a national people's lobby on neighborhood issues. One of the earliest agenda items of NPA was to get Congress to make redlining illegal.

In 1975, Congress responded to the growing concern about urban disinvestment with the first of two federal laws designed to stop the practice of redlining. The Home Mortgage Disclosure Act (HMDA) of 1975 requires all banks, savings and loan associations, and credit unions with over $10 million in assets and located in an SMSA to disclose the number and dollar amount of their residential lending by census tract. This disclosure provides the information necessary to determine patterns of residential lending by banks and savings and loan associations. In 1977, Congress went a step further by passing the Community Reinvestment Act (CRA) that established the responsibility of each bank and savings and loan association to serve credit needs within its local community and to pay particular attention to the credit needs of low- and moderate-income residents of that community. These laws recognize the importance of credit in the health of neighborhood economies and the role credit plays in creating a stable neighborhood real estate market. The Community Reinvestment Act establishes reinvestment as a national policy objective and HMDA provides the tool for regulators and community organizations to monitor reinvestment performance by banks and savings and loan associations.

Today, around fifteen years since the passage of the HMDA, it is appropriate to examine what is known and has been written about residential lending trends and patterns and the influence of those patterns on neighborhoods. In the intervening time, the banking business has undergone enormous technological and regulatory change that has affected both the way residential credit is provided and the types of institutions that provide that credit. Now more than ever, it is critical to understand the flow of credit within communities and the role of lenders in regulating that flow.

Tracking the Lending of Banks and Savings and Loan Associations

The first attempt to collect and analyze information on the residential lending patterns of depository institutions was made in 1973 before the passage of HMDA by the Federal Home Loan Bank of Chicago. In response to continued pressure from Cincotta and the West Side Coalition, the Federal Home Loan Bank of Chicago sent a questionnaire to every savings and loan association in metropolitan Chicago requesting voluntary disclosure of the number and dollar amount of residential loans and the total amount of dollars in savings accounts by zip code for the period June 1972 to June 1973. One hundred and twenty-seven savings and loan associations responded to the voluntary survey.

There were clearly problems with the information disclosed: not all institutions complied with the Federal Home Loan Bank's request; it was difficult to draw neighborhood conclusions from zip code information; and the information was available only to the Federal Home Loan Bank that tabulated the results and protected the confidentiality of individual lenders. However, the results clearly demonstrated a pattern of disinvestment and evidence of redlining in older urban neighborhoods. For the first time, data from a large number of financial institutions showed that, despite an increase in deposits from residents of the city of Chicago, mortgage lending had decreased, particularly in those zip codes that had complained of redlining problems.

The second major study of residential lending patterns was an eight-city study done by NTIC in 1978, three years after the passage of HMDA and one year after the first HMDA data were publicly available (Przyblski 1978). Using HMDA data collected directly from individual banks and savings and loan associations, NTIC examined the geographic distribution of residential lending done by a sample of the largest financial institutions in eight cities across the country.

Again there were problems with the information disclosed: the information was not centrally available; it was not computerized; inconsistencies and errors in reporting by lenders were widespread; and many lenders reported lending information by both zip code and census tract within the same report. But once again, the analysis demonstrated a clear pattern of disinvestment by some banks and savings and loan associations within urban neighborhoods. NTIC found that large areas of each of the central cities studied received very few or no conventional mortgages and that the majority of conventional mortgages were concentrated in a few parts of each metropolitan area. In this study, demographic data on race and income were used for the first time to describe the characteristics of neighborhoods that were disinvested and their reinvested counterparts. It concluded that "disinvestment of an area appears in many cases (especially in Columbus, Chicago, and Oklahoma City) to be more closely related to racial characteristics than to income characteristics of neighborhoods."

HMDA was passed with a five-year life that could be extended only by Congress. The 1980 extension of HMDA included several improvements that had a positive effect on the availability and usability of the data. First, the extension legislation established municipal depository institutions within each SMSA that would receive HMDA data for all institutions within the SMSA from the federal regulators and make them publicly available. This change meant that community organizations and researchers no longer had to go to each institution to collect the data. Before this change, HMDA data collection required enormous effort. Although banks and savings and loan associations were required to make their HMDA data available to the public, it was often difficult to find anyone at the institution that knew about the law or where the data were kept. In addition, making the data publicly available did not mean that institutions routinely provided a copy. Many charged high rates for photocopies of the data and others refused copies, forcing the collector to copy the data by hand, an arduous task when involving a large lender.

The second significant change was a requirement that the federal regulators provide the municipal depositories aggregate data by census tract for all lenders within each SMSA. These data provided a benchmark by which individual lender performance could be measured. In addition, in order to compile aggregate HMDA data, the data from each lender had to be computerized. Beginning in 1980, the Federal Reserve Board began collecting HMDA data for all SMSAs in the country from regional bank regulators. The Federal Reserve computerized these data annually and prepared a tape of the data for distribution by the Federal Financial Institutions Council. Thus HMDA data within any SMSA could be analyzed and compared with computerized demographic data, aggregate lending patterns could be determined, and individual lender performance could be monitored.

The first analysis using HMDA data collected and computerized by the Federal Reserve under the 1980 amendments was the three-city, multi-year study done by Woodstock Institute that was released in 1985, 1986, and 1987. The Institute analyzed residential lending patterns for two or more years in Washington, D.C. (Shlay 1985a), Chicago (Pogge, Hoyt, and Revere 1986), and Denver (Pogge 1987). In each city, demographic information including income levels, number of single family and multi-family housing units, and age of housing stock were used to determine the influence of market characteristics on lending. Racial characteristics were also used to determine the correlation between race and residential lending.

The information used in this study was more complete and accurate than that available for previous studies. The results showed a pattern of disinvestment by banks and savings and loan associations in urban neighborhoods that could not be explained by normal market factors. The number of loans and the amount of loan dollars per housing unit in the older central cities was far less than that of the suburbs. Despite significant differences among the three cities in the age of the housing stock, the dynamics of the housing market and the percentage and concentrations of low-income and minority residents, each of the three cities demonstrated disparities between the number and amount of loans made in predominantly white areas and those areas with a higher proportion of black residents.

The level of analysis possible with computerized data allowed the institute study to draw detailed conclusions about the characteristics of census tracts that received varying amounts of lending from banks and savings and loan associations and to discover a correlation between race and lending in urban areas that had long been suspected but never conclusively demonstrated. Regression analysis of data from the Washington area demonstrated that, in the suburbs, income, a normal market factor that should influence the amount of residential lending, was the primary predictor of where loan dollars went. However, in the central city, income had almost no effect as a predictor of lending. Instead, the most important characteristic influencing lending in the central city was race. Those census tracts with the highest percentage of black residents received fewer loan dollars from banks and savings and loan associations regardless of other characteristics including income level, percentage of homeownership, or number of other single family homes.

In Chicago, the suburbs/city differential was very evident, as were differences between community areas which correlated with race. The suburbs received more loans of every type and more loan dollars than did the city—an average of $5,345 per housing unit compared to the city's $2,179 per housing unit. The thirty-three predominantly black and Hispanic communities fell in the two lowest categories of lending. Factors and characteristics normally considered indicators of demand, such as the number of single family housing units, owner occupancy levels, turnover, and income did not explain the disparities in lending levels.

The housing market in Denver was very different than that of the other two cities in the Woodstock study. During the period studied, 52 percent of the housing stock was less than fifteen years old. In addition, unlike the older cities of Chicago and Washington, new construction was happening throughout the suburbs and the central city. Denver had one other key difference: it did not have concentrations of poverty in its central city on the same scale as Chicago and Washington. In addition, blacks did not compose the majority of residents in any of the Denver metropolitan area census tracts.

The Denver study concluded that the disparity between city and suburbs was far less than in the other cities studied, although there were differences between neighborhoods. Despite the substantial difference in the concentration and level of income of black residents in Denver, examination of the racial characteristics of seven focus areas revealed that a clear and inverse relationship existed between the percentage of black residents within a focus area and the amount of residential lending from banks and savings and loan associations that the area received. Again, market forces could not explain this difference.

The most well publicized, recent analysis of residential lending patterns of banks and savings and loan associations was done in 1988 by the *Atlanta Constitution.* "The Color of Money" looked at bank and savings and loan association lending patterns in the Atlanta SMSA (Dedman 1988). It too reported huge disparities between lending in predominately white communities and lending in predominately blacks ones. Spurred by the Pulitzer Prize won by the reporter who wrote "The Color of Money," this series has become a model for other reporters to emulate, and several other newspapers across the country have reported on lending patterns in their communities.

Another key multicity analysis of residential lending is the fourteen-city study released by the Center for Community Change (CCC) (Center for Community Change 1989). Using computerized HMDA data, the CCC analyzed the residential lending patterns of banks and savings and loan associations in fourteen cities. This study also found a correlation between race and lending in each of the cities studied. CCC also moved the research process a step closer to the community level by developing the capacity to make the data for each city available to local community-based organizations on floppy disk. This innovation will make possible the kind of neighborhood-by-neighborhood analysis necessary to monitor reinvestment over time at the community level—something envisioned by community organizations when they first began fighting redlining.

In September 1989, a residential lending analysis of the city of Boston prepared by researchers at the Federal Reserve Bank of Boston was released (Bradbury, Case, and Dunham 1989). This study was not only the first major residential lending analysis conducted and publicly released by a banking regulatory agency but also provided analysis of data on nondepository lender loans and seller financing.

The Boston study used regression analysis to control for normal market factors that might influence lending. Its conclusion was that there was a substantial discrepancy in mortgage originations between white and black neighborhoods. This discrepancy was evident in the lending patterns of banks and savings and loan associations and in the lending patterns of nondepository lenders. The only source of mortgages that was more prevalent in black neighborhoods than in white neighborhoods was seller financing.

Since the first attempt to analyze residential lending patterns, this type of lending analysis has been used by community organizations to demonstrate the problem of disinvestment so that action to promote reinvestment could be taken. The Federal Home Loan Bank of Chicago's analysis was one of the factors that led to the passage of HMDA and CRA. The NTIC analysis led to renewal and strengthening of the HMDA. Later analysis has been used to formulate city and state policy on reinvestment and to negotiate CRA agreements with individual lenders.

The level of interest in reinvestment combined with criticism that CRA was not being effectively enforced by regulators led directly to Senate Banking Committee hearings in April 1988 on the effectiveness of the regulators in enforcing CRA. Since those hearings, regulatory enforcement of CRA has increased dramatically. There is evidence that for the first time banks and savings and loan associations are actively and aggressively marketing to community organizations and developing special lending programs to meet the unique needs of low- and moderate-income communities. This trend toward more effective enforcement of CRA was given a further push by an amendment to the CRA passed in the S&L bailout bill in the fall of 1989. This amendment requires that the regulatory agencies' rating and assessment of each bank's CRA performance be available to the public effective July 1, 1990. The fear of bad publicity from a poor rating has heightened banker interest in strengthening their reinvestment performance.

Unfortunately, just as banks and savings and loan associations have begun to take CRA seriously, a major shift in the way that residential lending is done is under way. In 1979, Congress deregulated interest rates on deposit accounts and liberalized restrictions on the kind of loans that savings and loan associations could make. The resulting competition for deposits combined with sometimes wild and unpredictable loan interest rate swings has made the management of the interest rate match between loans and deposits a difficult and unrewarding task. One key response by financial institutions has been to move away from making mortgages funded by deposits to making mortgages that are quickly sold on the secondary market to investors.

During the process of this change, mortgage banking firms have been able to be flexible in moving money from region to region and use their experience with the secondary market to increase their market share and to compete head-on with S&Ls and banks in the most profitable markets. With the current savings and loan crisis threatening to put many savings and loan associations out of business, the mortgage banker share of the residential mortgage market is bound to increase even more. It now seems clear that the model of a mortgage banking firm, either as a stand-alone corporation or as a subsidiary of a holding company including bank and thrift holding companies, will be the standard delivery mechanism for the provision of residential mortgage credit in the future.

MORTGAGE BANKERS—OPPORTUNITY OR THREAT

The emerging importance of mortgage bankers as residential lenders promises to have an effect on the availability of mortgage credit in all types of communities. Because of the ease with which mortgage bankers can enter and leave particular markets and their dependence on Wall Street for capital to fund loans, there is no guarantee that the future supply of credit from mortgage bankers will be constant or competitively priced. Analysis of regional trends in mortgage banker lending indicates that mortgage bankers enter only those markets that promise significant volume and leave markets that are experiencing economic slowdowns. What this means for low- and moderate-income and minority communities is not clear. In the past, mortgage bankers have played a prominent role as a source of FHA/VA mortgage loans in these communities. However, the experience in some communities with inadequate underwriting of borrowers by mortgage bankers has raised the question of whether mortgage bankers are able to serve credit needs appropriately.

Little research has been done to analyze the lending patterns of mortgage bankers or to trace how economic factors and the opening of new markets affect either the quantity or quality of their lending in disinvested communities. Because mortgage banker lending is not tied to either office location or deposit solicitation, the amount of marketing and lending they do in particular communities is based solely on their assessment of the quantity and profitability of business within those communities. Whenever other communities, states, or regions offer better profit opportunities, it can be assumed that the pattern of mortgage banker lending will reflect those opportunities. This could have significant results for low- and moderate-income communities. The effect on black communities, already shown to be receiving less residential credit from banks and savings and loan associations, could be even more serious. The linkage of mortgage credit to secondary market underwriting and loan pool standardization requirements and to the preferences of securities traders raises additional concerns about the future availability of mortgage credit for urban communities.

Research in Chicago provides evidence to support these concerns. Since 1985, Woodstock Institute has annually released a *Community Lending Fact Book* that provides information on the number and dollar amount of residential loans made by banks, savings and loan associations, and mortgage bankers. In the majority of communities that have predominantly minority populations, mortgage banker lending has exceeded that of bank and savings and loan association lending combined. However, the percentage share of mortgage banker lending in minority communities has not increased over the four years, even though the percentage share of mortgage banker lending in white communities has increased.

While access to residential credit is critical to the maintenance of a viable neighborhood economy, mortgage banker lending has been a mixed benefit to black communities. Beginning in the 1970s, there has been a continuing problem with foreclosures in many black communities as a result of sloppy or fraudulent underwriting by mortgage banking firms. Often used as the lenders of first choice by unscrupulous realtors fostering panic peddling and rapid racial change, some mortgage bankers have profited by making FHA/VA mortgages to unqualified borrowers. Mortgage bankers profit on each mortgage loan transaction they complete, which includes loan originations, servicing, and foreclosure. They have no financial or institutional stake in the communities where they lend, so many look to increase the volume of transactions to increase profit, even if it means abandoned and boarded-up homes as a result.

Both the Roseland and Austin communities in Chicago demonstrate the results of inadequate mortgage underwriting. Both are predominantly black communities that have received vast amounts of residential credit from mortgage bankers and have seen home after home become abandoned because of foreclosure. Sometimes these foreclosures have happened as soon as three months of the date the loan was made. According to the Chicago Roseland Coalition for Community Control, a community-based organization that provides foreclosure counseling services and monitors foreclosure and abandonment in the Roseland community, there are currently over one hundred foreclosed and abandoned houses in Roseland, owned by HUD, caused by foreclosures. These boarded-up houses demoralize community residents, bring property values down, and serve as havens for criminals.

Despite the importance of mortgage bankers in low- and moderate-income and minority communities, little analysis has been done of their lending patterns. This is primarily because of the scarcity of accurate, computerized data on mortgage banker loans at the census tract level. It is also because mortgage bankers are difficult to see. They do not have offices in communities, they market almost exclusively to realtors who refer borrowers to them. In addition, not all mortgage bankers service the loans they make and, as a result, have no continuing contact with the borrower after the loan is made.

The following sections of this chapter describe the emerging role of mortgage bankers in the residential lending market; the availability and quality of data for studying residential lending including mortgage banker residential lending and, in the conclusion, a discussion of the research agenda for the 1990s.

MORTGAGE BANKERS IN THE RESIDENTIAL LENDING MARKET

When a potential home buyer finds the right house, the next step is to find the right lender for a mortgage loan. There are some situations where the right lender is the seller. In those situations, the seller agrees to finance the sale of the house, and the house is sold on contract. But most often, the home buyer needs to find an institutional lender to finance the purchase.

There are three basic types of institutional lenders that make single family mortgage loans: savings and loan associations, commercial banks, and mortgage bankers. Savings and loan associations were created by Congress in the 1930s to provide long-term mortgage financing for individual home buyers. They were given preferential operating status under federal law in recognition of their unique mission. This preferred status has been diminished somewhat with the deregulation of interest rates that began in 1980. However, in the years since their creation, savings and loan associations have originated the vast majority of home mortgages and, despite the well-publicized problems of the S&L industry, they continue to be the leading originators of single family mortgage loans.

Although commercial banks have always been able to make single family mortgages, residential lending has never been a large part of their business. However, with the recent rise in prominence of the secondary mortgage market, many commercial banks have increased their single family mortgage originations, often through mortgage banking subsidiaries that operate in much the same manner as independent mortgage bankers.

Mortgage banking firms specialize in originating single family mortgages for sale to investors. They are intermediary institutions that do not accept deposits but instead serve as a link to the funds controlled by major capital accumulators like insurance companies and pension funds.

Mortgage banking companies are not new to the mortgage credit market. They first developed in the latter half of the nineteenth century, in conjunction with the industrial growth of major cities on the east coast and the simultaneous expansion into the western United States. Surplus capital accumulated in the East was used to fund loans to home buyers, farmers, and businesses in the West. Mortgage bankers were the major conduit for this investment capital. The lack of truly national banks or savings associations that could do business across state lines made mortgage bankers an important link in the residential credit market of that day.

Today, mortgage bankers continue to serve as intermediaries between investors and borrowers. Mortgage bankers use corporate capital or bank loans to fund mortgages that they quickly sell either to private investors or to one of the federal mortgage agencies such as GNMA or FNMA. They make a profit on the fees charged to borrowers. After selling their mortgages, mortgage bankers often continue to "service" these mortgages for the investor by collecting payments of principal, interest, taxes, and insurance, in exchange for a fee.

Mortgage bankers rely on a network of relationships with realtors and mortgage brokers to identify borrowers. Mortgage brokers, who are often realtors, receive commissions for each mortgage they assist in arranging for a mortgage banker. To a large degree, realtors themselves serve as the sales force for both mortgage bankers and mortgage brokers.

There are thousands of mortgage banking companies in the United States, ranging from large national companies to very small localized lenders. However, a small number of large national mortgage bankers account for most of the industry's lending. In 1988, the *American Banker* conducted a survey of the top two hundred mortgage companies in servicing loan originations. This survey showed that of the $110 billion in single family mortgages originated by mortgage banking companies in 1987, the ten largest lenders accounted for $36.3 billion, 33 percent of the total.

Many of the large national mortgage banking companies are subsidiaries of bank or thrift holding companies, insurance companies, or diversified financial companies. However, several are subsidiaries of national manufacturing or retail corporations. According to the *American Banker* survey, among the top twenty mortgage banker loan originators are Citicorp Mortgage Inc. (no. 1), a subsidiary of a bank and thrift holding company; Sears Mortgage (no. 3), a subsidiary of a retailer; GMAC Mortgage Co. (no. 7), a subsidiary of an automobile manufacturer; and Traveler's Mortgage Co. (no 15), a subsidiary of a life insurance company.

As more of the mortgage market is serviced by these large national corporations, mortgage lending is characterized less by local community relationships between lender and borrower. Several companies, including the mortgage banking subsidiary of Prudential Life Insurance, market their mortgages nationally with a toll-free number and a computerized pre-approval system. Ford Motor Company's mortgage banking subsidiary has developed a similar computerized pre-approval system that is marketed nationally in K Mart retail stores. Metropolitan Life Insurance Company uses both its national network of Century 21 real estate brokers and its subsidiary, Crossland Financial Mortgage Company, to market its loans. Sears uses its national network of department stores, Allstate Insurance offices, Coldwell Banker real estate brokerage offices, and the Dean Witter securities brokerage and financial services chain to market its mortgage loans nationally.

Unlike banks and savings and loan associations, mortgage banking companies are not subject to federal regulation or legislation including CRA or HMDA. Rather, mortgage banking companies are licensed and regulated at the state level and state legislators have not yet addressed community concerns about disinvestment. Before 1988, mortgage banking subsidiaries of banks and thrift holding companies were also able to avoid HMDA disclosure requirements, but a 1988 regulatory amendment made by the Federal Reserve Board ensures that banks and thrifts must also report mortgages originated by mortgage banking subsidiaries.

With the potential decline in lending from thrifts as a result of the S&L crisis, mortgage bankers may provide even greater amounts of single family mortgage credit lending in the future. This will result in an even larger share of residential lending being done by lenders without legal reinvestment obligations or close ties to particular communities. Finally, the expected fallout from the savings and loan crisis and the growing pace of mortgage banking companies raises concerns regarding the vulnerability of mortgage credit. The growing dependence on the secondary

TABLE 5.1. NATIONAL MARKET SHARE OF SINGLE-FAMILY HOME MORTGAGE
LOANS BY TYPE OF LENDER, 1987

(Millions of dollars)

Type of Institution	Amount	% of Total
Commercial banks	124,025	27.6
Mutual savings banks	34,232	7.6
Savings and loans associations	173,822	38.7
Mortgage bankers	110,093	24.5
All other lenders	6,899	1.5
Total	$449,071	100%

Source: HUD Survey of Mortgage Lending Activity

market may link residential lending too closely to the whims of Wall Street and the demands of mortgage securities markets.

In 1987, $449.1 billion in single family mortgage loans were originated in the United States. Of these loan dollars, $110.1 billion or nearly one-fourth of all single family mortgage dollars were originated by mortgage banking companies (table 5.1). In comparison, banks originated $124.0 billion or 28 percent of loan dollars, and savings and loan associations originated $173.8 billion or 39 percent of single family mortgage loan dollars (table 5.1). The vast majority of single family mortgages are conventional or not government-insured mortgage loans. Conventional mortgages made up 84 percent of all single family mortgage loan dollars compared to 11 percent for FHA and 5 percent for VA loans (table 5.2).

Mortgage bankers have historically been the major delivery system for FHA and VA loans. Mortgage banking companies accounted for 72 percent of all FHA/VA mortgage loan dollars lent nationally in 1987 (table 5.3). Nationally, the mortgage banking industry devoted 48 percent of its single family loan dollars to FHA and VA loans and 52 percent of its loan dollars for conventional mortgages in 1987 (table 5.2). By comparison, commercial banks and savings and loan associations devoted only 10 percent and 4 percent of their loan dollars, respectively, to FHA/VA loans and 90 percent and 96 percent, respectively, to conventional mortgage loans (table 5.2).

However, there appears to be a shift toward conventional mortgage loans among mortgage bankers. As the volume of mortgage banker mortgage lending has increased, there has also been an increase in the proportion of their lending for single family conventional mortgages. During the

TABLE 5.2. National Distribution of Single-Family Loan Dollars by Loan Type and Type of Lender, 1987

(Millions of dollars)

Loan Type	Commercial Banks		Savings and Loans		Mutual Savings Banks		Mortgage Bankers		All Lenders*	
	$	%	$	%	$	%	$	%	$	%
Conventional	111,855	90.2	166,567	95.8	33,720	98.5	57,578	52.3	375,943	83.7
FHA	8,099	6.5	5,003	2.9	397	1.2	37,225	33.8	51,240	11.4
VA	4,072	3.3	2,252	1.3	114	.3	15,290	13.9	21,888	4.9
Total	124,025	100	173,822	100	34,232	100	110,093	100	449,071	100

Source: HUD Survey of Mortgage Lending Activity
*Includes institutions such as pension funds and insurance companies.

TABLE 5.3. National Market Share of FHA/VA Loans by Type of Lender, 1987

(Millions of dollars)

Type of Institution	Amount	% of Total
Commercial banks	8,099	15.8
Mutual savings banks	397	.8
Savings and loans associations	5,003	9.8
Mortgage bankers	37,225	72.6
Others	516	1.0
Total	$51,240	100%

Source: HUD Survey of Mortgage Lending Activity

1970s, according to the U.S. Department of Housing and Urban Development's annual survey of mortgage lending activity data, the dollars lent by the industry for conventional mortgages, as a percent of total lending, ranged from a low of 4.7 percent in 1970 to a high of 32.3 percent in 1973. The percentage remained below 20 percent from 1970 through 1972 and rose above 30 percent in only one other year in that decade (30.5 percent in 1978). In 1985–1987, the last three years for which data are available, the percentage has been 45.4, 39.9, and 52.3 percent, respectively.

Not only are mortgage bankers making proportionately more conventional single family mortgages; their market share of this type of loan has also increased. The HUD mortgage lending data showed that, during the 1970s, the percentage of conventional single family mortgage loan dollars provided by mortgage bankers ranged between a low of 1 percent in 1970 and a high of 8.3 percent in 1979. By 1987, that had grown to 15.3 percent.

From 1984 through 1987, mortgage bankers lent over $1.5 billion in single family mortgages in the city of Chicago, accounting for 28 percent of all single family mortgage lending in the city during that period (table 5.4). Mortgage bankers accounted for 15 percent of the conventional single-family mortgage dollars, and 88 percent of the FHA/VA loan dollars (table 5.4).

Mortgage banker lending has a similar profile in the suburbs. During that same four-year period (1984–1987), mortgage bankers lent $6.7 billion for single family mortgages in the suburban areas outside the city of Chicago (but within the six-county Chicago metropolitan area) (table 5.4). Mortgage bankers therefore, provided 28.9 percent of the total

TABLE 5.4. MARKET SHARE OF SINGLE-FAMILY HOME MORTGAGE DOLLARS OF BANKS, THRIFTS, AND MORTGAGE COMPANIES IN CHICAGO CITY AND SUBURBS BY TYPE OF LOAN, 1984–1987

	Conventional Loans		FHA/VA Loans		Total Single-Family Loans	
	$ (000's)	% of Total	$ (000's)	% of Total	$ (000's)	% of Total
City of Chicago						
Banks	874,996	19.2	63,767	6.6	938,763	17.0
Thrifts	2,983,829	65.5	48,983	5.1	3,032,812	55.0
Mortgage companies	697,603	15.3	851,024	88.3	1,548,627	28.0
Suburbs						
Banks	3,962,749	18.4	75,898	2.7	4,038,647	17.5
Thrifts	12,258,943	61.2	157,164	5.6	12,416,107	53.7
Mortgage companies	4,087,001	20.4	2,593,833	91.8	6,680,834	28.9
Metropolitan Area						
Banks	4,837,745	19.5	139,665	3.7	4,977,410	17.4
Thrifts	15,242,772	61.3	206,147	5.4	15,448,919	53.9
Mortgage companies	4,784,604	19.2	3,444,857	90.9	8,229,461	28.7

Source: Federal Reserve Board, Home Mortgage Disclosure Activity data

single family mortgage loan dollars received by the suburban portion of the Chicago metropolitan area (table 5.4). Mortgage bankers accounted for 91.8 percent of FHA/VA loan dollars and 20.4 percent of conventional mortgage dollars received by Chicago area suburbs during this period (table 5.4). According to the Illinois Savings and Loan Commission's Residential Mortgage Licensee Act disclosure data, mortgage bankers lent 81.2 percent of their single family mortgage dollars to the suburbs and 18.8 percent to the city. HMDA data show a similar pattern for banks and thrifts which both lent 80 percent of their single family mortgage loan dollars to the suburbs and 20 percent to the city.

Residential Lending Disclosure Data Bases

There are two residential lending disclosure data bases available at the federal level. Both contain information only on residential lending by banks and savings and loan associations. The best-known and widely used comprises the data collected under the federal Home Mortgage Disclosure Act (HMDA). HMDA data are required of all banks, thrifts, and credit unions with assets of $10 million or more that are in metropolitan areas. The other data base, which has only recently become publicly available, is the Federal Home Loan Bank Board's data submission reports on savings and loan association's loan applications and rejections by race, income, and gender.

Three states (Illinois, Michigan, and California) collect residential lending data from mortgage banking companies. The Illinois Mortgage License Act of 1987 and its forerunner, the Illinois Mortgage Banker Act of 1977, require all mortgage banking firms operating in the state to disclose the number and dollar amount of their residential loans by census tract. Michigan collects lending data from mortgage bankers with assets of $10 million or more under its 1977 anti-redlining act. In 1986, California passed a law requiring lending disclosure by nondepository lenders including mortgage bankers.

In addition to those required by the federal and state disclosure laws, Chicago has collected residential lending data analogous to the HMDA from financial institutions applying for City deposits under the Chicago Municipal Depository Ordinance since 1974.

Following is a description of these data bases and an evaluation of their quality and usefulness.

THE HOME MORTGAGE DISCLOSURE ACT

The Data   The Home Mortgage Disclosure Act was passed in 1975. It requires all banks, savings and loan associations, and credit unions with assets of $10 million or more located in metropolitan statistical areas to report the number and dollar amount of their conventional and FHA/VA single family mortgage loans, multifamily mortgage loans, and home improvement loans by census tract. Institutions must report loans by tract within MSAs in which they have facilities but are allowed to report in aggregate all loans made in MSAs in which they do not maintain facilities.

Data Quality   Over time, the HMDA data have become very accurate and reliable. Initially, both regulators and reporting institutions had difficulty interpreting HMDA requirements, and there were substantial problems with the data's uniformity and quality. By 1978, data reporting had become fairly uniform, and overall data quality had improved. In 1980, with the renewal of HMDA, several important improvements were made, including standard formatting of the data, central collection of data within each MSA/SMSA, and centralized collection and processing of all national data in a machine-readable format by the Federal Reserve Board.

A study of the quality of HMDA data from 1980 to 1982 by the Woodstock Institute (Shlay 1985a) found HMDA's data quality to be comparable to U.S. Census data, which are widely used for academic research, government policy and program development, and congressional district apportionment. The Federal Reserve "flags" data-reporting errors on its computer tape to call attention to data reported for nonexistent census tracts and for statistically implausible loan amounts. Using both the Federal Reserve's and its own data-cleaning program, Woodstock Institute found that only 0.2 percent of loans in the Chicago six-county metropolitan area in 1987 had to be deleted because of reporting errors.

Usefulness of the Data   HMDA data have been very useful in monitoring the reinvestment performance of financial institutions under CRA and in tracking credit flows within particular communities. HMDA serves as the major source of evidence in CRA challenges and has been instrumental in nearly every CRA lending agreement to date. By relating HMDA data to census data, one can chart lending for particular institutions or particular geographic areas by racial, income, and other relevant characteristics to analyze patterns of discrimination or disinvestment. While HMDA does not establish the actual race or income of individual loan recipients, it does allow for community-based analyses of lending practices that are both meaningful and appropriate because of the patterns of segregation along lines of race and class in most metropolitan areas. Because redlining is a practice that discriminates against and adversely affects the economic viability of entire communities, a community-level analysis is perhaps the most relevant type of analysis possible.

The Financial Institutions Reform Recovery and Enforcement Act (FIRREA) of 1989 expanded HMDA to include reporting by mortgage companies effective January 1990. These data are to be collected by HUD. Under an expanded HMDA format, institutions—mortgage companies, banks, and savings and loan associations with $10 million or more in assets—that lend in metropolitan statistical areas will be required to report data on mortgage loans, applications, and denials by census tract and by the race, gender, and income of individual loan applicants. The new requirements will enable a more comprehensive analysis of lending patterns and acknowledge the role of mortgage bankers.

FEDERAL HOME LOAN BANK BOARD LOAN APPLICATION DATA

The Data   In 1979, as partial settlement of a discrimination suit by the National Urban League, the FHLBB agreed to collect data on mortgage applications and their disposition by race and income.[1] These data were collected by the FHLBB for ten years but never analyzed or made available to the public. In 1988, in response to a Freedom of Information Act request, the FHLBB released these data aggregated at the metropolitan level, showing the number of applications, approvals, denials, application withdrawals, and nondecisions by race. A study of data for 1983–1988 conducted by the *Atlanta Constitution* found that loan denial rates for black applicants were more than double the rates for whites nationally and were nearly four times as high in some metropolitan areas.

Currently, these data are available only at the metropolitan area level. The FHLBB has refused to disclose information for individual institutions or for geographic units below the MSA level, although there are ongoing efforts to force public disclosure of such data.

Data Quality   To date, no work has been done on assessing the quality of these data. They are self-reported by the institutions and compiled by the Federal Home Loan Bank Board. Because of the nature of the relationship depository institutions have with their regulators, there is reason to believe the data are very good. However, researchers are only beginning to request and analyze them.

Usefulness of the Data   These data have been used by the *Atlanta Constitution* in its series "The Color of Money" and by a few other newspapers for stories on national and metropolitan comparisons of turndown rates by race.

The availability of application data by both race and income characteristics allows for comparison of higher-income minority applicants and areas to similar or lower-income white applicants and areas as a method for controlling, to some extent, for disparities in creditworthiness. The *Atlanta Constitution* study of application and turndowns from 1983 through 1988 found that high-income blacks were rejected at a higher rate than low-income whites in eighty-five of one hundred metropolitan areas in at least one of the five years studied and in thirty-five of the areas in at least three of those five years.

The FHLBB, itself, has assumed that some of this disparity is due to difference in creditworthiness and has defined as acceptable disparity minority approval rates of 80 percent of white approval rates. With minority approval rates being approximately 50 percent of the rate for whites and as low as 25 percent in some areas, existing disparities clearly exceed FHLBB defined levels of acceptability, controversial as they may be.

Such findings sufficiently establish differences in loan rejection patterns by race that add to the evidence of continued redlining and discrimination in lending. These data may therefore be considered an important supplement to HMDA for tracking patterns of redlining and disinvestment in low- and moderate-income and minority communities. The availability of these data at the individual census tract and institution level would add significantly to its usefulness.

ILLINOIS MORTGAGE BANKER DATA

The Data   In 1977, Illinois passed legislation to regulate mortgage banking companies. The legislation included loan disclosure data-reporting requirements similar to HMDA. The Mortgage Licensee Act (formerly an Act to Regulate Mortgage Bankers) requires all mortgage banking companies licensed to originate loans in the state to disclose by census tract the number and dollar amount of their FHA, VA, and conventional mortgage loans and their home improvement loans. The act also requires the disclosure of the number of foreclosures by census tract.

These data are collected by the mortgage banking division of the Illinois Savings and Loan Commission on standardized reporting forms similar to HMDA reporting forms. While the regulator is required to analyze and issue a report on state foreclosure rates, it does not computerize or analyze data on lending. The Woodstock Institute annually photocopies these disclosure reports, keypunches, computerizes, and cleans data for the Chicago six-county metropolitan area, and publishes data for the city of Chicago in its annual *Community Lending Fact Book*.

There are two significant limitations to this data base worth noting. First, finance companies licensed under the Consumer Installment Loan Act are regulated by the State Department of Financial Institutions and are exempt from the Residential Mortgage License Act. Many of these exempted companies are active mortgage lenders, including national firms like Household International. Because of this exemption, there are no disclosure data available on the lending activities of these companies. Second, multifamily (properties with five or more units) lending is not regulated by the Residential Mortgage License Act; subsequently, no data are collected on the multifamily lending of mortgage companies.

Usefulness of the Data   These data are analogous to the HMDA data reported by depository institutions and can be used in the same ways that

HMDA has been used. The Illinois mortgage banker data, therefore, serve as a supplement to HMDA to illustrate the role of these financial institutions in providing housing credit. As such, they can be used to document patterns of withdrawal of conventional mortgage loans in minority or racially changing communities and a resulting predominance of subsidized loans (part of the process of redlining). These data also offer insight into the viability of housing markets abandoned by depository institutions. With the growing use of mortgage banking subsidiaries by depository and nondepository institutions alike, the availability of lending data from these institutions will be essential for understanding overall patterns of investment in housing.

Quality of the Data   To date, the regulators have done little to address the quality of the data submitted by mortgage banking companies. In 1987, the latest year of Illinois data analyzed by Woodstock Institute, a handful of companies known to originate loans had no data reports on file, while several others reported by zip code rather than census tract. Of the data that were actually reported in the proper format, 4.7 percent of all mortgage banker loans reported in the six-county Chicago metropolitan area were deleted from the data base because of erroneously reported census tracts or implausible loan amounts. This is substantially higher than the 0.7 percent of loans deleted from the HMDA data base for the same area in the same year. By comparison, however, it is still considerably more accurate than U.S. census data. The 1980 census data had at least one missing or inconsistent value for 10 percent of all persons surveyed, and the Annual Housing Survey was found to contain inconsistent values on important items for 1 to 9 percent of the sample from 1974 to 1979 (Shlay 1985a:ii).

The foreclosure data collected under the Illinois Act have never been analyzed; therefore their quality is unknown.

MICHIGAN ANTI-REDLINING ACT DATA

The Data   Michigan passed the Anti-Redlining Act in 1977. The state began collecting data in 1979. Any person or institution making mortgage loans, including banks, thrifts, and mortgage banking companies, is required to report its lending activity to the state Department of Commerce in a form similar to HMDA. Lenders with less than $10 million in assets are exempted from these disclosure requirements. This somewhat limits the comprehensiveness of the mortgage banker data base because it is common for mortgage bankers to have less than $10 million in assets.

Legislation sponsored by the Michigan Department of Commerce to eliminate this asset-based exemption for mortgage companies is pending in the Michigan state legislature.

The Department of Commerce, charged with enforcement of the anti-redlining act, has been issuing annual reports of compliance, enforcement activity, and findings from these data since 1980. The data compiled in these annual reports include the number and dollar amount of loans, applications, denials, and foreclosures by loan type for each metropolitan area and several large cities in the state. Tables of the total lending and percentage of lending in low-income (less than 80 percent of median family income), moderate-income (between 80 and 100 percent of median family income), and moderate/high minority (more than 5 percent minority) tracts by each reporting institution are provided for all metropolitan areas and some cities.

More detailed reports are also available from the Department of Commerce. These include the dollar amounts of loans made by particular institutions according to census tract, which makes this data base analogous to HMDA. In addition, data on foreclosures, loan denials, and average term and interest rate are available by institution at the census tract level.

Usefulness of the Data   These data are potentially very useful for analyzing the lending patterns and practices of mortgage banking companies in a variety of types of communities over time. Because the data base includes lending by depository institutions as well as mortgage bankers, comparisons can be made between these institutions for each metropolitan area and city as well as for the state as a whole. The foreclosure data are unique in that they include foreclosure data from depository institutions as well as for mortgage bankers. These data allow for the analysis of lending, denial rates, down payment amounts, terms, rates, and foreclosures by institution at the census tract level.

Quality of the Data   According to the Michigan Department of Commerce's 1989 annual report, less than 7 percent of mortgage banker dollars were not reported because of reporting errors. The most common error was the use of invalid census tract numbers, 72 percent of which were in the Detroit SMSA. As a result of its mandated use in publishing reports and informing state public deposit decisions, this data base is probably superior in quality to the Illinois data, which have yet to be used for any public policy purposes.

CALIFORNIA MORTGAGE BANKER DATA

The Data   In 1987, Senate Bill 1556 amended the Senate Health and Safety Code (35–814) to require nondepository institutions including mortgage bankers, insurance companies, and finance companies to report their mortgage lending activity in a form analogous to HMDA. The first year for which the submission of these disclosure reports will be required is 1990. Annual lending reports for 1990 are due to be filed in March of 1991. These data will be collected by several different state agencies depending on the type of institution and its licensing agency, although apparently most mortgage bankers will report to the California Department of Corporations.

Usefulness and Quality of the Data   Potentially, these data could be useful in the same manner as HMDA and the Illinois mortgage banker data. Because the data are yet to be collected, their general availability and the form in which they are made available from the various agencies collecting them are unknown.

CHICAGO MUNICIPAL DEPOSITORY ORDINANCE

The Data   In 1974, the Chicago City Council passed the Chicago Municipal Depository Ordinance (CMDO) as a means of tying reinvestment performance to the awarding of public deposits. Although this goal was never realized, data on the geographic distribution of both deposits and loans by those institutions requesting city deposits have been collected for fifteen years. In addition to requiring disclosure of data analogous to HMDA, the CMDO requires banks and savings and loan associations applying for city deposits to report by census tract the number and dollar amount of their checking and savings deposits and consumer and commercial loans. These data supplement residential lending data and have been used by community groups in several CRA challenges. In 1986, Woodstock Institute conducted a study of the CMDO and the commercial lending patterns of banks applying for public deposits (Flax-Hatch 1987).

The residential data disclosure required by CMDO was a forerunner to HMDA and requires exactly the same information. The additional information on residential lending collected under the CMDO is the average weighted, down payment, the average effective interest rate, and the weighted average term of residential loans for each census tract in the city of Chicago in which loans were made as well as for the entire city of

Chicago and the entire metropolitan area outside the city. These data allow for comparisons of rates, terms, and down payments between tracts and neighborhoods within the city and between the city and the suburban metropolitan area.

The Usefulness of the Data   As outlined above, the residential lending data can be used in the same ways as HMDA, and in addition for comparing differences in terms, rates, and down payments between neighborhoods and between city and suburbs by specific institutions or sets of institutions. They also allow for the analysis of the ratio of deposits collected from communities to the amount of credit returned to those communities in terms of housing as well as commercial and consumer loans.

The drawback to CMDO data is that they contain only data from those banks that have bid on city deposits. Therefore, they do not constitute a complete data base. However, historically, between twenty and thirty banks bid on city deposits each year, including six of the seven largest.

Quality of the Data   For many years, the CMDO data were collected without any screening or analysis. Woodstock Institute's study, *Tracking Chicago's Business Bucks: Commercial Lending and the Chicago Municipal Depository Ordinance*, outlined a number of problems with missing and erroneously reported data. Beginning in 1988, the Office of the City Comptroller announced new reporting guidelines to clarify reporting requirements, standardize the data being reported, and compile lending profiles of the applicant institutions. These initiatives have greatly improved the quality of the data base. Data collected prior to the 1988 bid process vary greatly in quality, depending on the submitting institution.

The Research and Policy Questions That Remain

The history of central city communities in the last decades has demonstrated that there is a clear cycle of decline that follows disinvestment by capital and credit providers. When access to affordable credit is limited, homes and apartment buildings are not maintained and improved, the market for the buying and selling of houses slows, and prices drop. At the same time, rapid investment by outside developers without input from local residents has also proved to be harmful to communities. This type of misinvestment is usually a tool of the gentrification process that causes displacement of existing community residents.

The most appropriate strategy for community-based organizations seeking to stabilize and improve their neighborhood is the promotion and management of reinvestment that benefits community residents. However, community-based management of reinvestment is virtually impossible without accurate and timely information on aggregate lending patterns and the lending performance of individual lenders.

The growing body of research on the residential lending patterns of banks and savings and loan associations has identified distinct patterns of disinvestment in central city areas and in minority communities that cannot be explained by normal market factors. In communities across the country, evidence from this research has led to the negotiation of community reinvestment act agreements with banks and savings and loan associations. In addition, the research findings have attracted the attention of policymakers and led to proposals to strengthen enforcement of CRA and the expansion of the scope of disclosure legislation. State and local policymakers have become concerned with local disinvestment, and there have been numerous proposals developed to address discrepancies in the lending performance of banks and savings and loans and to require additional disclosure and set reinvestment standards for public deposits.

In the coming years, there will be major changes in the sources for and nature of residential mortgage credit—as the savings and loan association industry, which is currently the major supplier of single family mortgages, changes, shrinks, and reorganizes. It will be essential to track changes in the overall residential lending patterns by type of lender and examine some of the effects of those changes over the next few years. This requires continuing analysis of existing data sources as well as the identification of key data not currently available. To the extent that trends become apparent, new policy initiatives might be indicated to ensure the availability of mortgage credit throughout communities.

The emerging importance of mortgage bankers as well as evidence that existing mortgage bankers are very significant lenders in many predominantly minority communities means that it is important to look more closely at the nature of mortgage banker lending and its influence on the supply of credit in low- and moderate-income and minority communities. No analysis of mortgage banker lending patterns analogous to that of banks and savings and loan associations exists.

Without a serious analysis of mortgage banker lending patterns, it is not possible to determine how mortgage banker market shifts affect low- and moderate-income and minority communities. Mortgage banker lending may be decreasing in these communities as mortgage bankers compete aggressively for the more affluent suburban markets. Different products may be marketed in low-income communities, and there may be differences in the rigor applied to the underwriting of conventional mortgages opposed to and FHA or VA mortgages.

Any of these differences could affect negatively low- and moderate-income and minority communities. The effect of this may compound problems caused by bank and savings and loan association disinvestment.

It is also possible that mortgage bankers have become a cost-efficient delivery mechanism for one of the most common standardized loan products needed by homeowners, the home mortgage. Since interest rate deregulation forced banks and savings and loan associations to rethink their fee structures, the cost of credit delivery has been labeled a barrier to lender interest in lower-income communities. However, in Chicago, the volume of mortgage banker lending in lower-income communities suggests that it is possible to make a profit on mortgage origination in these communities.

The case for research on mortgage banker lending patterns is compelling. While the data base on mortgage banker lending is extremely limited, census tract data do exist for two key states, Illinois and Michigan. Both of these data bases could be correlated with demographic information from the United States census to produce information similar to existing studies of HMDA. From this analysis, emerging trends and disparities in lending patterns could be identified to inform public policy development that further enhances the ability of local communities to manage reinvestment and avoid both the serious deterioration that can result from disinvestment and the displacement that results from gentrification fueled by misinvestment.

NOTE

1. Loan applications, denials, and other dispositions are reported by a number of gender, race, and income categories. At the census tract level, data are aggregated for lending in tracts that are substantially minority according to three income categories: low-income, moderate-income, and above-moderate-income. Data are reported by lending to tracts that are not substantially minority for each

of these three income categories as well. Data are also reported for individual applicants by race under the category of white, black, Hispanic, Asian, or Pacific Islander and Native American. Individual applicant data are also collected according to gender and marital status.

Substantially, minority tracts are defined as tracts with 25 percent minority populations. Low income is defined as below 80 percent of the metropolitan area's family income, moderate income is defined as between 80 percent and 100 percent of the metropolitan area's family income, and above moderate is defined as anything above 100 percent of the metropolitan area's family income.

If the applicant is a couple or group, and one of the applicants is minority, the application is designated by minority applicant. Female is designated only when there is no male involved in application. Marital status is reported by categories of married, single, and divorced.

REFERENCE LIST

Bradbury, Katharine L., Karl E. Case, and Constance R. Dunham. 1989. "Geographic patterns of mortgage lending in Boston, 1982–1987." *New England Economic Review*. Boston: Federal Reserve Bank of Boston.

Center for Community Change. 1989. *New Research Shows S&Ls Shun Lower Income and Minority Neighborhoods*. Washington, D.C.: Center for Community Change.

Dedman, Bill. 1988. "The Color of Money: Home Mortgage Lending Practices Discriminate." *Atlanta-Constitution Journal*, 1–4 May.

Flax-Hatch, David. 1987. *Tracking Chicago's Business Bucks: Commercial Lending and the Chicago Municipal Depository Ordinance*. Chicago: Woodstock Institute.

Pogge, Jean. 1987. *Vista of Opportunity: An Analysis of 1983 and 1984 Residential Lending in the Denver/Boulder SMSA*. Chicago: Woodstock Institute.

Pogge, Jean, Josh Hoyt, and Elspeth Revere. 1986. *Partners in Need: A Four-Year Analysis of Residential Lending in Chicago and Its Suburbs*. Chicago: Woodstock Institute.

Przyblski, Mike. 1978. *Perception of Risk—the Bankers' Myth: An Eight City Survey of Mortgage Disclosure Data*. Chicago: National Training and Information Center.

Shlay, Anne. 1985a. *Using HMDA: Evaluating the Quality of Disclosure Data from 1980 to 1982*. Chicago: Woodstock Institute.

———. 1985b. *Where the Money Flows: Lending Patterns in the Washington, D.C.-Maryland-Virginia SMSA*. Chicago: Woodstock Institute.

Jean Pogge is president of the Woodstock Institute; **David Flax-Hatch** is an Associate Researcher at the Institute. The Woodstock Institute, a not-for-profit corporation established in 1973, is a nationally respected pioneer in applied research, program design, and policy development that fosters reinvestment in low- and moderate-income and minority communities. Through its work, the Institute seeks to promote reinvestment by private sector institutions such as banks, savings and loan associations, insurance companies, and pension funds. Woodstock has been a leader in using computerized Home Mortgage Disclosure Act data and other census data to track the patterns of loans made by banks and savings and loans association in a number of cities, including Washington, D.C., Chicago, and Denver.

6 DEVELOPMENT EFFECTS OF THE ASSESSMENT AND PROPERTY TAX SYSTEM
Arthur Lyons

Property Tax Mechanics: Some Background

The property tax is often the only local tax available to boards of education, park districts, public libraries, and other similar units of local government. For cities, especially ones that are middle-sized and smaller, it
can be the largest single generator of local taxes, although its share of
total revenue has gradually declined during recent decades.

This centrality of real estate in local finance arises because real estate is
tied to local government in ways that other tax bases are not and cannot
be. Sales taxes, for example, migrate from one municipality to another
when shopping patterns change. Local income taxes, where they exist,
suffer when job or residence locations shift. Transfer payments from
higher levels of government cannot readily be influenced by local voters
or their locally elected officials. In addition, transfers usually come with
"oversight" commissions or other accountability requirements that reduce local control. Even ostensibly unconditional grants eventually reduce local autonomy, since a higher level of government can always take
away what it has previously given. Federal General Revenue Sharing is a
recent example. Local budgets throughout the country had to be scaled
back when it was cut—not in response to local citizens, but because federal legislators had decreed it.

Real estate alone cannot flee. It is thus a uniquely local tax base, even
though its value and its owners' incomes, on which assessments and realized tax revenue ultimately depend, are only partly under local control.

For example, federal housing and other programs encourage people and jobs to move out of established cities. State and federal road construction have a similar effect.

Nevertheless, among the most important determinants of real estate value are local government activities, including the provision of local services (see American Institute 1987:40). Various studies confirm that high taxes in themselves do not reduce real estate prices or induce flight from a city, but taxes without services do (see Birch 1987; Howland 1985; Nealon 1978). Both common sense and common appraisal practice recognize that the total mix of all local taxes must be measured against the total mix of services to determine whether investors find an area attractive (American Institute 1987:169–170). Property taxes are crucial to this calculus because they undergird the financial security needed to support independent spending decisions that can be uniquely tailored by and for the specific residents of each locality.

The remainder of this chapter deals with the development effects of property taxes. Whenever appropriate or necessary for a complete understanding of the topic, information about the taxation of residential real estate is included, but the primary focus is on matters that more directly affect commercial or industrial real estate. Taxes are imposed on such property by localities in all states and the District of Columbia.

DIFFERENT BUT NOT DIFFICULT

If the property tax is so important, why is it perhaps the most misunderstood and maligned of all taxes? At least five reasons can be suggested:

1. In most places, it requires periodic large payments, which make it much more visible than, say, a sales tax. It is also paid with money that has already been in people's hands, unlike the withholding that can make income taxes appear less onerous.

2. Precisely because it is so clearly tied to local services, it is a natural target when citizens are dissatisfied with any aspect of their local officials' behavior.

3. The property tax uses asset ownership, rather than current income or expenditures, as its measure of ability to pay.

4. Real estate values, which form the base for the property tax, are neither directly observed nor static. They are only estimated, and they must be periodically revised.

5. Special administrative and legislative actions are required each year

to set a tax rate, thus constantly drawing attention to the property tax. Other taxes have rates that simply continue from one year to the next.

These characteristics make the property tax different from all other taxes. They sometimes create an impression that the tax is difficult to understand, but it is not—it is only different. The first two characteristics do not need further elaboration here, but the last three are so important for a full grasp of property tax policy that they are more thoroughly explained.

Ability to Pay   The property tax is not, and never was, directly based on the current income of taxpayers. Rather, it is based on the value of the real estate they own. Tax equity, therefore, means that (a) people who own similarly valued property pay the same amount in tax, and (b) people who own more expensive property pay more than people who own less expensive property.

This type of equity poses a genuine hardship for some people, even though the value of real estate holdings is highly correlated with income. On average, in fact, real estate ownership is even more concentrated than income, that is, the richest people in terms of income own more than their income-based share of real estate (Heilbroner and Galbraith, 1987:63–64). Nevertheless, the property tax alone, when considered in isolation from the overall system of taxes and relief measures, simply cannot meet an income-related ability to pay criterion in all cases.

The issue of ability to pay is more complex for businesses because all business expenses are eventually passed on as higher prices or lower wages or dividends. Although theories abound, the question of who pays business taxes of all types, including property (see Aaron 1975) is difficult to answer.

Determining the Tax Base   Other taxes are levied on something whose value is determined with relative ease because the liability arises when a measurable transaction occurs. Income, for example, is counted when it is disbursed. Sales taxes are measured by cash register prices. Excise taxes are so many cents per cigarette, gallon of fuel, or other known quantity.

The property tax, however, is imposed on real estate that simply remains in place from year to year, with no transaction to establish an unambiguous taxable value. Furthermore, values constantly change, often moving at varying rates or even in opposite directions in different parts of the same jurisdiction. If taxes are to remain proportional to these changing values, that is, if the tax is to be fair, someone must assign values to all the taxable real estate.

The ways in which this is done vary significantly across the country. In some places, an assessor is elected, while in others he or she is appointed. Sometimes there is a board of assessors, sometimes an individual, and sometimes a hierarchy in which the work of local assessors can be changed by a supervising individual or commission, even without taxpayer appeals. Depending on the state or locality within a state, assessments are made by city, township, county, or state level officials. Assessments may be periodically revised according to a specified temporal cycle, or decades may intervene between reassessments. In some states and localities, reassessments in recent years have occurred only as a result of court orders.

Annual Rate Setting   The property tax requires a new law for its collection each year, whereas other taxes do not. In other words, if public officials were to approve the annual budget without a single word about the sales, utility, or host of other taxes and fees, those imposts would continue to be levied at the same rates as in the past. But if the budget is not accompanied by an ordinance explicitly calling for a precise rate or dollar amount of property taxes, no property taxes will be collected that year.

The procedure for establishing tax rates in Illinois is typical of that used in most of the rest of the country. It begins with a determination of total projected expenditures for the coming year. Then total anticipated revenues from all sources except the property tax are subtracted. These other sources include not only local nonproperty taxes and fees, but also transfers from other levels of government. In a handful of cities, mostly suburbs with very large sales tax generators, nonproperty tax revenue is enough to meet all spending plans, and there is no property tax. In most jurisdictions, however, there is a difference between planned spending and estimated nonproperty tax revenue. This difference is called the "levy."

Independently of the budget process, participants in the assessment system are determining the taxable base for that year.

When both processes have been finished, the county clerk divides the levy by the taxable base to derive that year's property tax rate. There are no binding levy limits in Illinois, but nonhome rule units are subject to maximum tax rates set by the legislature. If the clerk's calculation produces a rate in excess of the limit for that particular type of government, the maximum legal rate is substituted for the calculated rate. Separate calculations are made for each unit of local government, and the aggregate rate extended against any individual parcel of property is the sum of the separate rates for each of the overlapping jurisdictions within which the parcel lies.

When other revenue sources remain roughly constant and services are unchanged, the tax levy does not vary much from one year to the next— while in times of rapid change or instability, levies may go up or down by relatively large amounts. Frequently, especially in years when reassessment occurs, local officials attempt to back into a levy that will leave the calculated tax rate similar to the prior year's. This creates an erroneous impression among taxpayers that tax increases should be blamed on the assessor.

Property Tax Equity

The preceding section provides a background for analyzing several aspects of property tax equity.

Assessments, Tax Rates, and Tax Bills   The most important relationships among individual assessments, total assessments, tax levies, and tax bills can all be understood by considering only two parcels of property. Thus, imagine a city with only two taxable properties, A and B. For simplicity, assume they both have the same value, $100,000. Now suppose property A is assessed at $20,000, or 20 percent of its value, whereas B is assessed at $40,000, or 40 percent.

Disparities larger than these are found in almost all assessment districts. To see how they affect taxpayers, note that total assessments are $60,000. If public officials extend a levy of $6,000, the tax rate will be 10 percent (6,000 divided by 60,000). Owner A owes $2,000, while B owes twice as much, or $4,000.

Because both owners have the same market value, they should each pay the same tax; but in this case they do not. Instead, B pays twice as much as A. In other words, both A's and B's taxes directly depend on the assessment of the other.

This last point, which is crucial to understanding all discussions related to real estate assessments, becomes even clearer if we review various ways to remedy the unfairness. Equity requires both properties to be assessed at the same percentage of value. The exact percentage is far less important than that it be the same for both owners, since the interaction between the levy and total assessments will compensate for variations in the overall average level of assessment.

For example, suppose both properties are reassessed to 20 percent of value. The total tax base declines, but the rate compensates, jumping to 15 percent. A's tax bill increases, while B's decreases, so that both owners now pay the same.

Fairness has been achieved, and total revenue is the same as before. Even though the tax rate is higher, B's taxes are lower than they were because her assessment went down by a greater percentage than the rate went up. A's taxes are higher, but they are now the same as B's. Owner A may complain that her taxes have been raised, as indeed they have; but this merely corrects the imbalance of prior years. However, a complete correction is never made, since B is never compensated for prior overpayments and A is never billed for the past years in which she paid less than her share.

Alternately, suppose the governing authorities want to shield A from a tax increase. The only choice is to reduce the levy to $4,000. When combined with the new tax base, this keeps the rate at 10 percent. Again, both owners now pay the same. Owner B enjoys a substantial tax cut, while A's taxes remain unchanged; but the price of this method for achieving equity is that the governing body has less to spend.

In short, once inequitable assessments are allowed to exist, there is no solution that does not impose a hardship on someone. Either total tax revenue must decline, which reduces public services for everyone, or the previously underassessed people must pay higher taxes. The best that can be done is to correct the problem in the present and then to initiate strong, impartial oversight of assessments in the future—so that the problem does not arise again.

Assessments and Taxes When Market Values Differ   The previous section assumed that all properties have the same value. That assumption is relaxed here in order to illustrate equity when property values differ. As before, only two properties, C and D, need be analyzed. Let C be worth $40,000 and D, $80,000. Assume, however, that the assessor puts the same assessment on both, $12,000.

This type of behavior—placing similar assessments on properties with different values, so that lower-valued properties are overassessed relative to higher valued ones—has been found in almost all jurisdictions where research has been conducted, and it leads to clear inequities. In this case, owner D should pay twice as much in taxes as C, but both pay the same amount.

The only equitable solution is for D's assessment to be twice that of C. Total government revenue can be maintained at or above its original level only if D's taxes are higher than they were before. A phase-in of the new assessments may seem appropriate from D's point of view; but it will not be looked upon kindly by C, who views it as only prolonging an unfairness that should not have occurred in the first place.

Assessment Equalization, or the "Multiplier"   Just as relative individual assessments within a jurisdiction are important for equity, so also are relative aggregate assessments among jurisdictions. For example, suppose properties A and B are in the same taxing district but different assessment jurisdictions, as occurs, for example, in many school districts. The assessor on one side of the line could arbitrarily shift taxes to owners on the other side by assessing at a lower fraction of market value than her counterpart on the other side. If the second assessor compensated by reducing assessments on her side, a fruitless and unending competition would result. In order to avoid this and promote equity on both sides of the line, states with local assessors frequently have a process for equalizing assessment levels.

A second reason for equalizing is that formulas for distributing state aid rely on per capita or other assessments as a measure of local need. Without equalization, jurisdictions with low assessments relative to real estate market values would receive more than their fair share, at the expense of poorer jurisdictions in which assessments were at a higher fraction of market value.

Third, equalization gives a uniform meaning to legislatively established tax rate or levy limits. Most state legislatures have now established such limits for some or all of the localities in their state (Raphaelson 1981: 129). Recurring anecdotal reports suggest that local assessors sometimes try to "help" taxing district officials who are their political allies by raising assessments, and at other times to thwart officials who are their opponents by lowering, or refusing to raise, assessments. In any case, if a limit is to have a uniform effect throughout the state, then all taxing bodies must have the same average assessment level.

Thus, equalization promotes interjurisdictional equity, but it does not affect relative tax bills within an assessing district. In districts without rate limits, often called "home rule" units, if the equalizer doubles assessments, the tax rate becomes half what it would be in the absence of equalization. Even in rate-limited jurisdictions, an increase in assessments or the equalizer only leads to larger taxes if the taxing body seeks a higher levy than it had obtained with the previous lower figures.

Nevertheless, assessors and the officials of taxing bodies often refer to state-mandated equalization factors as "tax multipliers." This suggests that the state is responsible for "multiplying" people's taxes, but it is not. Only a higher levy can effect a genuine tax increase, in the sense that the total amount collected from all taxpayers is higher than it was. Thus, local officials determine the overall level of taxes through their budget process, while assessors determine the distribution of those taxes among property owners through the assignment of relative assessments.

CONCLUSION

The property tax system outlined above is composed of many parts; but when properly understood, the parts fit together in a straightforward manner. However, the tax is confusing both because public officials do not present information about it in a straightforward manner and also because they frequently change parts of it. Some of the provisions that undergo the most frequent amendment are discussed in the next section.

Classification of Real Estate

Classification is the practice of assessing different types of real estate at different percentages of value, based on the property's use. As implemented in most places that use it, classification shifts tax burdens away from residential, especially owner-occupied, property. Cook County's system provides an example.

The history of its six basic classes is summarized in table 6.1. A reduction of more than one-fourth in the assessment level for one-six unit residential properties and smaller reductions for commercial and industrial property have resulted in a significant shift of the county's tax burden onto apartment buildings with seven or more units. Some implications of this are discussed later.

A special type of classification occurs when assessment or tax reductions, sometimes called "abatements," are given to specific property owners for particular types of investment. Cook County's five abatement classes are described in table 6.2, which also summarizes their eligibility requirements, application procedures, and assessment levels.

Revisions over the years have softened or eliminated earlier restrictions. For example, a prohibition against relocating within the county to get tax benefits has been removed. A location restriction for the previous class 6 (industrial property) was entirely eliminated for the new class 6.a. Nor is there a location requirement for manufacturing property under class 6.b. Reoccupied property now qualifies under eligibility criteria

TABLE 6.1. HISTORICAL EVOLUTION OF COOK COUNTY'S BASIC ASSESSMENT CLASSES

		Assessment as Percent of Market Value						
Class	Description	1972	1976	1977	1986	1987	1988	1989
1	Vacant land	22%						
2	Small residential (1–6 unit buildings, condominiums, cooperatives, farms)	22	17%	16%				
3	Large residential (residential not in Class 2)	33						
4	Owned and used by a nonprofit for its chartered purposes	30						
5a	Commercial not in any other class	} 40			39.5%	39%	38.5%	38%
5b	Industrial, not in any other class				39	38	37	36

Source: Cook County. 1988. Real Property Assessment Classification Ordinance (June 20).
Notes: Years are the tax year for which the assessment level was first legally used.
A blank means no change in assessment level from the prior year.
Prior to 1986, commercial and industrial property (5a and b) were in an undifferentiated Class 5.

TABLE 6.2. REQUIREMENTS AND APPLICATION PROCEDURES FOR COOK COUNTY'S REDUCED ASSESSMENT CLASSES

Class	Type of Property	Requirements	Procedures	Assessment Level
6a	Industrial	Used for industrially zoned purposes.	Taxpayer applies to assessor.	30% (17% reduction) for 8 yrs.
6b	Industrial	If manufacturing, no location requirement; if other industrial, must be in enterprise zone. City law declares project merits reduction.	Taxpayer applies to assessor.	16% (56% reduction) for 8 yrs.
7	Commercial	Located in area designated by federal, state, or local agency as blighted or otherwise in need.	Taxing bodies may sign income or profit sharing deals with developer. Governing body applies to assessor.	16% (58% reduction) for 8 yrs.; 30% (21% reduction) next 4 yrs.
		Area's property taxes have declined, remained stagnant, or potential not fully realized due to its depressed condition.	County Economic Development Advisory Committee reviews and makes recommendation to assessor.	
		Project is viable and likely to go forward on a timely basis if tax cut is granted.	Assessor holds public hearing.	
		Tax cut will materially assist development and project would not go forward without it.	Assessor decides.	
		Ultimate result will be increase in property tax revenues and employment.		

Class	Type of Property	Requirements	Procedures	Assessment Level
8	Industrial or commercial	Located in area defined by city law as depressed or otherwise in need. Private development in area not economically feasible without public assistance. City law declares project consistent with some overall plan.	City asks assessor to certify that the defined area actually is depressed.	16% (56% reduction [industrial] or 58% [commercial]) for 12 yrs.
9	Apartment building with 7 or more units	Located in Census tract or block group with 51% low or moderate income persons. Extensive renovation of primary building components, as defined by assessor. 50% of units have rents no higher than 80% of HUD "fair market rent" (no tenant income limit). Building satisfies all local codes.	Taxpayer applies to assessor. Recipient files annual report with assessor.	16% (52% reduction) for 8 yrs.

Note: Except for Class 9, property must be new, substantially rehabilitated, or reoccupied after abandonment.

which formerly required new construction or substantial rehabilitation. This tendency toward frequent amendments reflects the experience of most jurisdictions that classify: Once the classes begin, it is difficult to stop their proliferation (Gold 1979:148).

Classification and the Equalizer   Classification systems have an important but poorly understood effect on equalizers. Cook County's class ratios, for example, range from 16 to 38 percent, whereas the state-mandated overall assessment level is 33 percent, toward the upper end of this range. Furthermore, small residential property, which is assigned the lowest class ratio, constitutes more than 60 percent of the county's market value. Commercial and industrial real estate, the only groups assessed higher than 33 percent, represent only a little more than a fourth of total market value.

As a consequence, even if the assessor assigned values perfectly in accord with the classification ordinance, total assessments would be only about 23 percent of total market values. This means that the classification ordinance itself guarantees a county equalizer no lower than about 1.4, the number needed to bring 23 percent up to 33 percent. The fact that the actual equalizer has hovered around 1.9 is due to underassessing at the county level, but the underassessment is not as severe as it appears from the 1.9 figure alone.

CAPITALIZATION OF THE PROPERTY TAX

As a transition to discussing the property tax's development effects, a few words about tax capitalization are in order. Capitalization, of course, is the process by which future incomes or expenses are converted to present value.

When commercial and industrial real estate investors calculate their asking price, in the case of sellers, or bid price, in the case of buyers, they begin with projected gross income. From this are subtracted two broad types of cost. Operating costs vary with the level of activity, such as the occupancy rate for office buildings or output for factories; they are sometimes computed simply as a percentage of gross income. Fixed costs, primarily debt service and property taxes, are subtracted as lump sums, since they are not so dependent on the activity level. They are, however, dependent on the final price paid, and more complex methods for valuing real estate include mathematics by which the price and these costs are simultaneously determined.

In any case, the projected net income after both subtractions is combined with a discount, or capitalization, rate to obtain an estimated value for the real estate. The methodology can range from simply dividing a single year's net income by the capitalization rate to various procedures involving multiple rates for different parts of the income stream and an allowance for reselling the property at the end of a specified time.

Regardless of the specific methodology, however, property taxes are always accounted for in market transactions. This is the genesis of the observation that assessment or tax changes inevitably redound to the benefit or expense of the real estate's *current* owner. They are not passed on to succeeding owners because the purchase price compensates: When taxes are expected to be lower, a higher price must be paid; when taxes are expected to be higher, a lower price must be accepted.

Development Effects of Classification and Abatements

While classification shifts tax burdens away from residential property, reduced assessment classes generally shift taxes in the reverse direction. The shifts, however, do not offset one another, since existing commercial and industrial real estate get the highest ratios under classification, but only new commercial and industrial get the lower ratios of the special classes.

There are also other ways in which assessment practice is inconsistent. For example, using formal or informal "vacancy allowances" or "condition factors," many assessors grant relief to buildings that are less than fully utilized. This effectively subsidizes the speculative holding of property off the market, while owners await opportunities for higher returns in the future. On the other hand, reduced assessments are often used to subsidize reoccupied real estate. Other taxpayers thus pay twice: Once, while the property is being kept vacant, and again when it is reutilized.

EFFECTS OF CLASSIFICATION

Whenever considering the development effects of public policy, it is useful to isolate three groups of investors: (1) those who are already holding real estate for the purpose of developing it, or who make their living by buying and selling such real estate; (2) potential purchasers and developers of real estate; and (3) those who currently use real estate and who have no immediate intention to alter its use.

Speculative Holders or Dealers in Land   Because buyers pay more for real estate that has lower taxes, the current holders of land suitable for development face strong economic incentives to seek lower assessments. If they are planning to hold the land for a long time, they might also want lower current taxes; but for the most part, this is not an issue. What is most important is that low taxes be available to the property's future user, whether this be through low basic classification ratios or the availability of special tax abatements.

The same is true of those who broker or finance real estate. Since their incomes depend on the property's price, they gain from anything that increases prices, whether it be lower taxes or any other government program. Furthermore, because the rate of turnover can be important to this group of economic actors, they may favor policies which impose higher taxes on the current users of real estate than on different future users. This point is explored further in the discussion of current real estate users.

Investors and Developers   Investors seeking to buy real estate are largely indifferent to the level of property taxes, with one important caveat, namely, that the taxes be predictable. This indifference comes from the fact that taxes are capitalized into the prices they pay. Other things being equal, of course, they would prefer lower taxes; but the other things never are equal. Public services are better or worse, transportation facilities are better or worse, the labor supply is better or worse, and taxes are higher or lower. These and other factors are all part of the bargaining calculus. As long as the seller is knowledgeable, each factor will be capitalized. Thus, as soon as local officials try to gain a locational advantage by reducing taxes, the seller reacts by raising price.

Of far more concern to investors than the current or projected level of taxes is the accuracy with which predictions can be made. Whether taxes remain constant, rise and fall in concert with other costs faced by investors, or behave in any other way that can be forecast with relative certainty, they will be accounted for and are unlikely to have either a positive or negative impact on development. But if they are unstable, investors might lower their bids below what sellers are willing to accept. On the other side of the same coin, if instability takes the form not of unpredicted changes in government levies but of frequent enhancements in development incentives, sellers might increase their prices above what investors are willing to pay. In either case, as long as the assessment system continues to provide relief to owners who hold fully or partially vacant real estate, there is an incentive for such owners to engage in speculative holding rather than to sell for more intensive use.

Current Users of Real Estate   The current users of real estate "paid" for their tax situation when they first acquired the property. To the extent that taxes move roughly in line with their expectations relative to other costs they face, regardless of how long ago those expectations were formed, they have little incentive to engage in tax-induced behavior.

On the other hand, the progression of changes in Cook County's assessment system over about the last fifteen years has pressed on the current users of commercial and industrial real estate from many directions. Every time assessments were reduced for someone else who was holding a vacant building, reoccupying a formerly vacant building, or constructing anew, taxes were shifted onto them. When non-apartment residential assessments were reduced, commercial and industrial taxes were raised. As the state legislature continues to mandate cuts in taxable assessments for homeowners—a side of the tax system not yet discussed—commercial and industrial taxes are raised further.

In addition, the classification system itself contains subsidies for the premature conversion of property to other uses or conversion to uses that would not otherwise be feasible. For example, industrial space is assessed at 36 percent of its market value, while rental properties with fewer than seven apartments and all owner-occupied condominiums are at only 16 percent. To appreciate the effect of this, suppose an industrial owner is considering selling her property, and there are two bidders. One plans to keep the property industrial, while the other wants to convert it to one of the residential uses just described. Suppose, furthermore, that the net cash flow to both bidders, after all expenses except property taxes, will be the same. This means the cash flow after property taxes will be higher for the residential converter; and when this is capitalized, she will be able to outbid the industrial user. Even if the converter's expenses are higher, the assessment differential in favor of residential uses may permit her to make a higher bid.

The same thing has happened and is happening with respect to condominium conversions. A residential building with seven or more units is assessed at 33 percent of market value, but only if the units are rented. If the very same building is converted to condos, assessments drop to 16 percent, giving investors who want to convert a clear advantage in the market place.

Finally, there is a reduced assessment class for substantially rehabilitated multifamily buildings. But the eligibility and rehab spending requirements are drawn in such a way that the greatest benefits will go to rehabbers in gentrifying neighborhoods rather than to the community based nonprofit organizations that lent their political credibility to lobbying for it.

EVALUATIONS OF TAX ABATEMENTS

Many jurisdictions outside Cook County and Illinois have abatement programs similar in effect to the ones analyzed here, although few take precisely the same legal form because only a minority of jurisdictions classify real estate in the way Cook County does. On the other hand, many states, including Illinois, authorize taxing districts to engage in various sorts of tax forgiveness programs, usually subject to specified restrictions. Sometimes these restrictions bear the clear imprint of a particular interest group, as, for example, in Illinois, where counties with populations between 225,000 and 300,000 may grant property tax abatements to motor vehicle race tracks.

The discussion below is applicable to the tax abatement programs in most states, regardless of their specific form.

In Favor of Tax Abatements   Arguments commonly advanced in favor of using the tax system to promote development include the following:

1. Special tax provisions can be quickly enacted because they have low public visibility and may attract little attention during legislative sessions.

2. They can be quickly implemented because tax collection procedures are already established.

3. Once enacted, they rarely face further legislative or administrative scrutiny. This is especially true in states and localities that do not prepare an annual accounting of the cost of their various preferential tax programs, or a "tax expenditure budget."

4. Some targeting is possible.

5. Tax provisions entail no visible expenditure and so may be less controversial than proposals for direct expenditures.

6. Tax provisions can in some cases influence economic activity, even if only when the decision is a very close call.

7. Even if they have no direct economic effect, they have a symbolic value as indicators of public support for businesspeople.

Against Abatements   Arguments on the other side typically emphasize the following problems. In many cases, these are inherent in what have just been listed as advantages, suggesting that the conclusions on both sides depend more on perspective about the proper role of government than on factual disagreements.

1. Special tax provisions are bad public policy precisely because they have such low visibility. If subsidies are desired, it is better to provide them through direct expenditures, which are more likely to be fully aired and debated in public.

2. The fact that direct expenditures must be debated and reappropriated every year is an advantage, making it less likely that an ineffective program, one that has outlived its usefulness, or one that costs more than originally projected will continue unobserved.

3. Direct grant, subsidy, and other spending programs can be targeted much more closely than can tax provisions. In terms of pure economic analysis, they are demonstrably more efficient than tax breaks.

4. Local taxes are admittedly a small part of most firms' costs. Any economic activity whose success hinges on such a small difference either is too risky for public involvement or deserves a much larger subsidy—of a size more likely to insure success.

5. Although perhaps a small amount for most individual taxpayers, the total cost of tax expenditures to various local governments can be quite large, even interfering with service provision. The resulting prospect of unbalanced public budgets or new taxes is more harmful as a symbol to businesspeople than is the symbolic benefit of possible tax breaks.

6. Tax law provisions frequently discriminate arbitrarily, based on the particular tax situation of different firms in the same industry. In general, they create political divisions between new and existing plants, between businesses and individuals, and among political jurisdictions.

For a review of some of the literature on both sides, see Lyons et al. (1988:6–16).

THE STATED GOALS OF COMMERCIAL AND INDUSTRIAL ABATEMENTS

If the published literature on tax abatements teaches anything, it is the importance of determining from the outset who will bear the primary burden of proof: Should those who advocate abatements be required to show that the claimed results will be achieved, and in a cost-effective manner? Or should those who are skeptical of abatements have to demonstrate that tax breaks cannot under any circumstances have a favorable outcome?

Until recently, the burden seems to have been with those who doubt whether abatements are a cost-effective or wise public policy. In the absence of expressed public skepticism about tax breaks, public officials readily competed with one another to see who could offer the biggest incentives—despite the published academic evidence that the competition was largely futile. Media reports, however, are beginning to take a more critical stance toward such subsidies (see Glastris 1989), suggesting that the burden may be shifting to those who claim that abatements effectively achieve desired policy outcomes.

A second lesson is the importance of keeping in mind the distinction between *stated or desired* objectives and *actual* effects. It is not enough simply to assert that a particular goal is desired and that, therefore, tax abatements are appropriate. The real issues are (a) whether the revenue forgone by special tax provisions is actually being rewarded with the desired outcomes, and (b) whether the same or less money could be spent to achieve the outcomes more effectively.

With these lessons in mind, the goals commonly claimed for abatements can be examined. These are to promote employment, increase the tax base, and improve the business climate.

Promoting Employment   Reduced assessment classes are subsidies to capital. If they have any effect at all, it is in reducing the cost of capital relative to the cost of labor. Thus, property tax abatements encourage investment in capital-intensive processes rather than labor-intensive processes, even when the latter may be more efficient.

This does not imply that there is anything wrong with capital investment, nor that new labor-saving plant designs should not be introduced. But it does suggest that a property tax abatement, by directly subsidizing capital rather than labor, can lead to the premature displacement of workers, raising unemployment above what it would otherwise be. Even if new factories were built that would not otherwise have been constructed, their total addition to the work force will be less than could have been achieved by spending the same subsidy amount (or the same foregone taxes) directly on labor.

Empirical support for this conclusion is provided by Leslie Papke (1987), one of the strongest academic proponents of tax abatements. She found that lower taxes on business capital were associated with more capital per worker. This can happen only if workers are replaced by new plant and equipment or if investment in plant and equipment proceeds relatively more rapidly than investment in new employees. It suggests that subsidies to capital, such as property tax reductions, do not increase employment as much as would subsidies directly to labor.

Increasing the Tax Base   Those who advocate reducing assessments to increase the tax base subscribe, at least implicitly, to some version of the so-called Laffer curve hypothesis. Dating back at least to the fourteenth-century philosopher Ibn Khaldun (Adams 1981:415), and popularized more recently by economist Arthur Laffer, the hypothesis can be summarized as follows:

There are two tax rates at which government receives no revenue, 0 percent and 100 percent. Zero means no taxes are levied. At the other extreme, people will refuse to invest if all their return is taxed away; thus, there will be no tax base. As the tax rate is increased from zero, revenues increase until they reach a maximum; then they decline as continued increases in the rate are more than offset by citizens' reduced investment in taxable activities.

When applied to property taxes, this theory means that reducing assessment levels can increase the tax base if and only if real estate taxes were previously so high that revenue was on the declining end of the Laffer curve; but there is no credible evidence that this is so. However much taxpayers complain, revenues consistently increase when rates are raised, whereas they would decrease if we were on the declining end of the curve.

Furthermore, the construction increases that would be necessary to offset cuts in the tax base are so large as to be outside the realm of possibility. For example, consider an investor who would construct an industrial building in Cook County, even if she knew it would be assessed at the normal 36 percent. She now learns that it qualifies for the special 16 percent. Even with a discount rate as low as 5 percent, she would have to increase the building's size by 28 percent beyond what was originally planned just for the county's tax base to be the same as it would have been without the reduced assessment. If the discount rate were 10 percent, the building would have to be almost half again as large as planned.

Alternately, suppose the building is constructed as initially designed. Then someone else would have to enter the market, acquire financing, and construct another building worth at least 28 or 48 percent, respectively, of the first building's value. Furthermore, the second building must be one that would not have been constructed at all without the tax break.

Estimating whether construction increases of this magnitude are likely to occur requires an examination of real estate economics. The following example suggests that the desired construction increase would not, and probably should not, occur.

Begin by assuming that without special tax treatment, a $1 million building would be constructed. If a thirty-year mortgage were obtained at 12 percent interest for 80 percent of the building's cost, annual debt service would be $99,315. Using typical Cook County data, if the building were assessed at 36 percent, taxes would add $68,879, for a total annual cost of $168,194 for debt and property taxes combined.

Now suppose the building qualified for class 6.b's 16 percent. If the tax base is to break even, the developer must spend $1.28 million on it, instead of $1 million, assuming a 5 percent discount rate. Taxes for the first eight years at the reduced assessment level drop to $39,184, but debt service for the larger mortgage increases to $127,123. The total annual cost is virtually identical, $166,307.

The similarity, however, extends only to debt service and taxes. Maintenance and other operating expenses for the second building will be larger than for the first because the building is larger. But where will customers come from to pay the bills? Two principal alternatives must be considered, since the building can be either occupied by its owner or leased out.

If the new building is owner occupied, carrying costs for the additional space can be justified only if it can be used for more production. The property tax break, however, does nothing to increase consumer demand, so the added space is useless. The firm would make more money by constructing its building to the original specifications, paying reduced class 6.b taxes on the smaller facility ($30,613, rather than $68,879), and pocketing the difference as increased profits.

Now suppose the building is constructed for lease: Where will tenants come from? If the volume of new industrial space in any urban area increased by a steady 28 percent above the amount already coming onto the market, substantial rent concessions could be expected in the new buildings and possibly calamitous tenant losses in the older ones.

This has two property tax consequences. First, tax revenue from the new buildings will not be as high as projected, since assessors typically hold down assessments on recently completed property when rent concessions are being offered. Second, vacancies in the older buildings will provide the grounds for an appeal to reduce their assessments. The combined effect is that total assessments are likely to decrease, or not increase as fast as they otherwise would, even if construction were to increase.

Improving the Business Climate   Tax abatements operate by granting differentially low burdens to certain favored taxpayers. As a consequence, they create dissatisfaction among taxpayers who do not receive them. The resulting political divisions take at least three forms.

First, there are differences among plants. Reduced assessments are available only to companies that can build anew, rehabilitate, or reoccupy someone else's old space. If the plants are in industries already in the region, existing plants not in a position to expand or rehab—perhaps because they maintain their facilities so that major rehab is unnecessary—will rightly complain that they are paying taxes to subsidize their own new competition.

Divisions are also created between business and individual taxpayers as groups, especially when frequent amendments shift tax burdens back and forth between business and residential property owners.

Third, property tax abatements create dissension among units of government. This occurs whenever one government, usually the state or municipality, can abate taxes that would otherwise be collected by another jurisdiction. This problem exists in almost all states.

A forceful expression of these conflicts is offered by a member of the Illinois Manufacturers' Association: "Our employees are paying taxes to the state, which in turn is using that money to subsidize firms that will eliminate their jobs" (Veverka 1987:2).

In short, then, reduced assessment classifications, despite their stated goal of improving the business climate, foster instability in the tax code and divisions among taxpayers that actually achieve the opposite—a worsened climate.

Just What *Is* the Tax Base?

The most common measure of the tax base is "market value." In practice, most analysts agree that one of the best, if not the best, indicator of this value is the price actually paid for a recently sold parcel of property that is similar to the one being assessed (see American Institute 1987:313; IAAO 1977:41 and 108; and IAAO 1978:37 and 191). The American Institute of Real Estate Appraisers (1987:19) offers a technical definition frequently cited in assessment appeals and other legal proceedings.

For property types that are rarely sold, other indicators of market value must be found. For properties commonly leased, one approach is to capitalize net income. An unresolved question is whether assessing and appeal officials should use actual data for the specific property in question or "typical" data for a generalized property of the same kind. The latter is asserted to be more equitable under certain circumstances: A bad manager with poor cash flow should not be subsidized at taxpayer expense by having a low assessment, and an unusually good manager who derives a higher than "normal" rate of return should not have to pay a tax permium for his or her market prowess. In practice, however, there are no clearly written and publicly available statements of the actual procedures followed in most assessing districts.

SPECIAL PROBLEMS OF LONG-TERM OWNERS

Long-term owners of real estate are sometimes identified as being at the particular mercy of the assessor and market forces beyond their control. The definition of "long-term owner" in this context seems to be those who have not budgeted for what they perceive to be large tax increases.

133

However, for nonresidential property, market forces and capitalization of the property tax make relief through the assessment system almost impossible. When an individual assessment is increased relative to other assessments, or when it stays the same while assessment levels for other classes of property decrease, there is no question that a cash flow hardship can result. On the other hand, when low assessments are capitalized, they make it possible for developers to offer a higher price. This yields a capital gain for the current owner when he or she sells; but if the public purpose is to maintain the current use, the policy fails.

In some areas, most notably for farms, laws grant assessment relief to owners on the condition that back taxes be paid if the property is converted to another use before a specified time. These may have a limited effect, but they suffer at least two weaknesses. First, governing bodies are often loath to enforce the payback. Second, if market demand for the converted project is strong enough, back taxes are so small as a percent of total development costs that they provide very little disincentive. When laws do not incorporate payback provisions, they become merely subsidies to owners holding the real estate for the most opportune conversion date. If other laws provide tax abatements for rehab or conversion, the combined effect is even more perverse.

In this respect, classification may be a more serious problem than rising prices, since it provides an incentive for conversion from nonresidential to residential uses. Zoning could offset this, but only if maintained in the face of market pressure. Yet when zoning codes are strictly maintained, property owners who would like to convert complain that they are being deprived of their "right" to a capital gain on their real estate.

"MARKET" VALUE VERSUS "INVESTMENT" VALUE

Since at least the early 1980s, the owners of large commercial properties have engaged in a concerted effort to establish credence for a distinction between "market" value and "investment" value. (See Shlaes 1983; GFOA and Shlaes 1985; and McDonald 1987 for examples.) According to the argument, recent buyers of downtown office buildings have paid an investment price that is higher than the "true" market value. They thus have revealed prices that the assessor should not use as comparables.

The canons of professional appraisal, however, raise serious questions about the logic of using investment value in this way. The clearest illustration of this comes from the only example of investment value provided in the entire 750 pages of the American Institute of Real Estate Appraisers' text:

For example, an appraiser may be asked to consider whether a parcel of land that is adjacent to the client's industrial property is worth $500,000, the price being asked by its owner. Market analysis indicates that the property is overpriced in comparison with other properties and that its market value is $400,000. However, the client's successful business must be expanded and it will have to be relocated if the additional land is not acquired. If the existing operation is moved, disruption of business and other factors will create a loss of more than $100,000. Because this loss exceeds the difference between the property's market value and its asking price, it might be concluded that the property has an investment value of $500,000 or more to the client in question. [American Institute 1987:597]

There is no resemblance between the various elements of this example and the reported sales of downtown office buildings. The market for the latter seems to be defined precisely by buyers who consistently pay prices in a range well above what remaining owners want to be assessed at; but there is nothing to suggest that any one buyer is atypical of the rest of them or that they are acting under some duress that forces them to pay more than they would for any other property of a similar size, location, and quality. Nor is there evidence that current owners are willing to lower their asking prices below those being offered them.

On the other hand, many local assessors seem to have adopted at least some version of the investment value argument, since the assessments for large downtown properties are often on the order of half the actual sale price—in some cases, even after the sale price is known. Cumulative losses to the tax base, compared to assessments at actual market prices can be hundreds of millions of dollars per year in larger cities.

Assessment Discrimination

The types and extent of residential assessment discrimination have not changed much since Kenneth Baar (1981) wrote his excellent and thorough survey article on the subject. In general, assessment discrimination can take several forms:

1. Low-priced housing is assessed at a higher percentage of its market value than higher-priced housing. This is so widespread that property tax

135

research on individual cities now often only alludes to the finding in passing before moving on to other matters.

2. Lower-valued commercial or industrial property is assessed at a higher fraction of value than more expensive property. This is like the housing case above, except that it has not been studied as much—presumably because fewer data are available on nonresidential real estate transactions.

3. Some geographic areas or neighborhoods are assessed at higher percentages of value than others. The most favored neighborhoods tend to be those with concentrations of relatively high-income owners of single family detached homes. Although there is often overlap between minority neighborhoods and the parts of a jurisdiction with lower-priced housing, some reasearchers have been able to identify a racial bias that is independent of real estate values.

4. Some property types are consistently assessed at higher percentages of value than others. Business property tends to be highest, followed by apartment buildings, and finally single family homes at the lowest level.

These types of discrimination are not mutually exclusive, and it is common to find several of them simultaneously.

POSSIBLE REASONS FOR DISCRIMINATORY ASSESSMENTS

Although it is not possible to know the actual intentions of assessing officials, it is easy to speculate on some of the causes for these problems. The causes can be described as either methodological or political.

At least three methodological problems can be identified. In the first place, many assessments continue to be made by the so-called replacement cost method of determining value. Under this method, the same initial value is assigned to all properties of a given type. This value is then depreciated according to a formula for each property's age. The depreciated value, after something is added in for land, becomes the assessor's estimate of market value.

This method is still used in Cook County for most commercial and industrial property. It is also widely employed in many other jurisdictions, especially smaller ones, where it is applied to all types of property. Nevertheless, it is clearly inappropriate for older urban places. Even if land values are properly accounted for, and they hardly ever are, the method yields similar assessments for all properties of a given type and age—even though some are in neighborhoods where values have skyrocketed, while others are in poverty areas with declining real estate values.

Second, most assessors have a tendency to assess toward the average, or mean. They establish a range of values for an area, but the range does not extend all the way up to the highest actual values, or down to the lowest actual values. Even sophisticated computerized methods have some of this bias built in by the nature of the mathematics employed. Sometimes a formal floor is established below which assessments are not allowed to fall. The problem afflicts nonresidential as well as residential property, and it causes overassessment of precisely the lowest-valued real estate in the jurisdiction.

A final methodological difficulty is infrequent reassessing. In some states, several decades may intervene between reassessments. Results are predictable: In areas with rapidly appreciating prices, assessments as a percentage of current actual value drop precipitously. In less affluent areas, they drop less rapidly or hold steady. After a decade or so, it is not unusual to find assessment ratios in poorer neighborhoods at least twice the level they are in other neighborhoods.

Political reasons for discrimination are more difficult to isolate, but there are at least two that deserve mention. First, homeowners are more active politically than apartment dwellers. Middle- and upper-income owners are more organized than poor owners. Thus, it is not surprising to find these groups enjoying the lowest assessment ratios.

Second, despite a popular conception that all business people are "well connected" politically and routinely get whatever favors they want from government, most business owners do not protest their assessments. One reason is that property taxes, regardless of their dollar amount, are rarely more than a fraction of one percent of total costs for industrial firms. If labor or materials constitute, say, 50 percent of costs, it is much more productive for managers to work on obtaining even a 1 or 2 percent cut in those items than to seek a 50 or 75 percent cut in property taxes. For many commercial rental properties, part or all of real estate taxes are passed on to tenants. Finally, many businesspeople hesitate to make an issue of their assessments because of a concern that it might tarnish their image as good public citizens.

FACTORS HINDERING REFORM

Efforts to obtain assessment reform are hindered both by factors that relate to individual property owners and by institutional factors under the control of assessing authorities or other public officials.

With respect to individuals, most properties in virtually all jurisdictions are underassessed relative to the legally established target level.

137

Thus, when an owner looks only at her own assessment, the natural conclusion is that she has nothing to complain about. Only if she becomes aware of others' assessments can she realize that she is overassessed relative to them.

Even then, however, an overassessed owner might not take action if she believes that the only ground for a complaint is overassessment relative to the legal norm, rather than relative to other property owners. This opinion is not as uncommon as one might expect, especially since assessment and appeal officials do not always make their standards clear to the public.

On the institutional side is lack of effective oversight by the media or other levels of government. Because it can be difficult to collect the data necessary to complete a good study of discriminatory assessments, media investigative reporters rarely get involved. Skeptics also suggest that media executives do not favor such investigations because their property may be among the most favored.

In addition, academic researchers have devoted less attention to discriminatory assessments in recent years because they have been so well established already, that is, it is no longer cutting-edge research to establish the existence of discrimination. And in the absence of clear public support for state enforcement of local assessment uniformity, there is little basis for state officials to take strong action, even when they may be aware of irregularities.

Even after discrimination has become a public issue, there are important factors which hinder reform. Perhaps the most important is embedded in the genesis of the problem itself: The taxpayers most likely to be active in any reform effort are the same ones who are most likely to be active on other political issues—which means they are the ones with the lowest assessments. Taxpayers who are least active are also the ones with the highest assessments. Assessment reform, in other words, is not like dealing with other forms of discrimination, where enlightened members of a group not suffering discrimination can support a solution without necessarily incurring direct costs of their own. The only way to correct the problem, as illustrated in section two, is for a tax shift to occur. This limits political support to members of the group actually discriminated against and to those others who are explicitly willing to accept a larger tax share to correct what they recognize as an inequity. I am not aware of any jurisdiction where this latter group has been large enough to effect a change.

Furthermore, assessment officials themselves have a very strong tool to weaken reform efforts: They can simply invite people who feel they have been wronged to file an appeal. When relief is granted, an impression is created that the system really works and that the problem is not as severe as previously thought. In other words, the few people who complain most loudly are granted relief, thereby weakening their ability to continue in a leadership role; but the system itself does not change.

As a consequence of all these factors, solutions are usually limited to granting new forms of relief to identifiable groups of taxpayers who make a politically credible claim that they are overburdened. Genuine reform programs, with oversight to insure that similar problems do not arise in the future, are not implemented.

In some states, a measure of reform has been achieved when aggrieved taxpayers, usually including businesses suffering from de facto classification, have filed legal actions. Courts have consistently ordered reassessments to establish uniformity in accord with prevailing state laws; but as often as not—as in New York, Massachusetts, Connecticut, and other places—legislators have subsequently changed the law to enshrine the de facto classification and effectively nullify part of the court order.

Future Directions

Numerous problems are apparent from the preceding sections. What follows here is a list of suggestions for policy changes or research to clarify the program alternatives. Suggestions toward the beginning are probably more important than those toward the end, although a strict priority order is not realistic.

1. Engage representatives of all interested parties—the state, localities, school districts, high- and low-income taxpayers, large and small businesses—in a policy roundtable to establish clear and consistent policies with respect to new versus existing real estate uses. As it is now, assessment practices penalize existing uses for the sake of certain new investors. These and other implicit policies should be fully aired and resolved.

2. Related to suggestion 1 but sufficiently important to merit separate mention are questions concerning the so-called but-for clause in many abatement programs. This is the provision that requires a showing that the development would not be economically feasible but for a tax abatement. Tax increment financing (TIF), which was not discussed in this chapter, usually also has a similar provision. (See Staton and Lyons 1989 for a basic introduction to TIF.) Although popular in some development

circles as a means to target scarce public dollars to developments perceived as needy, the clause has several troubling aspects. Beyond the problem of measuring and proving need, which can be more difficult for small entrepreneurs without consultants than for well-heeled developers with consultants, there is the genuine economic contradiction of subsidizing what could not otherwise succeed on its own. That is, if the but-for provision has any meaning at all, it must mean that there is not enough market demand to support both existing businesses and the proposed new undertaking. If, under these circumstances, a new undertaking is subsidized, can it not succeed only by drawing customers away from the existing businesses? Is this an appropriate use of public funds? These questions deserve more study and discussion.

3. Declare a moratorium on all changes in assessment law until the discussions above are completed.

4. If reduced assessment classes (and tax increment financing) are to continue, methods should be sought to eliminate some of the ways they now threaten local government finance. One option is to give each governing body full control over its own share of the tax base.

5. Opportunities should be sought to expand the use of special service areas (SSAs) as an alternative to tax abatements. Taxpayers in an SSA pay more, not less, taxes; but they do it under a cooperative agreement with the municipality that precisely defines what the additional revenue will be used for. This provides tremendous opportunities to tailor development spending precisely to the desires of local property owners, whereas tax abatements reduce the resources available for public improvements.

6. All levels of government should prepare a "tax expenditure budget." This is a document that lists, each year, all the special provisions that reduce the taxes of specified groups of taxpayers. It also identifies the amount of revenue forgone as a result of each provision. With such a document in hand, public officials and citizens alike will be in a better position to determine whether the costs of various tax subsidy programs are really worth the benefits.

7. Assessors should publish clear assessment and appeal standards. As simple as this sounds, it is not done in most places. Published materials should include information about the extent to which typical market data are used, rather than property-specific data, in the income approach; typical expense ratios and income estimates per square foot or other measure for various types of property; and the capitalization rates used for different properties and neighborhoods. In addition, written opinions should be maintained on all appeals, whether granted or denied.

These actions will make assessing something less of a mystery to taxpayers and help to put them on a more even footing with one another.

8. Investigate various methods for introducing checks and balances into the assessment system. Since most taxpayers do not have the knowledge, time, or other resources to become familiar with the system and file appeals as often as appropriate, institutional remedies are called for. Of particular importance are measures that might correct serious underassessments, especially of large properties, since they have a direct effect on the tax rate for all other taxpayers. Remedies that have been tried in some places include giving to taxing bodies the right to file underassessment appeals and creating an independent government office, with members appointed to long terms, that is charged with educating taxpayers and filing both under- and overassessment appeals when appropriate.

Finally, no discussion of the property tax would be complete without at least some reference to individuals, especially those with lower incomes. They have not been explicitly discussed because of the focus on economic development, but they are crucial to the continued strength of the property tax as a local revenue source. If individuals cannot be reassured that the assessment system is fair and that provisions are made for low-income people who find the tax a burden, they may withdraw their support for the entire system. Then, as argued in section one, an important foundation for local government autonomy will be lost. Steven Gold (1987) has provided an excellent monograph that not only outlines the criteria for evaluating state and local tax relief but also summarizes numerous programs in effect throughout the country.

NOTE

This is an abridged version of a longer paper prepared for the Project for Chicago Research and Action in the 1990s. The complete paper is available for $7.50 (which includes postage and handling) from the Center for Economic Policy Analysis, 59 E. Van Buren St., 1716, Chicago, Illinois 60605; (312) 786-1825.

REFERENCE LIST

Aaron, Henry. 1975. *Who Pays the Property Tax?* Washington, D.C.: Brookings Institution.

Adams, Roy D. 1981. "Tax Rates and Tax Collections: The Basic Analytics of Khaldun-Laffer Curves." *Public Finance Quarterly* (October):415–430.

American Institute of Real Estate Appraisers. 1987. *The Appraisal of Real Estate*, 9th ed. Chicago: American Institute of Real Estate Appraisers.

Baar, Kenneth. 1981. "Property Tax Assessment Discrimination against Low-Income Neighborhoods." *Urban Lawyer* 13 (Summer):333–406.

Birch, David L. 1987. "The Q Factor." *Inc.* 9 (April):53–54.

Cook County. 1988. *Real Property Assessment Classification Ordinance* (June 20).

GFOA (Government Finance Officers Association), Government Finance Research Center; and Shlaes & Co. 1985. *The Property Tax in Chicago and Cook County.* Washington: GFOA (June).

Glastris, Paul. 1989. "Holdup in the Windy City." *U.S. News & World Report*, July 17:40–41.

Gold, Steven David. 1979. *Property Tax Relief.* Lexington, Mass.:Heath.

———. 1987. *State Tax Relief for the Poor.* Denver: National Conference of State Legislatures (April).

Heilbroner, Robert L., and James K. Galbraith. 1987. *Understanding Microeconomics*, rev. 8th ed. Englewood Cliffs, N.J.: Prentice-Hall.

Howland, Marie. 1985. "Property Taxes and the Birth and Intraregional Location of New Firms." *Journal of Planning Education and Research.* 4 (April):148–156.

IAAO (International Association of Assessing Officers). 1977. *Property Assessment Valuation.* Chicago: IAAO.

———. 1978. *Improving Real Property Assessment: A Reference Manual.* Chicago: IAAO.

Lyons, Arthur, Spenser Staton, Greg Wass, and Mari Zurek. 1988. *Reducing Property Taxes to Promote Industrial Development: Does It Work? An Evaluation of Cook County's Industrial Incentive Real Estate Classifications.* Chicago: City of Chicago Comptroller's Office (July).

McDonald, John F. 1987. *Assessment of Real Property in Downtown Chicago: A Review of Current Problems.* Chicago: Building Owners and Managers Association (December).

Nealon, Marianne. 1978. *Why Companies Stay—Why Companies Leave.* Chicago: City of Chicago Economic Development Commission.

Papke, Leslie E. 1987. "Subnational Taxation and Capital Mobility: Estimates of Tax-Price Elasticities." *National Tax Journal.* 40 (June):191–203.

Raphaelson, Arnold H. 1981. "The Property Tax." In *Management Poli-*

cies in Local Government Finance, edited by J. Richard Aronson and Eli Schwartz. Washington, D.C.: International City Management Association.

Shlaes & Co. 1983. *Real Property Appraisal in Downtown Chicago: Current Problems and Suggested Solutions*. Chicago: Shlaes & Co.

Staton, Spenser, and Arthur Lyons. 1989. *Tax Increment Financing: Is It Good Public Policy?* Chicago: Center for Economic Policy Analysis (April).

Veverka, Mark. 1987. "The Morning After: Critics Charge Incentives Make Poor Jobs Policy." *Chicago Enterprise* 1 (May):1–3.

Art Lyons has been director of the Center for Economic Policy Analysis (CEPA) since 1985. In addition to his role in establishing and running the Center, he has served as research associate at the Center for Urban Affairs and Policy Research at Northwestern University, administrative assistant to the Commissioner of the Cook County (Illinois) Board of Assessment Appeals, and assistant professor at the School of Urban Planning and Policy at the University of Illinois at Chicago. CEPA has been prominent in community organization circles in Chicago and in other cities.

7 THE EMPLOYMENT POTENTIAL OF CHICAGO'S SERVICE INDUSTRIES
Wendy Wintermute and Charles Hicklin

Background

Throughout the postwar period, the U.S. economy has undergone a massive structural transformation, resulting in a substantial loss of manufacturing jobs and a steady surge of growth in the service sector. Analysts began to talk of a new "postindustrial" society, in which Americans would swap a profusion of services for goods manufactured elsewhere. Original projections tended to be optimistic, predicting a general upgrading of work and standards of living, as the United States became the international center for highly skilled work and workers in finance, management and professional services, and information, leaving the "dirty work" of manufacturing to less developed nations.

Recently, however, more ominous reports warn that the shift to service jobs is creating a two-tier society by providing a small number of highly skilled and high-paying jobs and a much larger number of low-skilled, low-paying, part-time, and unstable jobs, with no apparent internal career ladders permitting upward mobility. The "middle," composed of the sort of well-paid unskilled and semiskilled jobs formerly provided by unionized manufacturing plants, was disappearing, along with middle-class incomes, middle-class life-styles, and, some argue, middle-class values (Bluestone and Harrison 1982; Kuttner 1983; Wilson 1989).

144

Some of the differences in prognoses may be explained by the fact that the service sector encompasses a very large and very disparate collection of industries, ranging from barbershops to wholesalers to railroads. These industries, in turn, exhibit very different occupational structures, employ a wide variety of workers, and offer a similarly wide range of wages and other employment benefits. Moreover, local economies throughout the country vary considerably in the structure of their particular service sector. Some cities have captured a significant number of headquarters and advanced corporate services. Others depend heavily on government or nonprofit service industries, such as education. Others may be centers of commercial activities, with wholesale and retail trade dominating (Stanback and Noyelle 1982).

Consequently, any analysis of the influence of the service industries on employment must, by necessity, examine specific service industries in specific localities. Unfortunately, the lack of substate data on employment-related data has made local analyses in most cases difficult. Chicago is fortunate in that its size and economic diversity provide a sufficient wealth of data to allow such an analysis. This report, in fact draws on relatively new data sources (post-1980) and several recent analyses of the Chicago economy which the data have permitted (Center for Urban Economic Development 1989; Allardice et al. 1990).

Having narrowed the focus to a specific local service industry, the scope of inquiry must of necessity be rather broad. This is because a number of factors influence the effect of a local service sector on a community and its workers.

Industry characteristics—such as average firm size, capital intensity, competition within the industry, stability of markets, and profitability—all affect the number, quality, and stability of jobs in that industry.

Occupational characteristics of jobs in service industries differ significantly in the skills required and the methods for acquiring such skills (e.g., on-the-job training vs. academic education), the opportunities for skill development and advancement, and the transferability of skills that promotes flexibility and stability of employment.

In any given locality, labor force characteristics determine how many and which workers are deemed qualified by employers to perform the jobs available. While job requirements include job-related training and skills, equally important are employer assessments of proper work "attitudes," which may include punctuality, deference to workplace authority, ability to "get along" with other workers, proper workplace attire, language, and etiquette. The problem is that work attitudes are difficult to estimate, and employers often rely on generalizations based on age, race, gender, and union membership, preferring to hire from those

TABLE 7.1. CHICAGO'S LARGEST SERVICE INDUSTRIES BY SERVICE INDUSTRY DIVISION

SIC Code	Industry Title	1986 Cook Co. Employment
Producer services/advanced corporate		
6020	Commercial and savings banks	50,142
6330	Fire, marine, casualty ins.	20,911
6510	Real estate operators & lessors	15,703
6530	Real estate agents & managers	21,422
7310	Advertising	12,805
7330	Mailing, reproduction, stenographic	12,424
7340	Services to buildings	17,872
7360	Personnel supply services	27,131
7370	Computer and data processing	23,909
7390	Misc. business services	64,675
8110	Legal services	28,999
Producer services/distributive		
4210	Trucking, local & long dist.	29,447
4510	Air transportation	30,682
4810	Telephone communication	21,490
4830	Radio and television broadcasting	4,118
5060	Electrical goods, wholesale	15,003
5080	Wholesale machinery equip. & supply	41,917
Social services		
8010	Offices of physicians	19,442
8060	Hospitals	99,793
8640	Civic and social associations	7,748
8660	Religious organizations	17,465
Consumer services		
5310	Department stores	38,467
5410	Grocery stores	46,546
7210	Laundry and garment services	9,969
7690	Misc. repair	4,169
Total, all selected industries		692,481

Source: County Business Patterns, Cook County 1986.

TABLE 7.2. PERCENTAGE OF LABOR FORCE BY OCCUPATIONAL CATEGORY FOR MAJOR SERVICE INDUSTRY DIVISIONS

	Producer Services		Social Services	Consumer Services	All Service Industries
	Advanced Corporate	Distributive			
Managerial & management rel.	13.2%	10.5%	5.6%	9.2%	10.0%
Marketing & sales	6.4	12.7	0.1	24.6	9.4
Admin. support & clerical	39.9	30.8	19.5	13.4	28.1
Service occs.	16.4	4.4	22.2	4.6	13.2

Source: Illinois Occupational Information Coordinating Committee 1984

clerical occupations; and service occupations. Employment in these four categories accounts for just over 60 percent of all employment in the selected service industries. Each of the major service industry divisions employs quite different proportions of these occupations (table 7.2).

Managerial and management-related occupations include managers and professional support occupations, such as accountants and auditors, inspectors, budget and credit analysts, and purchasing agents. Not surprisingly, advanced corporate services employ the highest proportion of managerial workers. Other managerial titles in the service industry include restaurant and hotel managers, health care administrators, education administrators, business executives, sales and service managers, financial managers, marketing managers, and advertising and public relations managers. Managerial occupations account for 10 percent of service industry employment.

The education and training requirements and the potential earnings of managers vary greatly. For instance, one may become a restaurant manager through on-the-job training after high school or with a minimum of formal training in a company program or at a community college. Earnings for restaurant managers in Illinois range from $17,000 to $44,000 a year. In contrast, people with jobs in health care, education, and public administration, as well as business executives and managers, require at least a bachelor's degree and experience or a graduate-level education. Salaries in these highly skilled positions range from $22,000 for junior

149

public managers to over $100,000 for chief executives of major corporations (Horizons 1989).

Marketing and sales occupations account for 9.4 percent of service employment. These occupations include cashiers, insurance sales workers, real estate agents and brokers, retail salespersons, and securities and financial services sales workers. Consumer services, which include retail establishments, are most likely to employ marketing and sales workers.

Advertising and business services salespeople are increasingly required to have college degrees, preferably in business administration, marketing, or another related field. Wages in this area begin at around $20,000. Because of the commission basis for most salaries, the range is quite large. Top salaries may be over $40,000 per year (Horizons 1989).

Real estate salespeople are also paid a commission, so earnings for this category vary widely, from around $20,000 to over $100,000 for successful commercial real estate brokers. One must obtain a real estate license from the state by passing a written exam. Although it is not required, most salespeople have some college education (Illinois Occupational Information Coordinating Committee (IOICC) 1988).

Securities salespersons earn much higher salaries than many other marketing and sales professionals. A college degree is usually required for these jobs. This occupation has a high turnover rate, but average earnings for experienced sales workers are from $64,000 to $156,000.

Cashier jobs normally require a high school diploma. Salaries range from about $7,000 to as much as $22,000 for union jobs. These jobs sometimes carry fringe benefits for those belonging to a union and employed by a large store on a full-time basis. However, many cashiers earn low wages, work part-time, and receive no fringe benefits. Store salespeople receive their training on the job. Earnings range from about $10,000 to about $16,000. Many store salespersons work part-time, and some are paid on commission.

Administrative support and clerical occupations claim the largest proportion (28 percent) of jobs in the service industries. The largest occupations in this category are bookkeepers, accounting and auditing clerks, receptionists, stock clerks, shipping clerks, secretaries, and typists and word processors. Advanced corporate services employ the highest proportion of administrative support and clerical workers.

Jobs such as general office clerks, file clerks, personnel clerks, secretaries, and receptionists do not require a college degree. One can enter these types of jobs with a high school education and skills in typing and word processing. These positions generally pay between $12,000 for a junior file clerk to about $25,000 for an executive secretary (Crain's 1989).

Typists and word processors require training similar to that for general office clerks. Most employers require a high school diploma and typing speeds between sixty and seventy words per minute. Many also require special word-processing training which can be obtained through a junior college or a private vocational training program (IOICC 1988). Some employers provide on-the-job training. Typist and word processor salaries range from about $12,000 to about $22,000 per year (Crain's 1989). Data entry clerk jobs require lower typing speed than word processors. Earnings for data entry clerks range from $12,000 to $20,000 (IOICC 1988).

So-called service occupations in fact account for only 13.2 percent of service industry employment. Service occupations include those of security guards, janitors, nurse's aides, food service workers, and personal service workers. Service workers are most heavily concentrated in social services.

Most of these service occupations require little or no formal training. Janitors, food service workers, and security guards learn their skills on the job, although many employers prefer applicants with a high school diploma or equivalent. Janitors and guards earn about $9,000 to $18,000 per year. Nursing aides are often required to complete a short-term training program to become a certified nursing assistant. Such training is a state regulation for those employed in nursing homes in Illinois. Nursing aides earn from $9,000 to $15,000 a year. Personal service workers include hairdressers, who must complete a 1,500-hour program and pass a state certification exam. Wages range from $12,000 to $25,000 (IOICC 1988).

Employment outside these four groups varies widely across different industries. Professional occupations are numerous. People in health-related occupations, such as physicians and registered nurses, are a large group, accounting for 6.8 percent of local service industry employment. These jobs are located in one of the largest (hospitals, SIC 8060) and one of the fastest-growing (offices of physicians, SIC 8010) service industries in Chicago.

While little firm research exists on career ladders in service firms, the general opinion is that movement from one level to another is difficult. Unlike the case in manufacturing occupations, opportunities for on-the-job training for higher-level jobs are not common in the service industries. Upper-level professional or management positions in many service industries require formal educational training, including college degrees or graduate training. It seems that career paths such as those in manufacturing, where someone can enter as an assembly worker and progress to a management job, are lacking in the service industries (Spilerman 1977).

151

It is not that career paths are entirely absent; more commonly they are truncated. For example, there is a career path for clerical workers, who may begin as receptionists or general clerks and advance to office managers. There is also a path for managers that begins in a sales or professional position and progresses to executive positions. But there is no intersection between the two paths. One cannot begin as an office clerk and advance to a professional or management position without further education.

Chicago's Service Workers

There are quite distinct patterns in service sector employment evident by race and gender. In general, women are much more likely to be concentrated in service industries than men. Nine of the ten industries with the highest percentage of women are service industries: private households; hospitals and health services; banking and credit agencies; general merchandise retail; public and private educational services; and social services. In contrast, of the ten industries with the highest proportion of men, only five are service industries: trucking and warehousing; repair services; utilities and sanitary services; automotive dealerships and gas stations; and railroads.

Employment in service industries also varies by race. One of the most striking findings is the underrepresentation of Hispanics in the service industries. None of the top ten industries for Hispanics are in service sectors. In contrast, eight of the ten industries with the highest proportion of blacks are service industries: U.S. postal service; private households, railroads; other transportation; communications; public administration; hospitals; other personal services. Whites are concentrated in a number of advanced corporate services—including legal, engineering and other services, business services, and finance, insurance, and real estate—as well as entertainment and recreational services, public education, wholesale trade, trucking and warehousing.

There are similar race and gender disparities among service occupations. Employment quotients for forty-eight service sector occupations were devised to measure the degree of concentration of workers by race and gender (table 7.3).

Of the three racial groups, whites are disproportionately employed in twenty-seven of the forty-eight occupations. These include most occupations at the top levels of educational requirements and earnings. Lawyers

TABLE 7.3. EMPLOYEMENT QUOTIENTS FOR 48 SERVICE-RELATED OCCUPATIONS BY RACE AND GENDER

	Whites	Blacks	Hispanics	Women	Men
Managerial occupations					
Public officials and administrators	0.94	1.32	0.23	0.77	1.19
Managers other than mfg. and retail	1.27	0.71	0.38	0.97	1.03
Management-related occupations	1.20	0.74	0.37	1.02	0.98
Professional occupations					
Health diagnosticians	1.22	0.38	0.36	0.50	1.41
Health assessment and treatment	0.92	0.81	0.31	1.91	0.25
Lawyers and judges	1.55	0.30	0.15	0.53	1.39
Natural scientists and mathematicians	1.24	0.54	0.33	0.76	1.20
Social scientists and urban planners	1.36	0.61	0.21	1.10	0.91
Architects	1.47	0.28	0.22	0.33	1.56
Engineers	1.25	0.44	0.33	0.17	1.69
Elementary and secondary teachers	0.87	1.47	0.36	1.66	0.45
Other teachers, librarians, and counselors	1.22	0.69	0.43	1.08	0.93
Bookkeepers and accountants	1.21	0.66	0.58	1.89	0.26
Social, recreational, and religious workers	0.87	1.37	0.58	1.22	0.82
Writers, artists, and athletes	1.39	0.42	0.44	0.95	1.04
Technical and paraprofessional occupations					
Surveyors and cartographers	1.75	0.00	0.00	0.27	1.60
Health technologists except LPN	0.84	1.16	0.35	1.55	0.55
Technologists except health	1.12	0.72	0.56	0.63	1.30
Licenced practical nurses	0.50	2.15	0.33	2.15	0.05
Clerical occupations					
Supervisors (administrative support)	1.03	1.13	0.53	1.20	0.83
Secretaries and typists	1.12	0.93	0.58	2.15	0.05
Financial records processors	1.05	0.96	0.60	1.79	0.35
Material recording and scheduling clerks	0.99	1.01	1.22	0.62	1.31

TABLE 7.3 (*continued*)

	Whites	Blacks	Hispanic	Women	Men
Computer equipment operators	0.96	1.10	0.55	1.25	0.79
Mail and message distributors	0.52	2.09	0.38	0.89	1.09
Other administrative support people	0.95	1.17	0.68	1.73	0.40
Sales occupations					
Sales reps (finance and business services)	1.39	0.51	0.23	0.84	1.13
Sales supervisors (not self-employed)	1.19	0.74	0.66	0.76	1.20
Sales (retail commodities and services)	1.18	0.74	0.70	1.28	0.77
Sales reps (commodities except retail)	1.39	0.45	0.38	0.56	1.36
Salaried retail employees	1.19	0.75	0.48	0.84	1.13
Cashiers	0.93	1.16	0.89	1.78	0.35
Sales workers (nonretail)	1.11	1.00	0.60	1.04	0.97
Sales supervisors (self-employed)	1.14	0.64	1.31	0.54	1.38
Self-employed retailers	1.03	0.64	1.00	0.62	1.31
Sales-related occupations	1.29	0.54	0.00	1.65	0.47
Service occupations					
Food service occupations	0.96	0.87	1.50	1.14	0.88
Health service occupations	0.57	1.74	0.65	1.90	0.26
Cleaning and building services	0.81	1.35	1.13	0.69	1.25
Personal services	0.82	1.40	0.79	1.46	0.62
Private household services	0.60	1.75	0.94	2.07	0.12
Miscellaneous occupations					
Auto mechanics and repairmen	0.98	0.91	1.40	0.03	1.80
Mechanics and repairmen except auto	1.06	0.88	1.19	0.14	1.71
Transportation except motor vehicles	0.84	1.47	0.81	0.07	1.77
Motor vehicle operators	0.87	1.37	0.81	0.12	1.73
Police and firefighters	1.30	0.64	0.27	0.11	1.74
Guards	0.79	1.53	0.56	0.51	1.40
Other protective services	0.85	1.50	0.24	0.37	1.52

Source: U.S. Census of Occupations 1980.
Note: The employment quotient is calculated by dividing the proportion of jobs in an occupation held by members of a group by the proportion the group comprises of all workers. An employment quotient greater than one indicates that members of the group are over-represented in the occupation; a quotient less than one indicates under-representation.

and judges, architects, managers, engineers, scientists, and health diagnosticians (e.g., doctors) all have high-paying occupations that require, at a minimum, a four-year college degree.

Black workers are overrepresented in twenty of the forty-eight occupations. However, few of these are in the upper levels of service occupations. Only public officials and administrators and elementary and secondary teachers require a college degree and offer opportunities for advancement. (These findings also underscore the importance of public sector employment for employment gains by blacks.) However, black workers also are concentrated in some middle-level service occupations. Black supervisors of administrative support, health technologists, and transportation workers may have mid-level jobs, although the level of data aggregation makes this difficult to determine.

Hispanics, again, show very low employment in service occupations. Only seven of the forty-eight occupations reflect a concentration of Hispanics. All of these, including food service workers, mechanics and repairmen, clerks, cleaning and building personnel, have the lower-level service occupations. Interestingly, Hispanics are more likely than other groups to be self-employed in sales occupations.

Women are concentrated in twenty-two of the forty-eight occupations, particularly as secretaries and typists, licensed practical nurses, and private household service providers. Like black workers, women are concentrated primarily in occupations at the middle and lower levels of service sector employment.

Unemployment among Service Workers   Another criticism leveled against many service sector jobs is that they are unstable, resulting in increased part-time jobs and high unemployment. Limited data are available measuring the likelihood of unemployment for particular industries or occupations; more work can be done in this area.

Seven of the ten occupations employing most minority workers in Chicago, according to the 1980 Census of Occupations, are service industry–related occupations, including secretarial and typing, other administrative support, cleaning and building services, food services, motor vehicle operation, elementary and secondary school teaching, and material recording and scheduling.

Similarly, of the ten occupations most frequently reported by minority applicants at the Job Service Offices in Chicago, seven are related to service industries: general clerk; cashier; cleaner; security guard; cook; truck driver; nurse's aide. Given some leeway in nomenclature, four of the ten occupations are found on both lists. Clerks, cooks, truck drivers, and building cleaners account for much of the employment among

155

minority workers. They also, however, account for much of the unemployment among minorities.

Among occupations employing the most women in Chicago, eight of the top ten are service related: secretaries and typists; other administrative support; food services; elementary and secondary teachers; health assessment and treatment; managers (other than manufacturing and retail); cashiers; bookkeepers and accountants. And, again, the highest number of occupations reported by registered unemployed women are service related, most notably clerical work of various kinds. Secretaries, typists, and receptionists (other administrative support staff) appear on both lists, accounting for much of the employment and unemployment among women.

Moreover, the service occupations with the largest number of unemployed minority and women workers are all growing occupations in Cook County, and most are projected to grow faster in the service industries than in the economy as a whole. For instance, employment for general office clerks is expected to increase by 5.6 percent between 1984 and 1995 across all industries. But employment for general office clerks in the service industries alone is expected to increase by 12.2 percent. The exceptions are that openings for nurse's aides are declining among the service industries, and openings for cooks are not growing as rapidly in the service industries as in other local industries.

However, employment growth does not guarantee a job for everyone who has experience or training as a cashier, general office clerk, guard, janitor, or truck driver. There may be more workers in these occupations than the market can absorb. The jobs projected could be in the suburbs, beyond the reach of inner-city residents who are unemployed. Or the jobs may offer such low wages that workers cannot live on the salaries they earn.

Even if the number of jobs available is sufficient to meet the demand of a growing labor force, one must consider the quality of jobs that employ large numbers of women and minorities. The service industries do provide many employment opportunities for unskilled workers, those without a college education. But these jobs offer low wages and few opportunities for advancement. Unless workers attain education beyond high school, they will have more and more difficulty maintaining a reasonable standard of living. Throughout most of the postwar period, the wages of Americans at different income levels rose at relatively the same rate. The rich and the poor became richer together. However, since 1978, the real wages of unskilled workers declined while the salaries of managers and executives increased (Reich 1989). The percentage of workers who earned low wages ($11,000 in 1986 dollars) was roughly 22.1

percent in 1963. This figure declined throughout the 1960s to about 13.5 percent, where it remained constant until the late 1970s. Since then it has increased again, to over 17 percent in 1985 (Harrison and Bluestone 1988).

MEDIATING INSTITUTIONS: JOB TRAINING AND PLACEMENT

We have suggested that many factors contribute to job numbers and quality, including industrial, occupational, and labor force characteristics, which have been examined briefly above. Another mediating factor is the presence and performance of education, training, and employment institutions, organizations, and programs, as well as related private and public policies.

A major mediating force in Chicago has been a network of community organizations with job training and placement programs assisting low-income, minority, and women workers. Most receive much, if not all, of their funding from federal sources, principally Job Training Partnership Act (JTPA) funds, administered through the Mayor's Office on Employment and Training (MET), and, more recently, funding from Project Chance, a welfare to work program administered by the Illinois Department of Public Aid (IDPA).

Over half (52.2 percent) of the adults and over three-quarters (77.1 percent) of the young workers recently served by MET programs in Chicago were placed in service sector jobs, including retail industries (table 7.4). The single largest sector for placements was eating and drinking places, accounting for 18 percent of all placements and the majority of youth placements.

During fiscal year 1988, IDPA's Project Chance spent $43.4 million on education, training, and social service programs to assist welfare recipients into education and training programs or into jobs. Of those placed in jobs, nearly half (47 percent) were placed in service occupations. Two-thirds (66 percent) earned $5.00 an hour or less (IDPA 1989).

We interviewed several organizations in Chicago that conduct job training, provide job referral, or actually employ community residents in their own enterprises. We found that the agencies are facing a serious problem. They attempt to help people find better, more secure, and higher-paying jobs. But their efforts are constrained because many low-income and minority residents lack the formal education required to obtain the quality service industry jobs.

Consequently, basic skills and English as a second language (ESL) are important components of community job-training efforts. Many of the

157

TABLE 7.4. Predominant Industries for MET Placements, Program Year 1989

| | % of All Placements | |
Industry	Adults	Youth
Manufacturing	30.4	13.8
Services	34.7	19.1
Retail	17.5	58.0
Eating and drinking places	17.8	
Business services	11.9	
General merchandise retail	8.8	
Food stores	6.9	
Electrical equipment mfg.	5.3	
Hotels and motels	4.9	
Food products	3.0	
Social services	2.8	
Miscellaneous retail stores	2.6	
Local passenger transit	2.5	
Health services	2.5	
Fabricated metal	2.4	

Source: Mayor's Office on Employment and Training 1989

city's unemployed have limited abilities in math and reading, which restrict their eligibility for JTPA-funded job training programs and referrals. Most of the MET programs require ninth-grade reading and eighth-grade math skills.

All of the community agencies we spoke with agreed that one of the biggest barriers to employment among Hispanics is lack of English-language skills. The ability to read and speak English at a functional level is a common job requirement. This is especially true in service jobs that involve contact with customers, such as those for cashiers, clerical, and sales-persons.

Often, the best the organizations can do is train residents for low-level service jobs and hope that, once employed, the workers will be able to continue education that will lead to better opportunities.

City College Learning Centers   The City Colleges of Chicago operate two Learning Centers in Chicago, one at Olive-Harvey College on the southeast side and one at Truman College on the north lakefront area. The Learning Centers offer day and evening classes in basic math and reading skills, General Education Diploma (GED) classes, and ESL. These services are provided at little or no cost to city residents.

The Learning Centers also conduct short-term job training for two service-related jobs. A twenty-four-week program in word processing and data entry aims to teach students basic skills in popular word processing software and to bring the student's typing speed to fifty-five words per minute. This is the minimum speed most employers require of entry-level typists. A sixteen-week course in basic electronics covers the principles of AC/DC electricity and an introduction to solid-state technology.

The Learning Center training programs do not require a high school diploma or a GED to qualify. The program does require ninth-grade reading levels and eighth-grade math skills. Those lacking these skills are referred to the center's basic skills training. The programs are largely targeted for the unemployed, underemployed, and Public Aid recipients.

Howard Area Community Center   Howard Area Community Center (HACC) serves the far North Side of the city. For the past three years, HACC has provided training for certified nursing assistants (CNAs). Although HACC's community orientation focuses on the Rogers Park area, the CNA training program draws its clients from throughout the city. Like the Learning Centers, the target population includes the unemployed, the underemployed, and Public Aid recipients. Generally, classes have been 60 percent black, 20 percent Hispanic, and 20 percent white. Roughly two-thirds of the students are women.

Participants in this MET-funded program are required to pass a reading and math test to qualify. Those with children receive free day care services while in the program, with the possibility of a short extension of these services once they start working. All participants receive a $120 stipend to help cover transportation costs and other related expenses. The program itself is provided free of charge.

Graduates of the program work with a job developer to assist in placement. Most placements are made in nursing homes, especially on the north lakeshore area in Chicago. The wages paid to CNAs by Chicago nursing homes are very low. Better wages are available from home health care agencies and nursing homes in the suburbs. However, few of those participating in the program own cars, so transportation is a major obstacle to graduates of the program. Besides the low wages, the working conditions in many nursing homes are poor, and job security is very low. Home health care agencies, for example, are often reluctant to guarantee full-time positions to their workers.

The HACC CNA training program has been discontinued for a period of one year. It will be reviewed during that time and may resume in 1990. Three problems led to the program's suspension. First, the low wages and poor conditions for those working in nursing homes made the program's director question this specific area of training. The director indicated that she is aware of a demand for CNAs in Chicago, but that nursing homes were unwilling to pay reasonable wages. Poor regulation and inspection by the Illinois Department of Public Health (IDPH) has contributed to the poor working conditions in nursing homes.

Second, HACC had difficulty finding a replacement instructor for the program. CNA training must be conducted by a registered nurse who has passed an IDPH-certified instructor's course. HACC found it hard to compete with registered nurse salaries in the private health care market. Third, HACC experienced many bureaucratic problems related to its funding from MET. MET requires its delegate agencies to keep detailed records in order to receive reimbursement. Requirements changed often, and HACC was not always notified of the changes and therefore lost opportunities for reimbursements. There were often delays in the award-ing of program contracts.

ASI   ASI is a community-based organization serving the Hispanic community on Chicago's Near Northwest side. ASI operates three employment and training programs in addition to other social service activities.

ASI's homemaker program directly employs community residents in a service industry. Homemakers provide services to homebound elderly and disabled residents in the community, helping them with meal prepa-ration, shopping, cleaning, and other household and personal tasks. The service is funded under contract from the Illinois Department on Aging, Illinois Department of Rehabilitation Services, and the City of Chicago. Currently, the program has about 1,600 clients and over 400 homemaker workers.

The agency runs a training class for homemakers about once every two months. Most of those involved in the program are recruited by word of mouth. ASI staff provides training in both homemaking skills and in basic skills in each five-week session totaling 100 hours of instruction. Once trained, the homemakers are employed directly by ASI at a starting salary of $3.90 an hour. Although the wages are somewhat low, workers also receive health care insurance, paid vacation, sick leave, and tuition reimbursement for continued education.

The fringe benefits make the work attractive to low-income residents. When the workers were asked to choose between increased wages or maintaining the fringe benefits, they voted to keep the health insurance. Few lower-level service jobs provide health insurance as a benefit.

According to ASI program director, language is the primary barrier to job placement among the Hispanic residents of the West Town area. ASI offers nighttime ESL classes. It also operates an amnesty class that helps residents to qualify for legal residency by offering ESL and civics classes. Transportation is another significant problem for all low-income residents in the city, because many of the better-paying service and manufacturing jobs are in the suburbs. ASI job developers are somewhat reluctant to refer clients to suburban jobs if they do not own a car. When clients are dependent on others for transportation to a suburban job, retention is problematic.

Some of the homemaker workers have been with the program since it started thirteen years ago. A recent survey of former workers shows that most of those who leave the program go on to continue their education or find better jobs with another agency. About 96 percent of the homemakers are minorities and 97 percent are women.

A unique aspect of the homemaker program is that it was developed to serve the needs of one group in the community, the elderly and the disabled, and has grown to also serve the needs of another group, the unemployed.

Summary and Recommendations

Service occupations appear to be the jobs of the future. However, Chicago's diverse service sector provides a wide range of jobs varying significantly in job requirements and job rewards. We need to know a great deal more about the characteristics of specific service sector industries and occupations, about the characteristics of workers who currently hold such jobs or are excluded from such jobs, about the effectiveness of mediating institutions, and about the effect of public policies in increasing the quality of both work and workers in Chicago's service industries. Additional research on the effect of service industries on Chicago's workers is needed to improve our understanding of the employment potential of specific service industries and occupations, to formulate more effective public and private policies and programs, and to help Chicago workers, particularly women and minorities, move into better-quality service industry occupations.

The following provide an initial list of recommendations for research and policies to better understand and mediate the effect of the service economy on work and workers in Chicago.

REFERENCE LIST

Allardice, David, Wim Wiewel, and Wendy Wintermute. 1990. "The Strength of Size and Diversity: Changes in the Chicago Economy, 1980–1986." In Richard Bingham et al., *Economic Restructuring in the Midwest*. New York: Kluwer.

Bluestone, Barry, and Bennett Harrison. 1982. *The Deindustrialization of America*. New York: Basic Books.

Center for Urban Economic Development. 1989. *Economic Audit of Chicago: An Identification of Target Industries*. Chicago: University of Illinois at Chicago.

Crain's Chicago Business. 1989. "1989 Wage and Salary Survey" (May 8):23.

Ehrlich, Elizabeth, and Susan Garland. 1988. "For American Business, New World of Workers." *Business Week* (Sept. 19):112–120.

Harrison, Bennett, and Barry Bluestone. 1988. *The Great U-Turn*. New York: Basic Books.

Illinois Commission on Intergovernmental Cooperation. 1987. *The Organization and Administration of Education for Employment in Illinois*. Springfield: ICIC.

Illinois Department of Public Aid. 1987. *Opportunities: Project Chance Annual Report*. Springfield: IDPA.

Illinois Occupational Information Coordinating Committee. 1988. *Horizons: Occupational Information 1989 Edition*. Springfield: IOICC.

———. 1989. Substate Employment Projections Data Tape, 1984.

Kuttner, Robert. 1983. "The Declining Middle." *Atlantic Monthly* 252:60–72.

Love, Lois. 1988. *A Job Is Not a Job . . . The Experiences of Job Training Partnership Act Participants*. Chicago: United Charities.

Ranney, David, and John Betancur. 1986. *Labor Force–Based Economic Development: University Center Challenge Grant Report to the Economic Development Administration*. Chicago: University of Illinois at Chicago, Center for Urban Economic Development.

Reich, Robert. "As the World Turns." 1989. *New Republic* (May 1):23–28.

Sheets, Robert, Stephen Nord, and John Phelps. 1987. *The Impact of Service Industries on Underemployment in Metropolitan Economies*. Lexington, Mass.: Heath.

Singlemann, Joachin. 1978. *From Agriculture to Services*. Beverly Hills: Sage.

Spilerman, Seymour. 1977. "Careers, Labor Market Structure and Socioeconomic Achievement." *American Journal of Sociology* 83:551–93.

Stanback, Thomas, and Thierry Noyelle. 1982. *Cities in Transition*. Totowa, N.J.: Rowman Allanheld.

Touraine, Allen. 1971. *The Post-Industrial Society; Tomorrow's Social History: Classes, Conflicts and Culture in the Programmed Society*, translated by Leonard Mayhew. New York: Random House.

U.S. Department of Commerce, Bureau of the Census. 1986. *County Business Patterns*. Washington, D.C.: GPO.

————. 1980. *1980 Census of Occupations Data Tape*.

Wilson, William J. 1989. *The Truly Disadvantaged*. Chicago: University of Chicago Press.

The two authors of this chapter were staff members of the University of Illinois at Chicago Center for Urban Economic Development at the University of Illinois at Chicago (UICUED) when it was completed for the project. UICUED has been a particularly active research voice in discussions about the changing urban economy. Because Chicago's economy has been traditionally heavily manufacturing, the trend toward service employment—in particular the extent to which this trend is occurring and the degree to which the transition has been beneficial to this industrial city—is being closely watched. **Wendy Wintermute** has been part of a research team conducting an economic audit of Chicago, targeting industries and occupations for Chicago's Economic Development Commission. **Charles Hicklin,** who now works for the Chicago Economic Development Commission, has been involved in researching a pilot project looking at new and effective ways of designing job referral services in Chicago.

8 THE GOVERNMENT'S PERSPECTIVE ON THE LAND DEVELOPMENT PROCESS
Jeffrey D. Reckinger, David Mosena, Charlotte Chun, and Raymundo Flores

Historical Background

Although land-use and development patterns in American cities are largely the product of private sector investment decisions, government plays a key role at a number of points in the development process. Local governments regulate zoning and building construction, establish application and review procedures for prospective developers, and control access to public resources (including land and financial assistance) that may be utilized for development.

Each of these processes represents a potential avenue for citizen input into the development process. Indeed, one significant outcome of the neighborhood empowerment movement of the last two decades has been a growing sensitivity on the part of government to the need for preserving and enhancing such opportunities.

This evolution has spurred a variety of locally initiated regulatory, procedural, and informational initiatives designed to open up the land development process to neighborhood input. Such input is being exercised in a number of ways. First, community-based organizations ("CBOs") can acquire developable land, enabling them to control its later use. Second, they can become better informed on current development matters, enhancing their ability to influence public and private decisions on land use and development. And third, they can offer input directly to public regulators who must review and approve development plans.

For its part, local government can and does play a significant role in each of these three areas. Gaining a clearer understanding of these roles—and their effects on neighborhood involvement—is the primary objective of this paper. By focusing on government's key roles as a landholder and as a regulator of development, this paper explores the major avenues through which neighborhood interests now have a voice in these decisions. Through a selective examination of initiatives in Chicago and (to a lesser extent) other cities, answers are sought to the following questions:

1. How can government most effectively encourage neighborhood-based ownership of usable land?

2. How can CBOs effect more meaningful input into the land-use regulatory process?

3. How can CBOs and neighborhood residents gain better access to information on development matters?

On the basis of this analysis, several directions for further research are proposed.

The Context for Local Government Intervention

Cities seeking to encourage neighborhood participation in the development process find three basic types of tools at hand: *public subsidies,* including real estate and financing; *regulatory and administrative powers;* and *dissemination of information.* This paper will cite examples of ways in which these tools are already in use in Chicago and elsewhere. Before beginning that discussion, though, it may be appropriate to touch on some of the factors that limit the capacity of cities to exercise these powers.

Public Subsidies

The decline in direct federal support (such as low-income housing subsidies) for neighborhood-initiated development projects has severely limited the capacity of most cities to fund CBOs seeking to acquire, bank, or develop real estate. Out of necessity, increased attention has been focused on the use of publicly held real estate to write down land costs for neighborhood developers. Several cities have set up specialized sales programs for city-owned land; others have focused on land banking and site assemblage for potential users. In Chicago, several city departments and public interest organizations have been looking at methods for improving the existing, state-mandated sales process for city-owned land.

REGULATORY AND ADMINISTRATIVE POWERS

Conventional zoning mechanisms have proved less and less effective in balancing the conflicting demands of established land uses and encroaching new uses in regentrifying neighborhoods. One well-publicized local example has been the accelerating pace of land-use conversions in historically industrial areas on the North and Northwest Sides. In such situations, the need for additional zoning controls must be weighed against their potentially inhibitory effects on desirable new development as well as the competitive standing of the city vis-à-vis the suburbs or other metropolitan areas.

DISSEMINATION OF INFORMATION

Under state law, the Chicago Plan Commission is the forum for citizen input into local government land-use decisions. To facilitate greater public involvement in the review of major project proposals, the plan commission recently codified and published its application and review procedures in a readily comprehensible public document. Meanwhile, the city's land management agency has begun the long-delayed task of preparing publicly accessible data on surplus land—a process that has already been completed in a number of other large cities.

Review of Current Initiatives

NEIGHBORHOOD LAND ACQUISITION

For several reasons, local government is a prime owner of vacant and derelict land in many cities. Chicago typically acquires vacant lots after it forecloses on liens filed to recover the cost of demolishing blighted buildings on the property. (In other cities that directly levy and collect property taxes, acquisition may occur in response to tax delinquency before demolition becomes necessary.) The scope of the city's inventory—now numbering over 8,000 parcels, most of them vacant—attests to the difficulty of restoring them to responsible private ownership. Chicago is among a number of cities that have set up specialized sales programs for this type of land.

ANLAP The Adjacent Neighbors Land Acquisition Program (ANLAP) —the prototype for similar programs in a number of cities—sells certain city-owned lots at reduced cost to owner-occupants of houses on adjacent parcels. Established in 1981, ANLAP was the culmination of the efforts of a coalition of Northwest Side community organizations to return derelict, city-owned residential property in low- and moderate-income neighborhoods to local control. The enabling ordinance states:

> It is the intention of the City of Chicago to convey certain city-owned parcels of vacant real property to adjacent neighbors for the purpose of returning said properties to the tax rolls and enhancing the quality of life in the city's neighborhoods. [Chicago 1981]

While neighborhood organizations embraced the program as a long-overdue tool for returning land to local control, city officials welcomed it for a different reason. The director of real estate pointed out that, although most of the lots had been owned by the city for years,

> developers or real estate speculators refused to buy them because they [were] too small or odd-shaped for any kind of significant development. Consequently, the city was losing money on these parcels because they were not generating any tax revenues and because the city had to spend money to maintain them. [Ziemba 1981]

Under the first ANLAP sale offering in 1981, no minimum bid was required, enabling properties to be turned over for as little as one dollar. At the time the elimination of the minimum bid was hailed as the most revolutionary provision of the ordinance. (Prior to ANLAP, the city would reject any bid of less than 80–90 percent of the appraised/fair market value.) In 1986 the Department of Housing (which at that time administered the program) made an administrative decision to raise the minimum bid to $300, hoping to discourage frivolous bidders and help amortize program costs.

Under the original ordinance, only unconnected vacant lots of less than twenty-five-foot width in R-1 and R-2 zoning districts qualified. Multiple lots and corner lots were excluded. In 1982 the City Council expanded the program to include "properties with thirty-five front footage or less in R-1, R-2, R-3, R-4, and R-5 zoning districts [and] corner parcels and parcels bordered on one side by an alley which meet these criteria, as well as irregularly sized parcels which meet the zoning criterion" (Chicago 1982). To speed up sales, the real estate office also revamped procedures to allow prescreening of applicants and quicker handling of bids. Sales began to be processed on a continuing basis rather than through mass offerings at widely spaced intervals.

Despite these changes, ANLAP's potential usefulness as a tool for strengthening neighborhood control over land use is quite limited. By its nature, the program is so restricted in eligibility criteria and in the kinds of future development permitted (in fact, construction of a new structure on the parcel is prohibited for a period of seven years after purchase) that it can never be applied to the majority of city-held lots in neighborhoods where development pressures are high. Open Lands Project, an advocacy group for open space preservation, has also pointed out the need for a system to track ANLAP properties during the bidding process, to systematically eliminate parcels that lack any qualified or interested bidders (Open Lands Project 1987).

On an ad hoc basis, the city has occasionally exercised its "home rule" powers to sell land at reduced prices (through so-called negotiated sales) for certain neighborhood development projects. In 1988, for example, the City Council established the Chicago Affordable Housing Program, enabling a limited number of lots to be conveyed to developers of low-cost housing at $1 each. But such arrangements are the exception rather than the rule. Partly for that reason, neighborhood groups and local government officials have sought systemic improvements in the process through which the city sells surplus land.

Streamlined Land Sales Process   Because so much vacant land is city-owned in many low- and moderate-income communities—including the same areas experiencing redevelopment and regentrification—some neighborhood advocates have pointed to the city's cumbersome sealed-bid sales process as an impediment to increased neighborhood control over land use. The existing process, which has never been codified in a single ordinance, is lengthy and complicated. Repeated City Council action is required—both before and after properties are put out for bid—and a year or longer may be required to complete the sale of a single parcel. In fact, Open Lands Project has estimated the average duration of the process at more than two years.

This is particularly detrimental to neighborhood interests for at least two reasons. First, the inability of CBOs and neighborhood residents to expeditiously acquire blighted vacant lots—which often attract unsightly fly-dumping as quickly as they deter reinvestment in nearby properties— means lost opportunities for development of affordable housing, recreational open space, or other much-needed improvements. Second, the complexity of the process—and especially the need for repeated City Council action—often places CBOs and residents at a competitive disadvantage compared with land speculators and others better versed in its intricacies.

By 1989 initiatives were under way in both the public and private sectors to address these problems. A special interdepartmental committee chaired by the Department of Planning in 1989 instituted a new computerized inventory system to assist the city in identifying surplus property and tracking it through the disposition process. That committee has also examined the sales process to pinpoint unnecessary steps that might be eliminated and to facilitate the creation of specialized sales programs for neighborhood concerns. Concurrently, Open Lands Project's City Open Lands Program has made a detailed analysis of the city's sales practices, with a particular focus on open space preservation needs. One encouraging development is that new lines of communication have opened between these two efforts, increasing the likelihood that a public-private consensus for action will emerge.

Tax-Delinquent Land Acquisition   The county's system for returning tax-delinquent property to responsible ownership is based on a three-tiered system of sales. Properties initially are offered at the annual sale (covering all tax-delinquent properties for the current tax year), then at the forfeiture sale (under which properties are continually offered to the public), and finally at the scavenger sale (a last resort for properties with two or more years of delinquency), which is normally held in alternate years. If no one bids on a parcel at its first sales offering, the parcel is then offered at the next sale.

The extreme complexity of the tax laws and sales procedures have rendered the entire tax sales process highly susceptible to manipulation by land speculators and other outside interests. For that reason, reforming the process has long been a high priority of neighborhood advocacy organizations, such as the Campaign for Responsible Ownership, that seek to prevent fraud and shorten the redemption period to reactivate properties more quickly. One successful outcome of this effort was the reduction of the scavenger sale eligibility period from five years to two under a law passed in 1987. (Because the tax sales are administered under Illinois statute, changes in eligibility or redemption requirements require legislation at the state level.)

171

The redemption period during which the owner can reclaim delinquent property upon which a bid has been made now stands at two years for most types of property, reduced to six months when these parcels are more than five years delinquent. A constitutional amendment that appeared on the November 1987 ballot would have reduced the period to one year for most properties and six months if only two years delinquent. Despite enjoying widespread expressions of support, the amendment failed (apparently because of reasons unrelated to the merits of the proposal); it was expected to be reintroduced at the next legislative session.

The city now plays a direct role in the scavenger sale through the tax reactivation program, which enables neighborhood developers to obtain delinquent land at minimal cost for siting of low-income housing or economic development projects. Under this program, the Departments of Housing and Economic Development review applications from developers, select eligible parcels, and refer them to the City Council for submittal to the County Board. The county then enters a "non-cash bid" on behalf of the city and the applicant at the scavenger sale. Following a six-month redemption period, ownership then is transferred to the new developer, contingent on the buyer's honoring the redevelopment agreement signed with the city.

On the whole, the tax delinquency system has not been particularly successful at reducing tax delinquencies. Over 31,000 parcels appeared on the 1985 scavenger sale list (when the delinquency requirement was five years), up from 6,500 in 1977. Meanwhile, uncollected taxes jumped from $21 million to a currently estimated $110 million. And records from the annual sale show that in 1985 just 27 percent of the 65,000 parcels put up for sale were sold (Ownership Transfer Working Group 1986).

A recently introduced senate bill would help tighten the process further. Included in the bill are measures that would deter unscrupulous owners from making "paper" transfers to third parties whom the county must then track down; prohibit owners or their agents from bidding on their own properties; toughen registration guidelines and impose a registration fee, to discourage fraud and abuse; and establish minimum bid requirements to weed out frivolous bidders.

Other Cities   A number of other cities have set up proactive programs to encourage local residents and neighborhood organizations to acquire surplus city-owned land (Chicago 1987a). Boston has established a special clearinghouse to facilitate sales under a "negotiated sale" process. New York and Rochester are among the cities that conduct regular auctions of surplus vacant land. Some cities set specific size or value limitations to determine eligibility of parcels for special sales programs. Milwaukee has set up a special procedure to give away property that fails to attract bids through the normal sales process. Several cities have also set up adjacent neighbors programs modeled after ANLAP.

One approach adopted by other cities that has not often been utilized in Chicago is leasing and "Adopt-a-Lot" programs. These have the dual advantage of preserving public control of potentially valuable property while allowing neighborhoods to make short-term use of the land for gardens, playgrounds, and the like.

Neighborhood Participation in the Regulatory Process   Although citizen input in the regulation of land use and major development projects is mandated by state and federal law, the record of local government in encouraging and recognizing this input has been poor. The mechanisms now in place are mainly of an advisory nature. The Chicago Plan Commission was established expressly to provide a vehicle for public review of major development proposals. And under the Urban Renewal Program, special citizens' councils have been set up to allow neighborhood input into all land-use changes in Urban Renewal project areas.

Conservation Community Councils   The Urban Renewal program incorporates one of the most long-standing mechanisms for neighborhood input into land-use decisions. Under Illinois law, the Urban Renewal Board, appointed by the mayor, is responsible for designation of "conservation areas" and approval of "conservation plans" (i.e., land-use plans) for each such area (Illinois 1985). (Conservation areas generally are larger and less intensely blighted than "redevelopment areas," which are designated for full-scale redevelopment projects.) In addition, the board nominates a Conservation Community Council (CCC) for each area, consisting of from nine to fifteen members representative of that community.

Though the CCC's powers are advisory only, subject to confirmation by the full Urban Renewal Board and City Council, it is the CCC that has the most direct voice in neighborhood land-use planning. CCCs prepare the conservation plans for submittal to the Urban Renewal Board and vote on any subsequent amendments. (They are not empowered to review public land sales or acquisitions.)

Consequently, the Conservation Councils have not always been an effective force for neighborhood-based planning. In one recent instance, a zoning change for a Hyde Park parcel was approved by the CCC only to be overridden by the City Council at the behest of the local alderman.

NEIGHBORHOOD ACCESS TO INFORMATION

Civic and business groups have frequently joined with neighborhood organizations in criticizing a perceived lack of public access to information on city programs and development plans. Access to information opens the door to public resources and to meaningful participation in the project review process. Conversely, when government neglects to make this information available, neighborhoods will find it difficult to participate as full partners in the decision-making process. This section highlights two local examples of recent initiatives designed to heighten awareness of public resources and of opportunities for input into the regulatory process.

City Land Inventory System   Development of a comprehensive inventory of City-owned land was the major recommendation of a 1988 report under the auspices of Open Lands Project. "A land use information system would provide the city with a comprehensive management and policy tool. . . . The data should be reliable, valid, updated and readily available . . . to city staff and the public" (Open Lands Project 1988).

This input played a major role in development of the City Land Inventory System that was brought on line in 1989. When fully operational, it will for the first time provide the public with access to comprehensive, up-to-date lists of surplus properties available for sale. Although manpower limitations have so far delayed complete implementation of the system, it should prove a boon for neighborhood planners seeking to identify both short- and long-range resources for development.

Planned Development Handbook   At the same time that the Plan Commission enacted new bylaws earlier this year, it published a public information document explaining the procedures for reviewing large-scale development proposals. The *Planned Development Handbook* (Chicago Plan Commission 1989a) responds to the oft-stated desire of both civic groups and developers for clearer information on how applications are to be prepared, how they will be reviewed by the Plan Commission and Department of Planning, and how the public can participate in the process. This is the first time these procedures have been codified and presented in a format that is readily comprehensive to the public; it is especially significant in that the Planned Development classification covers virtually all of the largest developments—those projects that have the greatest effects on neighborhoods and frequently demand the largest commitments of public resources.

Other Cities   Computerized inventory systems accessible to the public are already in place in several large northeastern and midwestern cities

(Chicago Planning Department 1987b). New York's system is generally considered the most advanced, providing a wealth of information to prospective buyers. New York supports its sophisticated auction program with a strong commitment to the aggressive dissemination of information on city-owned real estate; it even offers a detailed how-to booklet for making improvements to lots acquired at auction. Marketing brochures have also been published by Boston and St. Louis (where land management and disposition are housed in an agency separate from city government, the Land Reutilization Authority).

Conclusion and Recommendations

One product of the neighborhood empowerment movement has been a radical reshaping of the ways in which local government interfaces with neighborhood-based organizations. Examples of these changes have been a major focus of this paper. The final outcomes of this restructuring are far from clear; indeed, there are a number of programmatic areas where government policies are still adjusting to the rising role of communities in the development process. A strong need exists for further research on several of these policy questions.

Improving public land disposition, for example, has become a priority of many local governments, Chicago included. Several different approaches have been tried by cities in the 1980s, all with the aim of returning surplus land to the tax rolls and to productive use. Because these new programs are finally at a point where they have begun to demonstrate meaningful track records, it would be timely now to give them a closer look. *Just how effective have they been at permanently restoring property to the tax rolls and to productive use?*

Closer to home, Cook County's tax sale system suggests a whole range of potential research topics. Again, comparisons with other major cities—in particular those that, like Chicago, do not levy and collect their own property taxes—should be highly instructive. Just as important, the effects of recent scavenger sale reforms need to be closely monitored. *Have they been successful in blunting the upsurge in tax-delinquent properties that has occurred since 1977?*

Despite recent improvements in the availability of development information, Chicago's neighborhood development organizations lack access to some of the basic data that the downtown development community finds readily at hand. There is no regular report or compendium of development activities and trends for the city outside of the central area. A prototype for this type of publication already exists in the Planning Department's *Downtown Development* report (Chicago Planning Department 1989). *Could a comparable project be undertaken jointly by the City and neighborhood development groups and updated on a regular basis?*

If there is a single message that subsumes all of these policy questions, it is that the nature of the decision-making process on public development matters in Chicago has entered an era of fundamental restructuring. Public review bodies such as the Chicago Plan Commission, which historically has not been a prime mover of development policy, should see their roles continue to evolve as a product of more accessible administrative procedures. It is likely that other advisory planning agencies, including the Urban Renewal program's Conservation Community Councils, will feel the same winds of change. At the same time, policy areas in which there have been few avenues for neighborhood input in the past—such as public land disposition—will face growing pressures for meaningful public input. And whatever the outcome, we can expect that Chicago—where so much of the history of neighborhood empowerment has been written—will continue to play a leading role in the process of change.

Addendum

Since the completion of this article, Chicago has started two major initiatives aimed at streamlining the land sales process and making it easier for CBOs to acquire and recycle derelict properties. The new Accelerated City Real Estate Sales (ACRES) program not only simplifies and speeds up the sales process, but also enables organizations to acquire certain lots at $1 each for eligible neighborhood development projects. In addition, under the new Chicago Abandoned Property Program, the city now can take over abandoned buildings (using "quick-take" powers granted by the State of Illinois in 1990) before demolition becomes necessary and then convey them directly to qualifying buyers for rehabilitation. Input from CBOs and neighborhood advocates played a major role in the conception and design of these programs.

REFERENCE LIST

Campaign for Responsible Ownership. 1989. *Report of the Task Force on Tax Delinquent Properties.* Chicago: Campaign for Responsible Ownership.

Chicago. 1981. *Journal of the Proceedings of the City Council of the City of Chicago.* March 6:5584–5585.

Chicago. 1982. *Journal of the Proceedings of the City Council of the City of Chicago.* July 23:11830–11833.

Chicago. 1989. *Chicago Zoning Ordinance.* Chicago: Index Publishing.

Chicago Department of Planning. 1987a. *Report of the Mayor's Task Force on Neighborhood Land Use: Vacant Land.* Chicago: City of Chicago.

———. 1987b. *Vacant Land in Chicago: Current Conditions and Policy Options.* Chicago: City of Chicago.

———. 1989. *Downtown Development: Chicago, 1987–1990.* Chicago: City of Chicago.

Chicago Plan Commission. 1989a. *Planned Development Handbook.* Chicago: City of Chicago.

Chicago Plan Commission. 1989b. *Rules and Procedures of the Chicago Plan Commission.* Chicago: City of Chicago.

King, John. 1988. "Protecting Industry from Yuppies and Other Invaders." *Planning* 6:4–8.

Illinois. 1985. *Illinois Revised Statutes.* Chaps. 24 and 91.

Open Lands Project. 1987. "Adjacent Neighbors Land Acquisition Programs in Chicago and Five Other Cities." Unpublished draft. Chicago.

———. 1988. *The City of Chicago's Real Estate Inventories: Exploring the Opportunities.* Chicago: Open Lands Project.

Ownership Transfer Working Group. 1986. *New Strategies for Tax-Delinquent Properties in Chicago: Recommendations for Change.* Chicago: Ownership Transfer Working Group.

Ziemba, Stanley. 1981. "Program of selling lots to neighbors may expand." *Chicago Tribune,* October 19.

Jeffrey Reckinger is Assistant to the Department Commissioner for Neighborhood Planning in the City of Chicago Department of Planning. A researcher with the department since 1984, Reckinger has authored several reports on vacant land planning issues. Most recently he co-authored a chapter on "General Development Plans" for a volume published in 1988 by the International City Management Association (edited by Frank So). **David Mosena** is Commissioner of the Department of Planning. **Charlotte Chun** and **Raymundo Flores** both work at the Department.

9 THE COMMUNITY'S PERSPECTIVE ON THE LAND DEVELOPMENT PROCESS
Luther Kildegaard Snow

"Citizen input" is as American as the town meeting. "Land use" is as common to our everyday experience as a game of Monopoly. We want "citizen input in the land development process" because as Americans we want liberty and justice for all. After all.

Of course, it gets a little more complicated than that. We want to protect individual liberties and freedoms but are concerned when the most wealthy and powerful use their wealth and power in ways that restrict opportunities for poor and disadvantaged. We want justice for the disadvantaged, but we worry about sacrificing individual liberties. Though we distrust the political process, our "Research and Action" agenda for the 1990s must ultimately focus on these basic values. Our challenge for the decade is to communicate and demonstrate how justice underpins liberty, how fairness and equitable opportunity create development that is good for all of us.

Nowhere is this challenge more real and down to earth than in the dynamic political process determining land uses in communities. Land is the ultimate playing board, the focus for our human concerns about home and work and the quality of our lives. The use of land gives physical presence to the score in the game, to the size of the pie, to what is stable and what is changing. It is the hotel on Boardwalk, and the crowded little green house on Baltic Avenue.

Over the years, those of us working in community-based organizations (CBOs) have developed a more sophisticated understanding not only of land but also of equitable participation in decision making. As our

180

development capacity has increased, we have recognized that land is a key factor in the control over local economic decisions. At the same time, we have begun to realize the potential community role in the local politics of land development. By bringing the process out in the open, we can achieve greater equity in land-use decisions and increase the opportunities for development that builds on community resources.

These realizations have led to the emergence of a new approach in the field of community-based development. The approach is pro-active, calling for self-initiative among community stakeholders, rather than mere reaction to the decisions of others; forward-looking and cooperative, calling for the development and negotiation of a common vision for the community among the various local constituencies; integrative, calling for consideration of the connections between local land uses and other factors in the development of a community, or of the connections between communities; pragmatic, calling for partnership building with the public and private sector policymakers who can advance their agendas in union with community plans; just, calling for the real empowerment of the disadvantaged and the poor in decision making.

In short, the approach is economic democracy in action. We call it community-based planning.

What is community-based planning and how does it differ from the status quo, or from planning and community development practice of the past? How can community-based planning efforts best develop, and what are the obstacles in the way? The following discussion of the current problem—the process of community-based planning, the politics of support for community-based planning, and ways to put "teeth" behind community-based plans—indicates some solutions and some directions for further exploration.

The Existing Pattern of Waste and Inequity

Most land-use decisions are made without even the pretense of community input. Property owners are free to do what they want with their property within existing zoning, building, and sanitation regulations. Indeed, private property rights are individual liberties, and some developers object to even the basic governmental provisions on land use, characterizing these provisions as "government intervention in the free market."

However, the government's authority and responsibility to regulate land use have long been upheld in the law as an appropriate provision for the public good. What value would land have without public "intervention"? Zoning provides for the compatibility of nearby uses. Roads and infrastructure and geographically targeted public investments provide for the access to and usefulness of land. Land uses also depend on community services and trade that are provided for by government market making and public expenditures. It is not a question of whether the government will or should "intervene" but of what value the government will create in land, and to whose benefit. This is the basis for citizen input in the land-development process.

Direct and specific land-use controls such as zoning and the power of eminent domain are the province of local government. But community input into uses and changes in such land-use controls is limited in practice.

In Chicago, City Council ordinance requires that property owners within two hundred feet be notified of any application for a zoning change, however small. Further improvements in the systems of communication of planned projects can help improve citizen input. In some other cities, for example, proposed zoning changes are posted by prominent signs at the location, which informs a broader "community" than just property owners within two hundred feet.

In Chicago, zoning changes must be approved by the City Council, and council tradition respects the wishes of the local alderman in ward matters. A few aldermen have established constituent panels to review zoning change requests, but there is no formal or required mechanism for community input, so input depends on the style of a particular alderman. For the largest private developments, citizen input is allowed through the Plan Commission, an advisory public board. One problem lies with the development of medium-sized projects that do not receive much attention through the Plan Commission process but nevertheless have a significant effect on the land uses of a community.

The use of eminent domain by local governments to acquire private property for "fair market value" is regulated in more detail. Citizen advisory panels and meetings are created for input on public land development projects, such as Conservation Community Councils for Urban Renewal districts.

The Plan Commission, Conservation Community Councils, and the like can provide information and some access to citizens. But do the existing land-use processes really provide for democratic decision making? In the tradition of "citizen input" of the 1960s and 1970s, community participation in local decisions has often been considered a mere formality, something to satisfy requirements of federal funding programs. Even where the process is taken seriously by government officials and/or developers, citizen participation in land-use decisions is still basically reactive and piecemeal.

Private developers put together development concepts, garner business and political support, and present the concept. The community, and often even the public officials, are forced to react. But the best land uses are not apparent from examination of a single project. Without a broader vision of what could be, communities cannot fairly consider how a project "piece" fits the whole. And yet, to oppose a particular development because of a lack of broader vision is seen as obstructive. Communities and public officials are stuck; we must either approve land-use changes, or appear antidevelopment.

What are the effects of the current system of land-use controls? The answer is clear in the results *between* and *within* communities.

In Chicago, great inequities *between* communities exist. Massive and broad-scale development near downtown and the airport dwarfs the development in all other parts of the city, while suburban development has created a "collar" of affluence around the city. The pattern is not dissimilar in other urban centers around the nation.

Racially, Chicago is the most segregated city in the nation. When combined with the related concentration of economic disadvantage in particular poor communities, the existing pattern of land-use development does not provide for the equitable or just distribution of economic opportunity among the citizens.

Lopsided land-use development between parts of the metropolitan area is not only inequitable; it is also inefficient. Inner-city communities hold the greatest proportion of residents, the greatest proportion of consumer demand, the greatest proportion of the available work force, and the greatest potential for economic enterprise that can increase national productivity and competitiveness in today's global markets. To underallocate public and private resources to these communities is not efficient policy.

The role of land uses in the changes that take place *within* neighborhoods is also revealing. There is a generally accepted paradigm of negative change in neighborhoods which lack strong community-based planning and development: A prosperous neighborhood will be affected by unanticipated technological or demographic change, such as the development of suburban shopping malls or the migration of local residents. The neighborhood loses economic strength, which results in the loss of local and outside investment, which decreases economic strength, and so on in a vicious cycle of disinvestment and abandonment. Eventually, changing in-city development pressures nearby create conditions that encourage speculation in local land and property. New residents are attracted to the area at higher prices, which eventually results in the displacement of the existing residents. Gentrification and "revitalization" complete the negative cycle.

Much of the urban studies literature focuses on the causes of neighborhood change, on resident and investor perceptions of neighborhood vitality, and on the extent of the shifting that occurs through the process of change. Usually the assumption is that "poor" neighborhoods are the problem and "growth" is the cure. Not much attention has been given to the question of who benefits from change and who loses, or to the contribution of land-use changes to the problem.

A few individuals can make extraordinary profits at each stage of neighborhood change, particularly by controlling land. When a neighborhood starts to "slide," for example, real estate professionals can employ blockbusting tactics to scare existing residents into selling cheap, while charging a premium to new residents for the opportunity of moving into a new neighborhood. This practice has been common in changing neighborhoods despite legal sanctions, especially where race is a factor.

In disinvested neighborhoods, developers are able to acquire land at deflated prices. As speculation fuels outside interest, property values may appreciate without any real improvement to the property itself, allowing the speculators to earn extraordinary profits but making it too expensive for existing residents and businesses to remain.

Thus, at each stage of the cycle, disadvantaged people lose. The largest costs are suffered by the poor and disadvantaged who do not control or own land. The disadvantaged see their personal investments of energy and resources penalized by declining property values at one time, then absorb the costs or dislocation and displacement at another time, while living or doing business under the least desirable neighborhood conditions throughout.

And the cycle itself is certainly costly and inefficient, as alternating concentrations of poverty and affluence move from neighborhood to neighborhood. The result is public spending on local improvements and provisions that increase private property values, followed by the waste of those resources in the pattern of private disinvestment. This is a sort of "planned obsolescence," neighborhood style, that costs all taxpayers in the long run.

Thus, existing land development patterns have a disproportionate economic effect both *between* and *within* communities. With only limited, piecemeal, and reactive community input, the greatest burden is imposed on those who can least afford to pay the costs. This is not only unjust, but unwise. The public costs of lopsided development between communities and of the "boom and bust" cycle of change within communities are paid by everybody.

It does not have to happen this way. With community-based planning and development, the negative cycle of neighborhood change can be replaced with a positive, regenerative cycle. Community members can anticipate change and act together to stay ahead of change. Local decisions can be made in ways that sustain the local economy and provide opportunities for low-income people to create and control wealth, thereby employing the capacities of all community members. Healthy, sustainable communities can be the building blocks of a more healthy and more just national and global economy.

The Process of Community-based Planning

Along with people and investment, the use of land is a key to the development of communities that are healthy, sustainable, and just. But CBOs have learned that equitable land-use control depends on community planning.

Nationally, CBOs have developed an impressive track record in "hard" development projects, and Chicago leads the nation in the number of organizations active in project development.[1] These developments range from community-sponsored businesslike enterprises, called community ventures, to CBO-developed residential, commercial, and industrial real estate projects. The benefits of these projects are significant, not only in terms of the direct influence on local employment and affordable housing, but also in terms of the capacity and understanding they generate among community leaders for the complexities of development and business.

Still, direct sponsorship of development projects is not the only appropriate community-based development approach. Project development is limited by the capacity and resources controlled by the CBO and by the development opportunities available.

Unlike project development, traditional community organizing has focused on broader policy decisions. Community constituents often are mobilized by changes proposed from outside, such as a new development project, or by a lack of responsiveness to community needs, such as red-lining or inadequate government services. The benefits of such organizing are also significant, particularly for increasing the awareness by constituents of the decisions that affect their lives and of the control they may exercise over those decisions through community-based action.

But existing land development processes have determined a response from communities that is piecemeal and reactive. Reacting to a development proposal or to a government-sponsored advisory process, organized community action can make communities appear antidevelopment when they are not.

Community planning offers an alternative and a complement to both development and organizing. Like organizing, community planning is broad in scope. Like development, community planning is pro-active. And community planning is special in the extent to which it provides a vehicle for building a common vision among community stakeholders.

Communities differ widely, and the methods communities use to plan and to influence land uses differ also. Consider these examples of community-based planning.

THE LEED COUNCIL PLANNED MANUFACTURING DISTRICT

On Chicago's North Side, near the Chicago River and west of one of the city's most affluent neighborhoods, lies an industrial area that contains businesses that employ hundreds of workers from all over the city. Skyrocketing property values in the nearby neighborhood have attracted developers to the area with plans for loft conversions and retail developments. But the factories and the lofts conflict; new residents find the existing industrial uses noxious, and some environmental regulations are more strict when the nearest distance to residential property is recalculated.

A local CBO, the Local Employment and Economic Development (LEED) Council of the New City YMCA, works to accomplish community economic development by retaining relatively high-paying manufacturing jobs and developing linkages to these jobs for disadvantaged residents of the nearby low-income and public housing communities. The displacement of local industries because of land-use pressures was seen by the LEED Council as a threat, so they organized a community-based planning effort to provide for stability in industrial land uses.

The planning effort brought together local manufacturers, concerned residents, and workers and unions. The plan itself focused on land-use areas, indicating where industry would continue to locate, where residential development would be allowed to occur, and where a "buffer zone" of retail and office uses would exist. The plan took authority and formal structure in the form of a city ordinance that established a planned manufacturing district, a land-use control that goes beyond zoning to encourage compatible uses according to the plan. The local alderman brought a tradition of public participation to the issue and helped negotiate a plan that was acceptable to the local residents. The city administration recognized the significance of the issue to the entire city's economic base and supported the planning effort.

The effort to plan in this community has led to the recognition of the need to identify and plan for industrial uses in other communities, with the participation and involvement of CBOs. Efforts by the LEED Council to extend the PMD within the industrial area but across a ward boundary have run afoul of a different alderman.

THE DUDLEY STREET NEIGHBORHOOD INITIATIVE REVITALIZATION PLAN

The Roxbury community of Boston is a community of low-income residents, located not far from downtown. The population is minority and racially mixed. Here the neighborhood dynamic has been one of disinvestment, characterized by property abandonment, sanitation problems, unemployment, and vacant land. Responding to a request for community involvement in a planning effort sponsored by a private foundation, local residents and community organizations decided instead to prepare their own community plan.

The effort came to be spearheaded by a new organization broadly representative of local constituencies, called the Dudley Street Neighborhood Initiative (DSNI). With support from the Riley Foundation, a planning process was developed and managed that involved constituent committees, interviews, and meetings over four years. A key aspect of the planning was the development of a "development concept" that incorporated a common community vision. During the process, organizing work on neighborhood needs continued.

The plan goes beyond land-use mapping. It addresses the process of land development, calling for local ownership structures and anti-displacement programs. Human services and economic development components of the plan address important community needs and values, including the racial, ethnic, and cultural identity and diversity of the community.

The adoption of the plan carried the support of a substantial base of local constituents. The city administration embraced the plan fully, and proved its commitment by the extension of two land-use controls to

DSNI and the implementation of the plan: the city donated all city-owned vacant land in the area to the CBO and ceded to the group the power of eminent domain over privately owned vacant land. DSNI formed a community land trust to own and hold land for community-based development.

These two examples of community-based planning efforts illustrate the range of strategies used to meet different needs. The LEED Council faced the neighborhood dynamic of gentrification and displacement and sought to manage growth and empower disadvantaged workers, while DSNI faced disinvestment and sought to stimulate appropriate and accountable development. LEED's efforts targeted land uses for their effect on economic development; DSNI took a comprehensive approach, including human services and economic development as a part of the plan.

But while these two examples demonstrate the diversity of community strategies, they also illustrate some of the common principles of the new community-based planning approach:

The approaches are pro-active. Both plans were initiated by community stakeholders. Both plans were formed to "specify how the City and private sector should address development in the neighborhood."[2]

Both approaches are forward-looking and cooperative. Each built a consensus among stakeholders who had not previously worked together by focusing on the long-term prospects for the community.

The approaches are pragmatic and action oriented. Both LEED and DSNI sought the support of elected and appointed officials and worked to communicate the broader benefits of the community-based plans.

Both plans are integrative, although in different ways. DSNI's plan integrates land use with human services and economic development. LEED's plan created a movement toward community planning for industrial protection around the city.

The methods promote more just and equitable participation in decision making. LEED worked to include the participation of workers and small business people as well as local residents in the planning; DSNI strove for broad participation of the disadvantaged residents from among the racial and ethnic constituencies in the community.

Because community-based planning seeks to encourage democratic decision making, the process is as important as the results. Often the early stages of the effort are dedicated to building relationships among community stakeholders, to establishing a level of comfort and trust that can make negotiation and compromise possible.

In the middle stages of the effort, emphasis is on the match between community need and development possibilities. A balance is struck between the "stretch" required to reach a vision for a better community and the "realism" that is required to make the plan credible and to fore-stall disillusionment among the constituents in implementing the plan. It is here that expertise in the various technical areas of development is helpful, and where community-based project development experience provides significant capacity.

In the latter stages of planning, priorities must be finally set, hard decisions must be made, and choices must be reduced to concrete work plans by which efforts can be guided, monitored, and evaluated. Here, skills in group process, conflict resolution, and constituent motivation come into play. While the earlier work can reduce the potential for conflict and delay at this stage, most community groups seem to feel that usually some dissent is unavoidable.

The planning process can be long, and "planning" itself is not a good motivator of participants. It is important that participants are working on common goals in the meantime, in projects that more directly address short-term self-interests. DSNI continued to organize around sanitation issues during planning, and this helped keep interest and motivation high.

The Politics of Community Input and Land Uses

Community-based planning puts the shoe on the right foot. It sets the challenge for those who are most affected by land uses (and by other development factors) to reach a common vision and set priorities by which uses can be evaluated and promoted. It addresses the problem of having to react to development proposals and of appearing antidevelop-ment in opposing projects or efforts that do not fit with community values and goals.

The process of community-based planning is the process of reaching a dynamic balance between liberty and justice, between the initiative of individuals and the equitable participation of all. Ultimately it is in the interests of everyone involved to reach this balance of mutual, long-term, collective interests. But along the way, more narrowly defined, short-term self-interests must be negotiated. Issues and potential conflicts will come up between local stakeholders and between the community and others. Through community-based planning, stakeholders within and outside the community negotiate their self-interests to reach the collective interest. Thus planning does not remove politics from the picture but brings it out in the open and up front.

INTERNAL POLITICS

Basic conflicts often surface around the question, "Who is the community?" In other words, "Who decides?" This question relates to *scale and physical boundaries* as well as to the legitimate *standing* of various participants. There are no single common answers to these questions, but there are real lessons to be drawn about *equitable participation* in the community process.

In both the community plans developed by DSNI and LEED, establishing *physical boundaries* was important, especially on land-use questions. One may draw a border on a map, but are the interests of stakeholders on one side of that line really different from the interests of stakeholders on the other? Sometimes natural boundaries alleviate this problem, but where they do not exist, CBOs may design "secondary" or "buffer zones" around a primary area, as did both LEED and DSNI. For LEED, the buffer zone had tangible, physical consequences in separating competing land uses—allowable commercial and retail land uses "buffer" industrial uses within the zone and residential uses outside the zone. For both plans, the intermediate zones had political uses as compromise solutions to the question of community boundaries.

Physical boundaries do not completely determine "who" is the community. Often, the question of legitimate standing comes up. Who has what standing to contribute to community decisions? A strong appeal may be made on behalf of residents: "This is our home," is an appeal based on the values we associate with homes and the communities we live in. But workers and representatives of local businesses will point out that their economic livelihoods are affected by community land uses. Among residents, homeowners will appeal for standing based on their economic stake in property appreciation, as in "I am concerned about my property value." But this stake extends to absentee owners as well, and renters will maintain that their economic and personal stake can be as high and even higher than homeowners, as in "I cannot afford to move." Long tenure in the community will be cited as demonstration of commitment and stake. And the standing of participants based on race, gender, ethnicity, age, and culture will be at issue, whether implicitly or explicitly.

Clearly, there are many kinds of stake in communities, and community-based planning involves negotiation around self-interests arising from these stakes. The tough question is not legitimacy, but equity. To reach the goal of democratic decision making, planning must involve the equitable participation of all stakeholders in the process, including those who have been left out of decision making in the past and those who are disadvantaged and unfairly powerless.

"Equitable" participation means something different in each community, depending on the historical inclusion and exclusion of stakeholders and the relationship of stakeholders to the neighborhood economy and land uses. Where there are pockets and concentrations of residents along lines of racial and economic disadvantage, the scale of boundaries can have different implications for equity. For example, in integrated or majority neighborhoods near minority neighborhoods, large retail shopping developments and franchises are sometimes opposed by some local residents because they will attract "outsiders" to the community. A more equitable, inclusionary result can be reached by including the nearby minority residents in the decision-making process.

Equitable decisions can also relate to the standing of local stakeholders. In Roxbury, equitable participation meant a strong resident focus, while in the LEED Council's planning it was the workers and small manufacturers who were viewed as historically excluded from land-use decisions.

Equity in community planning does not have to be a zero-sum game around boundaries and standing. The benefits and costs of land development in communities can be negotiated around factors that go beyond simple zoning categories. A shopping center may be more acceptable if the stores hire local youth. A residential development may gain support if affordable units are available to residents in need. Communities can plan for nonprofit, community-based, or cooperative ownership structures. Local control and benefit can be negotiated through contracts for property management, local purchasing, or local employment.

The tensions and conflict around internal politics are the most painful and difficult aspects of community planning for local leaders and participants. Is it worth it? Although imperfect, inclusionary community-based efforts provide some of the best methods for empowering the disadvantaged. Through community-based structures, individuals may develop new skills and capacities which can extend existing capacities and enable individuals to represent their own needs and interests. Some key factors in the success of managing equitable decisions include affirmative recruitment and development of leaders, established formal and informal methods of representing constituent interests, and fair but decisive group processes.

EXTERNAL POLITICS

Community-based planning relies on the capacities and sense of community constituents, but it is critical that the plans attract and channel appropriate and responsible outside resources to the community. The politics of land development and community-based planning also extend to those who control or influence those resources. Chief among these are local elected officials, city administrators, developers, and representatives of large outside institutions.

In times of scarce financial resources, the ability to shape the use of land is perhaps the most significant remaining power of local governments. It is not surprising, then, that local elected officials are sensitive to the process of land-use planning and to the roles that they play.

For some elected officials, community-based planning is competition. After all, the election of politicians is itself a democratic decision, and the exercise of control over land uses by the local alderman, the City Council, and the mayor and the city administration is an extension of that decision. Community-based plans that focus on democratic processes that are independent of the government represent an alternative definition of democracy which can be threatening to some officials. Some see community-based planning as a platform for potential opponents in the next election. And of course, those politicians who seek to exploit control over land use for illegitimate personal gain will find any democratic process counterproductive.

But many elected officials realize the potential benefits of community-based planning. Planning efforts take the "heat" off officials who are besieged by conflicting proposals for development and by ad hoc community opposition or support. By developing a consensus over a common vision, community-based plans offer a politician a platform and a position to champion that will have the support of a significant and active portion of the electorate. Under such plans, politicians can respond to development interests by encouraging land uses that are consistent with community needs and goals. And the positive results of community-based planning efforts create a community track record that a supportive politician can run on.

Officials of the city administration who report to the mayor have some of the same concerns as local politicians, and they share the potential benefits as well. In addition, city officials have the job of allocating scarce resources, so they have a self-interest in the plans that may form the basis for the allocation of resources within and between communities. These officials may also suspect competition from community-based planning, because of a concern over community misperceptions of technical or financial considerations. For example, a community plan may result in a consensus to build affordable housing that officials think is financially not feasible, or to install a traffic light that officials think will upset the technical ability to time existing lights for optimal traffic flow.

But generally city officials stand to benefit from a process that negotiates priorities among constituents and enables the government to use resources in ways that respond to agreed-upon needs. A plan gives officials something to stand on, something to measure results by, and something to cool periodic "hot spots" of political pressure. And to the extent that plans help attract private support for responsible development, they help multiply public support for greater effect.

Developers, investors, and financiers may also be leery of community-based plans. Time is money, and anything to do with democracy and process sounds like costly delays and obstacles to development. In practice, the reverse may be true. Development and investment in the absence of a community consensus around a plan always carries the risk of community opposition. Vocal community constituents have often delayed projects that are not worked through community process. Development and investment consistent with a previously developed plan tap the support of a built-in constituency. In fact, the time and energy spent by the community on its plan may be seen as a replacement for the work in "community relations" that would otherwise be necessary to a developer—a sort of "research and development" effort in advance of project conceptualization. And to the extent that community-based planning efforts empower disadvantaged people, public subsidies may be available for the implementation of these plans.

Finally, the role of outside institutions in community-based planning is a tricky one. On the one hand, outside institutions may provide a neutral ground on which local constituencies may come together. And the prospect of support for the process and results may help forge consensus, as with the Riley Foundation in the Roxbury neighborhood. But outside institutions cannot replace community initiative. Planning processes sponsored by governments or large corporations or institutions will not carry the same legitimacy or weight as community-based plans. Even the same decisions made by the same local stakeholders will not have the same support with outside sponsorship that they would have if the process is "owned" by those local stakeholders.

For elected officials, community-based planning offers an opportunity to respond to community needs while supporting responsible development. For government officials, it offers direction to the tough choices of setting priorities within and between communities. To developers, it offers development opportunities that provide for public needs and that carry community support. And for community residents, workers, small businesses, and other stakeholders, it offers an opportunity to contribute fairly to significant decisions and to work toward a vision for the future.

Putting Teeth into Plans

A plan is one thing. Results are another. While there may be benefit and empowerment in the process of community-based planning, the final measure is in the translation of the results of the plan into tangible differences in the lives of community stakeholders.

There are three sources of power communities can tap and develop to implement plans: government authority, private ownership, and public pressure and promotion.

Both DSNI and LEED tapped government authority to put teeth into their plans. The Planned Manufacturing District is a creative form of governmental land-use control, and the acquisition of public land and the power of eminent domain by DSNI are a new twist on traditional government authority. There are obviously a wide range of public subsidies for projects and programs that implement community plans and develop appropriate land uses. Less often considered are taxing policies such as special service areas, special assessments, and tax increment financing that can be put to the service of community-based plans. Another creative use of government authority is referendum zoning, which puts community land uses on the ballot.

In contrast to government authority, private ownership of land provides for greater control of individual parcels. When land is privately owned by CBOs or by community land trusts, the community stakeholders continue to have decision-making power over the use of that land through the development process and through changes in the community situation over time. Community land trusts can be structured so that ownership of the land itself is retained under community control, while the building or "improvement" on the land may be privately owned.

Community land trusts can also be structured to limit the appreciation in the value of the properties held, thus providing for permanent affordability and a hedge against speculation and displacement while making small but structural changes in the way we view the value that the government and the community create in property. In Suffolk County on Long Island in New York, the government purchased the development rights of farmland to prevent further suburban sprawl and preserve open space while retaining private property ownership. The purchase of development rights could be implemented by CBOs or community land trusts as well.

There are problems with relying on private land ownership, however.

Whenever plans for the development of land are publicly surfaced, the cost of acquiring that property goes up. Plans can be developed in a more general way and specific parcels negotiated confidentially, but there can be leaks and holes in this process. This is why eminent domain is a critical power in the development of land in the public interest. Also, implementation of community-based plans takes time, and land that is "banked" in the meantime costs money to maintain and insure. Public ownership can shift some of these costs away from CBOs or land trusts while retaining public control and preventing speculation.

While direct government authority and private ownership can provide significant control to communities, both ultimately rely on the third power, the power of public pressure and promotion. A well-publicized, widely supported plan can attract compatible resources for appropriate projects and programs. A plan can catch the attention of individuals and institutions and channel that interest into areas of matching need. On the other hand, development at odds with the goals and values of the plan will be highlighted and subject to adverse publicity and delay that can sink the project. Even without government authority or private ownership, this public power can strengthen the position of community stakeholders who have been shut out of the process in the past.

Conclusion and Directions for Future Exploration

The most promising direction for community input into land use today is community-based planning. These planning efforts bring to the front the political negotiation of self-interests, both within and outside communities. Although the politics are complex, the process can strike a balance between liberty and justice that empowers the disadvantaged and develops communities that are sustainable and contribute to the growth of freedom and prosperity for all of us. To make plans work requires a sensitive management of process as well as the development and application of creative uses of governmental authority, private property ownership, and the power of public pressure and promotion.

The most important area for further exploration is the support and development of specific community-based planning efforts. These efforts are new and relatively untried, and participants must cover new ground and build new relationships while avoiding the pitfalls of old planning models that were "top-down" or merely "window dressing." Support for community-based planning must also be sensitive to the need for local initiative.

Every community is different, but at the Community Workshop on Economic Development we find that there are common lessons in community-based planning that may be shared between communities. Our Local Development Issues Working Group provides a good way to support the sharing and developing of methods in managing the community planning process. Like community-based planning efforts, permanent coalitions are democratically controlled by the stakeholders who are most affected by development decisions, and are therefore appropriate to and consistent with the goals of community-based planning.

We need to develop models and policies for the application of the three powers tapped by community-based planning efforts. How successful are creative applications such as PMDs and the administration of public land and eminent domain by CBOs? How can community land trusts be adapted to various community situations? How can community constituencies from multiple communities work together with partners in the public and private sector to develop and promote priorities that support community-based planning?

And if partnerships and the negotiation of self-interests are an integral part of community-based planning and democratic-decision making, we need to know more about the players in the game. We know a good deal about the results of existing land-use processes, but we know less about how these results are achieved. To what extent are a few developers well connected with government officials making things happen? To what extent is the currently lopsided pattern of development a matter of policies and practices that are simply expedient? Who sees self-interest in the status quo, and how can we begin the process of educating and negotiating that interest?

Liberty and justice, community and partnership, economic resources and equity, land and control. Our democratic political goals can be achieved if we bring the process out into the open. Community-based planning offers a promising new approach. With hard work and the right support, the Boardwalks and Baltic Avenues can all be prosperous and vital. Otherwise communities may continue to find land development a throw of loaded dice.

NOTES

1. National Congress for Community Economic Development. *Against All Odds: The Achievements of Community-Based Development Organizations,* March, 1989.
2. Dudley Street Neighborhood Initiative, *Dudley Street Neighborhood Initiative Revitalization Plan: A Comprehensive Community Controlled Strategy,* 1988, p. 2.

Luther Snow is the director of the Community Workshop on Economic Development (CWED). CWED is a coalition of community organizations that wa˞ formed in 1982. Their primary interest was to provide a platform for a balanced growth, pro-neighborhood agenda. Many CWED members went on to be part of Harold Washington's administration when he was elected in 1983. CWED continues to present an alternative to the blindly pro-growth interests that have often ignored Chicago's many neighborhoods. Prior to joining CWED in 1989, Luther Snow was director of Real Estate and Membership Development for the Chicago Association of Neighborhood Development Organizations (CANDO), a coalition of seventy neighborhood economic development groups. Prior to that he was director of economic development for Bethel New Life, Inc., an innovative community-based economic development organization serving Chicago's low-income Westside community.

10 EFFECTIVE STRATEGIES FOR COMMUNITY ECONOMIC DEVELOPMENT

John J. Betancur,
Deborah E. Bennett, and
Patricia A. Wright

The history of commnity economc development (CED) is rich and con-flicted: it gets things done, but suffers setbacks and failures. CED has almost as many directions as organizations that identify with it. In prepa-ration for writing this essay, the authors reflected on their own ex-periences, read and discussed prominent articles on the subject, and conducted thirteen interviews with CED practitioners and analysts. The essay is presented in four sections. This first section gives an overview of the main evaluative literature on community economic development identified for this paper; the next section lays out a brief historical sketch of the rise of CED in Chicago; the third section discusses effective CED strategies over the years, followed by a section on the roles of different players in the process.

Review of Evaluative CED Literature

The future success of CED requires systematic documentation, not only to justify further funding but to enrich the theory and practice of

CED as well. Few evaluations of CED have been conducted because of the difficulty in defining and quantifying evaluation standards. Those that have been conducted have many limitations.

The first major study in the United States was conducted by the Westinghouse Learning Corporation for the Office of Economic Opportunity (OEO) in 1968. It was a qualitative evaluation comparing a community development corporation (CDC) with three other types of economic development projects, all funded under a single congressional mandate, the Special Impact Programs for deteriorated inner-city areas and impoverished rural areas. (CDC is used here as a generic term for all nonprofit community-based organizations involved in development activity.) The study assessed projects run by four different government agencies using four discrete approaches to job creation in low-income communities. Two of the projects, the CDC-sponsored project and a rural project, involved local people in their design and execution. The other two did not. The study concluded that the two indigenously controlled projects were the most successful. It attributed this success to commitment and knowledge of the local area (Perry 1987:185–87).

An 1973 Abt Associates study also found successful OEO grantees. Abt concluded that business and social goals could be successfully combined and found "strong evidence for the positive effects of community participation and control on CDC performance" (Perry 1987:188). Community control was measured by the percentage of representative and resident community board members versus outsiders.

In 1974 the Ford Foundation commissioned a study of its CDC grantees. The study, conducted by the Urban Institute, measured each CDC's performance against its own goals and projected outputs. It concluded that self-selected goals resulted in higher performance (Perry 1987:189–190). In 1976, a study of the leadership of CDCs found a positive statistical correlation between high performance of CDCs and strength of community boards (Kelly 1976:191).

A 1980 study by the National Center for Economic Alternatives, using a cross section of fifteen CDCs, confirmed the Abt study findings on business development, concluding that "the (non-real estate) ventures had a business survival rate of about 50 percent, but it pointed out that CDCs tolerated a level of loss in ventures that would not conventionally be accepted" (Perry 1987:192).

Despite many methodological problems (i.e., measuring variables that are more meaningful from a long-term perspective in a short-term time frame), these early evaluations recognized that lasting improvement in the quality of community life depends on the full involvement of residents in defining and solving their own problems. These evaluations also acknowledged the trade-off between social and economic goals, and that success cannot be measured only in economic terms.

CDCs employ a gamut of strategies to transform their communities into viable places to live. The effectiveness of these strategies must be judged on a community-by-community basis. Each low-income community has unique characteristics, and a community economic development strategy must incorporate the needs, capabilities, and resources at the disposal of a community. A CDC pursues a particular strategy based on these characteristics. One interviewee for this analysis suggested that we look at the following questions when measuring the effectiveness of community economic development:

What happens to the development of the capacity of the people involved?

What happens to the development of organizational capacity in the community?

What is the effect of this activity on the neighborhood economy? Is the community transformed? Are there rising expectations of what the community can become?

The above set of questions reflects a comprehensive approach that many analysts and practitioners think is necessary to truly turn depressed communities around. Unfortunately, many CDCs move away from comprehensive planning in favor of the "quick fix." Funding requirements often force CDCs to take this more pragmatic route. As a result, emphasis is increasingly placed on quantifiable rather than on qualitative results. Empowerment gives way to projects taken as "end products." Strategies to integrate social, physical and economic activities have been largely abandoned (Shiffman and Motley 1989).

More recent evaluations of CDCs reflect this shift in emphasis. In its 1988 survey of 834 CDCs across the country, the National Congress for Community Economic Development (NCCED) found that:

CDCs have built nearly 125,000 units of housing, over 90 percent for low-income occupants.

CDCs have made loans to 2,048 enterprises, equity investments in two-hundred eighteen ventures, and own and operate four-hundred twenty-seven businesses.

CDC commercial/industrial and business enterprise development activities have accounted for creation and retention of almost 90,000 jobs in the last five years (NCCED 1989:1).

NCCED acknowledged, however, that these accomplishments must be viewed within the context of the less tangible products of effective community economic development—capacity building, leadership development, and community participation.

Conversely, interviewees cited these less tangible elements of effective CED as the key elements. They consistently acknowledged those CDCs that have been able to involve community residents in the development process as the most effective. They linked a CDC's ability to sustain development projects with the level of community participation. One housing developer described it as "the community having a stake in the dwellings they live in." Most of them acknowledged the serious limitations of the current emphasis on quantifiable results.

Practitioners and other analysts of community economic development suggest that if the aforementioned achievements are to be sustained, if CDCs are to become more than marginal players, then "the movement which spawned CDCs must be reformed and reinvigorated" (Keating and Krumholz 1988:16). CDCs must again attempt to address the economic, social and cultural needs of a community as well as the physical. "Physical development and people development, and economic and political development must all occur, each at its own pace, each with its own integrity" (Shiffman and Motley 1989:36).

Another school of thought asserts that the critical factor is not comprehensiveness but scale. The challenge of the future is to increase the scale, and critical influence, of CED efforts (Peirce and Steinbach 1987). According to these analysts, there are three principal ways to move CDCs to greater scale: (1) by large, symbolic projects that begin to reverse a community's negative image; (2) by the numbers: catalyzing CDC activity to a point where the efforts in housing rehabilitation or job creation reach a cumulatively massive scale; and (3) by strategic political and economic intervention (Peirce and Steinbach 1987:38).

The notion of scale is further explored in a national survey assessing the organizational characteristics and work of 130 urban CBOs in twenty-nine cities across the country. According to this study, there are several ways to expand the scale of community development activity: increase the number of community development organizations; increase the output of existing CDCs (e.g., undertake more projects or larger projects); or increase the efficiency of CDCs (Vidal 1989).

An interesting finding of the assessment is the speed with which younger CDCs move into production activity. Older groups that came out of an organizing tradition operated for an average of six years before engaging in production activity. Newly established CDCs enter into production after an average of eight months. While these CDCs are growing in staff and budget, their expansion (and subsequent increased production) is hindered by the lack of affordable long-term financing and support for overhead costs. Again, this assessment reflects an emphasis on quantifiable results.

This selected literature review reflects many different approaches to community economic development. The era of Reaganomics and severely restricted federal budgets that once supported local initiatives have forced CED practitioners to become more "creative." This creativity often means more partnerships with the government and corporate sectors. Many times these partnerships result in CDCs becoming more project oriented and more market oriented. Sometimes partnerships result in the loss of an equity stake or the loss of control in a project. The very nature of the relationship discourages advocacy. On the other hand, these partnerships allow CDCs to "get the deal done."

Accounts of specific CED efforts abound in the literature. A national compilation of these has been developed by the Community Information Exchange in Washington. They reflect a gamut of choices, a variety of projects, and differences in emphases and variables used to assess the work. Effectiveness in each case is determined according to the task, the goal, and the perceptions of those involved.

The Rise of Community Economic Development

Two related historical trends contribute to what we know today as community development. One is the change in our nation's political climate at the end of the protest movements of the sixties. The other is the drastic shift in the U.S. economy from the booming sixties to the recession of 1975. Together these trends created an uphill battle for the success of community developments efforts. From its inception, the community economic-development movement has been reactive, first to the decline of the social movements of the sixties and later to the restructuring of the economy. Beginning in the late seventies, this economic restructuring is what caused economic development to take a more defined role in community-development activities.

For the most part, community development occurs through not-for-profit groups organized at the neighborhood level to work on quality of life issues such as better housing, street improvements, social services, and schools. Each neighborhood group strives for its fair share of government programs. Many groups also fight for other issues affecting their neighborhoods, such as nondiscriminatory regulations in the banking and insurance industries. Generally, community groups concentrate their efforts on issues within the neighborhood and look mostly to government programs for solutions.

Community development efforts follow an earlier stage of resistance when community groups fought against government programs such as urban renewal and highway expansions that destroyed many neighborhoods in the sixties. After opposing these government programs in the sixties, the seventies found community groups trying to wrest control of many of these programs away from government. People wanted to set up alternative community development institutions to develop their own plans as to how government monies should be spent in their areas. In a change from the beliefs of the civil rights, black power, antiwar, and other protest movements, some people now thought that social change could be furthered from within the community without directly challenging the overall system.

In many communities there was resistance to this approach of building alternatives within the system. The civil rights and black power movements of the 1960s had aimed for more radical changes in the system. Although these movements were sabotaged and leaders such as Martin Luther King, Malcolm X, and Fred Hampton were assassinated, many people were not willing to give up the visions for change that these leaders and the movement as a whole were striving for. Many took a wait-and-see attitude about accepting government money to build alternative institutions within the community. Some rejected it outright as selling out. This conflict within the black community and other minority communities has made community involvement and support for development projects a continuing problem.

The political stagnation that set in after the sixties caused frustration and had many people rethinking their political activities. Some people were attracted to community development because it concentrated on concrete issues that would improve people's lives on a daily basis. Others joined in community development efforts because they had lost faith in the government and decided to rebuild their communities themselves.

While community groups were refocusing their efforts to respond to the changed political climate, economic changes were also afoot. In Chicago, one of the first manifestations of the economic changes was the unveiling of the Chicago 21 Plan in 1973.

The Chicago 21 Plan was the corporate vision for Chicago in the twenty-first century. It was sponsored by the Chicago Central Area Committee, an organization of the downtown corporate interests. In 1973, this plan anticipated the economic trends that would shift the growth areas of Chicago's economy from manufacturing to the service sector.

The Chicago 21 Plan was a vehicle whereby these downtown interests were asking the city government to support this restructuring of Chicago's economy with public policies and expenditures.

The main concept of the Chicago 21 Plan was a fortress city. It aimed to redevelop the land that circled a booming service sector downtown for middle- and upper-class residents. This redevelopment was to create an ever-increasing buffer zone to protect the downtown investments from the growing number of poor and minority people living in Chicago's surrounding neighborhoods.

The unveiling of the Chicago 21 Plan created a storm of protest from community groups. The focus of the protest was on the lack of community participation and review of the plan before it was published. As in the days of urban renewal, decisions were being made downtown about future city developments that would affect the neighborhoods. A coalition of community groups drawn from across the city challenged the concept and vision of the Chicago 21 Plan. This challenge was a turning point for the community groups looking at building alternative community institutions as the approach for the seventies. The Chicago 21 Plan gave these groups the rationale to pursue this agenda. The argument was: "if we don't take control of our communities and fight for the resources to develop them ourselves, the resources will continue to be concentrated in the development of the downtown."

The opposition to the Chicago 21 Plan was also important for other reasons. It challenged the pro-growth attitudes of the post–World War II era, which was centering its attention on the central business district and neglecting the other sectors of Chicago's economy. It was a direct confrontation with the corporate leaders instead of with the city government representing their interests. Unfortunately, the challenge to the Chicago 21 Plan ended as community groups became more and more consumed in the alternative institution building in their areas. The interrelationship of the neighborhood and downtown economic development policies were pushed to the background. Not until ten years later, with the opposition to the World's Fair, would these relationships be reexamined.

The Chicago 21 Plan was an early signal for the restructuring of the economy, but it did not foretell the resultant recession and economic upheaval that would hit in the late seventies.

The recession would take its greatest toll in the minority and other working class neighborhoods. Unemployment rates soared as the steel industry collapsed on the southeast side, and factories closed and moved to the sunbelt and eventually offshore seeking cheaper and cheaper labor. Most minority communities had been suffering economically even during the prosperity of the sixties. The recession of 1975 worsened these conditions, but also affected the city's white ethnic neighborhoods. The city's loss of jobs and commercial activity to the suburbs brought many white ethnic groups into the community economic development field.

By the end of the seventies and early eighties, economic conditions grew worse. As community groups struggled to maintain ongoing housing rehabilitation and other community programs, many took on the additional problems of unemployment, factory closings, and the effects of these economic changes on the commercial strips. This was when economic development became a more defined activity within community development activities.

Many groups overwhelmed by the problem realized that they were working too much in isolation. Coalitions like the Chicago Rehab Network (CRN, 1977) and the Chicago Association of Neighborhood Development Organizations (CANDO, 1979) were formed to share information and pressure the city government to allocate more funds to continue or expand the many programs started in many neighborhoods on shoe string budgets.

The main source of CED funding has been the federal government, particularly the Community Development Block Grant Program (CDBG) initiated in 1974 and the Comprehensive Employment and Training Act (CETA). Initially, the federal funds were tightly controlled in Chicago by the Democratic party under Mayor Daley. With his death in 1976, the Democratic machine's stranglehold not only on government funds but also on independent political activity loosened, just as many groups were beginning to form community development alternative institutions. This allowed many groups to be funded. Later, the four years of the Carter administration created additional programs like the Urban Development Action Grants and the self-help grants of the special neighborhood division in the Department of Housing and Urban Development. These programs were set up specifically to create investment opportunities in the northern cities most affected by the recession. The neighborhood office was quickly dissolved by the Reagan administration. Ironically, the UDAG program was used throughout the eighties to further the downtown development outlined by the Chicago 21 Plan.

Throughout the Reagan years, community development organizations struggled to survive on the dwindling federal dollars. In Chicago, community development groups were more fortunate than many groups in other urban areas. They helped bring to power the Harold Washington administration, which consequently increased city support for their activities. But the lack of federal dollars and the continuing strength of the downtown corporate interests split the attention of the Washington administration between supporting neighborhood development and fueling the growth demands of downtown with federal subsidies, land write-downs, and special favors. The subsidies to downtown development continued even into the late eighties when interest rates declined and segments of the economy experienced some recovery.

A turning point in the awareness of community groups of the relationship between the neighborhood economies and the larger economic picture was the defeat of the proposed 1992 Chicago World's Fair. The World's Fair was such an expensive and poorly planned development scheme, it awakened many community groups to oppose it, primarily as a waste of public monies. Unanswered environmental and displacement concerns also figured in the anti-Fair organizing campaign. The World's Fair issue, once again, brought community groups into direct confrontation with the downtown corporate interests, the same actors that supported the Chicago 21 Plan.

Since the defeat of the World's Fair in 1986 there has been more coalition building and awareness of the relationship between the changed economy of Chicago, investment decisions, and their effects on jobs and conditions in the neighborhoods. CANDO has developed a neighborhood investment campaign which targets $200 million for neighborhood development. The Community Workshop on Economic Development (CWED) and other community housing groups have lobbied and won the creation of low-income housing trust funds at the city and state level. The Campaign for Responsible Ownership fought and won legislative changes in the housing tax delinquency regulations. The Chicago 1992 Committee and the Chicago Affordable Housing Coalition have both done extensive research on linked development. These efforts demonstrate new approaches that coordinate organizing and development efforts. The economic relationship of the neighborhoods to the Chicago economy is being reexamined. But, there is still concern about the overall purpose of CED efforts and its relationship to not only the economic but also the political climate of the country. These concerns will be explored further in the next section.

Effective CED Strategies

What is the nature of CED and how does one measure the value of its alternative approaches? Assessing the effectiveness of specific CED strategies is an extremely complicated task, as our earlier review of CED evaluations indicates. Echoing almost every account of CED approaches and strategies, a recent compilation by UICUED asserts that these challenges are closely associated with the "social perspectives of those defining local problems and formulating solutions" (1987:1). In other words, approaches and strategies are not neutral. On the contrary, they gain meaning from the efforts within which they take place. Hence, their effectiveness cannot be measured independently of these efforts and circumstances. A few examples will illustrate this point.

CED is perceived by efforts such as the Chicago 21 Plan as a function of the expansion, support, and stability of the central business district (CBD). This perspective justified actions such as the razing of a viable neighborhood to the Southwest of the CBD for construction of the University of Illinois at Chicago. Similarly, CED has been synonymous with the gentrification of low-income neighborhoods, often through the use of public programs such as Urban Renewal in conjunction with the plans of private developers. More recently, the expansion of the CBD into neighboring communities has replaced many viable manufacturing firms with artist studios or offices (DED 1986). In these cases, effectiveness is measured by the ability of business interests to raze these neighborhoods or displace their current residents or firms with higher income groups or business tenants. The success and profits of these developments are made at the expense of others—namely, the firms or residents displaced, or the workers losing their jobs.

Similar considerations apply to community-based initiatives. Efforts that are exclusively centered around real estate development may improve the physical appearance and attract new businesses and tenants into a neighborhood. However, this may also happen at the expense of established businesses and long-term residents, who may no longer be able to afford to live in the area. Even identical strategies may have a different meaning and potential in different communities. As one of the interviewees for this paper suggested, we cannot properly compare the People's Bank of Lawndale to the South Shore Bank because the former bank is working in a much tougher environment. Finally, the director of a community group producing housing argued that the effectiveness of community-based housing organizations could not be properly measured by the number of units produced—it is often a drop in the bucket—but by the meaning of this effort to the community in terms of building local capacity, creating a sense of pride and collective achievement, or having a demonstrative effect beyond the units themselves.

Discussing all these issues as they relate to each of the CED models and perspectives is beyond the scope of this paper. Instead, we will concentrate below on issues concerning the effectiveness of community-based CED efforts. For this purpose, we will start with a brief analysis of the two overarching approaches to CED identified by UICUED researchers (Wright, Betancur, and Wiewel 1985; UICUED 1987), namely, the business development and the empowerment/organizing approaches.

CED groups may choose to pursue the business route and engage in facilitation of business activity or in direct business creation. In the first case, CED acts as a catalyst for business activity. In the second case, it assumes the role of developer. The assumption here, of course, is that business activity can create the economic opportunities and capital that are needed to improve a neighborhood. Assessments of these perspectives have pointed to a series of limitations and have made distinctions that are worth mentioning here.

The literature and our interviewees question the assumption that adequate business development can occur in the inner city without major structural changes. Further, the relationship between business development and adequate opportunities and benefits from this development for current residents is dismal. Issues such as lower disposable incomes, higher costs of running a business in the inner city, the availability of better business opportunities elsewhere, and perception explain our first assertion. Ownership, racism, job networks, availability of skilled labor and training opportunities, lack of local ties, and outside control explain the second.

Some efforts to develop neighborhoods in Chicago have succeeded at the expense of displacing current residents, as illustrated above. Other successes took place in neighborhoods that lost their business and population base to suburbanization, but underwent a successful replacement process of both residents and business owners. CED groups were often a factor in facilitating this transition. The ability of CED efforts to develop communities without sacrificing the needs of residents, however, is questioned in this paper both on the basis of structural factors and past experiences.

Many businesses located in inner-city communities are there only as a result of past location decisions that bear no relationship to the existing community. Even though local intervention can make a difference, the factors determining the location of these businesses are usually beyond the local realm.

Many community players and researchers in community economic development argue that corporations and other mid-size businesses manage to monopolize economic activity to the point where there is room for new players only in marginal sectors. Under these conditions, CED is left with low-end, less profitable small business opportunities. Similarly, others argue that there is a profit in disinvestment and that the interests tied to this process run counter to CED efforts.

Interviewees criticized local CDCs for becoming little empires of their own. Their institutional perpetuation, or the reproduction and growth of their assets, come before the community and dictate their priorities and forms of work, rather than the community's needs and struggles. Several analysts have also pointed to the heavy reliance of this business development approach on outside experts and its excessive focus on the improvement of places.

All these factors illustrate both the considerations needed in measuring CED effectiveness, and the general possibilities of strategies based on this approach. The specific strategies and results can vary immensely.

Interestingly enough, successes in this business development approach have been usually associated with non-business factors or with elements beyond the narrow business framework claimed by many of its advocates. The success of a well-known CED group in Chicago was attributed by some interviewees to its comprehensive approach of providing support and services along with job assistance and business opportunities. This group also set geographic boundaries that were reasonable and had the support of a local church with access to many resources. Correspondingly, many interviewees blamed the failure of many locally based CED efforts on their lack of comprehensiveness.

Interviewees also measured success by the ability of CED groups to involve the community, combining organizing efforts with economic development undertakings. The failure rate of business ventures by not-for-profit development corporations is much lower than that of the private sector; and CDCs tolerated levels of loss better (National Center for Economic Alternatives 1980). This could be explained by subsidies and cost savings—from volunteer work to the reinvestment of proceeds. However, the main explanation, we argue, is the social motive behind the venture that changes many of the strictly business elements into a different form. This is not to say that CED ventures are any panacea. On the contrary, measured by business indicators these activities confirm the structural limitations mentioned earlier. A study of twelve organizations reputed as most successful in Chicago concluded that they did "not yield sustained economic growth or generate(d) adequate jobs for the targeted Chicago communities and residents." (Brown-Chappell et al. 1988:31). Yet, the authors admitted to the important symbolic role of these organizations in their target communities (Brown-Chappell et al. 1988:1).

What this discussion suggests is that a business-as-usual approach cannot succeed in these communities and that the complex schemes being tried in many inner-city communities only produce marginal results from a conventional business perspective.

In sharp contrast with business indicators often used by funders, the government, or the private sector to measure the effectiveness of these efforts, the practitioners and analysts of community-based initiatives we interviewed more often use process-oriented, social change, or empowerment indicators to define success in these projects. These include: the creation of local capacity or building a base for expanded undertakings, increases in local control and self-reliance, awareness of interests and contradictions at stake in the development process, stalling further deterioration, and the development of leadership.

Again, the above indicators call for forms of CED work that are not fully ruled by business concerns. In fact, the measures of success mentioned above point to the roots of local initiatives: that is, spontaneous resistance to oppressive conditions, to a status quo that does not provide the opportunities needed by residents, and the search for alternatives. The business route, as suggested earlier, is not necessarily the end, or even the main, purpose of CED efforts, but a means to obtain some of these local aspirations or to stay in business hoping for better opportunities in the future.

The second approach to community-based CED, empowerment, has also many variations, inspiring philosophies, and styles. The best-known ones in the United States have been summarized in the UICUED compilation cited (1987:6–8). We will concentrate our analysis here on two empowerment models: those struggling for the redistribution of resources— the "fair share" form—and those interested in social change. Effectiveness and success, of course, have to be determined on the basis of their contribution to each particular form.

Organizing, another name for the empowerment approach, has been rated by many as more effective in general than business development. It has been argued that it can get results much faster at a much lower cost. The struggle for a fair share of jobs in the public sector in Chicago is a good example. There is every indication that the organizing efforts of minorities here have resulted in the allocation of more jobs for their constituencies than the business development approach.

This effectiveness, however, has serious costs, even from the perspective of the community and the approach. These jobs do not necessarily benefit those most in need. They may help some residents to move out of the community, hence losing the multiplier impact that these jobs could have for the community. More importantly, these jobs are taken away from other groups, thus becoming a source of tension among communities and minorities.

The "fair share" form has been extensively used in Chicago by communities and interest groups to fight City Hall over the distribution of CDBG, capital investment, IRBs, UDAGs, municipal jobs and contracts, and many others. Some redistribution has been achieved, even though not at the level and in the terms proposed. The process and allocation of the goods redistributed have many times set groups against each other. More often than not, gains are temporary and can be turned around or taken back by new administrations or new programs.

Such organizing requires large levels of participation, the continuous mobilization of people, and the use of confrontational tactics that involve risks for the participants and the organizations involved. Staff control and isolation from the community are frequent. This type of action is predominantly result oriented, and each undertaking consists of immediate, short-term, winnable projects. This approach looks for shortcuts, sacrificing issues of democratic process and community building along the way. Pragmatic leaders often lose track of the large picture and the real issues. As one interviewee suggested, these campaigns often address the symptoms, not the diseases.

Organizing has been also extensively used to push policies, to demand changes, or to protect the interests of consumers and residents. Opposition to the 1992 World's Fair by many communities and interest groups is an example, as are the struggles of consumers against the utilities, and residents of the West Side and South Side against sports stadium proposals. In many cases, groups and individuals consciously engage in these actions as part of their general struggle for social change. Others join the actions as a way to protect their particular interests.

Finally, it is important to mention that these approaches take on many variations, and that they often include different combinations of organizing and development. It is also important to add that the underlying drive of locally based CED efforts, particularly those by inner-city residents and the disadvantaged is their spontaneous resistance to existing conditions. The outcomes of these actions are determined by many factors beyond local control, some of which are mentioned throughout this paper. Very often these undertakings are manipulated by outside forces with other interests, by internal forces representing outside interests, or by existing programs with different agendas. As a result, the original need or demand is often lost, redefined at convenience, or turned into something else. In these cases, CED assessments do not measure the effectiveness of CED work per se, but the actions, priorities, and agendas of players that do not have local needs as their main goal.

Aside from these approaches, but closely associated with them is the entire issue of CBOs. While these organizations have been the central players in community-based CED efforts, many have become ends in themselves. In this way, their survival as institutions has absorbed a large part of the total community effort, at the expense of crucial CED tasks.

The needs of institutionalization often discourage the risk taking and opposition that may be needed in CED work. In the absense of other local institutions striving for local development, these organizations become key players in representation of their communities. However, they may easily become small bureaucracies of their own, controlled by professional staff, with their own self-defined agendas, often detached from the community. These institutions may preempt other work or may substitute for the comprehensive organizing efforts badly needed in these communities. What may be perceived as a success from one perspective—the growth and power of these organizations, for instance—may be alternatively viewed as a problem as it may preempt other efforts required for the deep changes called forth by local conditions and need.

This discussion illustrates the complexity and contradictions surrounding CED work. More specifically, it shows the multiple perspectives from which the effectiveness of this work can be established, and the uses to which the assessments can be put—assessments themselves become forces pushing in specific directions, opposing others, or condemning the entire effort. Judging the effectiveness of CED work can be one or another thing, depending on who is making the judgment.

Roles of Community Economic Development Players

This section examines the roles of the main players in community economic development, namely, government, foundations, the private sector, coalitions, technical assistance providers, and community based organizations as discussed by interviewees and as analyzed in the literature.

GOVERNMENT AGENCIES

In the last thirty years, the federal government has played a combined funding-programmatic role in a series of community development initiatives including: Urban Renewal; The Special Impact Program (SIP) of the former Office of Economic Opportunity (OEO) for deteriorated inner-city areas and impoverished rural communities; Community Development

Block Grants (CDBGs); Urban Development Action Grants (UDAGs); and the Special Neighborhood Division of Housing and Urban Development (HUD).

The city of Chicago had important participation in each of these programs. Urban Renewal was extensively used to clear land for development in projects such as The University of Illinois at Chicago Campus, Sandburg Village and others in Lincoln Park, and a number of developments around the University of Chicago in Hyde Park. The North Lawndale Economic Development Corporation (later the Pyramid West Corporation) and The Woodlawn Organization (TWO) received funding under the Special Impact Program of the OEO for development efforts in their communities. CDBG has been one of the main source of funding for CED initiatives in Chicago. UDAGs have been also widely used, particularly in the downtown area. With the exception of funding under the Special Impact Program of the OEO for CDCs, participation in the above programs has been controlled by the city government and has been largely used to clear low-income areas for institutional or middle income housing use, to subsidize the downtown office boom of the last twenty years, to fund many bureaucratic positions in city government, and to make up for extremely low funding levels for investment in the neighborhoods. In all of this, funding for CED and, more specifically, for inner-city development was very limited during the administrations of Daley (1955–76) and Bilandic (1976–79).

City government has played a much larger role in community economic development. First, it distributed federal funding and controlled participation in federal programs. Second, it controlled planning and resource allocation, particularly the distribution of capital investment and projects throughout the city. Third, the city controlled development activity via permits, licenses, codes, and similar powers. Fourth, it directed policy for undertakings with a crucial effect on community economic development such as development of the central business district and organization of the 1992 World Fair. Fifth, it assigned specific roles to selected players such as CBOs, private consultants, and contractors.

Historically, city government steered development in certain directions to the neglect of particular areas and sectors of the city. For instance, downtown development was strongly promoted during the Daley, the Bilandic, and the Byrne (1979–83) administrations. Along with this, real estate, middle-income housing, and the service industry received a strong boost from economic-development initiatives and priorities of the local government. This work was often conducted in close partnership with the corporate sector. Participants in our survey resented the role played by the local government in the 1960s and 1970s because it created a

213

dichotomy between downtown and the neighborhoods and was highly political.

The Washington administration (1983–87) tried to redistribute some of these efforts to include neighborhoods and sectors that had been previously neglected. As part of this, the administration engaged in partnerships with CDCs towards retention of businesses located in the neighborhoods, emphasized the retention of manufacturing jobs, and tried to influence policies and practice of community economic development.

CED is heavily dependent on government funding. The work of CED groups has been largely determined by the types of activities or approaches the government funded. In this way, CED work fluctuated from administration to administration, from federal program to federal program to federal program, a condition that negatively affected stability, scale, and continuity of efforts. Initiatives were expected to produce dramatic results too soon or were unfunded before they could mature. Funding was withdrawn from a group to be assigned to another group. Large sums were poured overnight into a community or group that was not ready to manage large projects. Agendas were pushed on organizations.

Community groups had no choice but to rush to produce the numbers they were asked to produce without much planning, and often without much relationship to previous and ongoing efforts. It was the government through its funding agencies and selection mechanisms, not the community, which decided who got funding for what and how to go about addressing local problems. Several interviewees commented that organizing, planning, capacity building and advocacy efforts usually received little attention, if any. As a result, the community was treated as merely a site for projects conceived and controlled by city or other government bureaucrats. Within these circumstances, CED efforts were deemed to fail but were not given much of an alternative.

In light of this, the following suggestions can be made:

1. The city should develop a comprehensive policy to determine the priorities and allocation of CED resources on a more objective and systematic basis. New concepts of enterprise zones, tax reactivation, energy efficiency incentives, recycling, reverse commuting, neighborhood workshops for planning and development of local initiatives, planned manufacturing districts, welfare reform, tenants bill of rights, and building code waivers were mentioned as examples.

2. Organizing and advocacy work should get a greater share of funding.

3. Local administrations should play a more active role in advocating for increased funding for neighborhoods on the part of the state and the federal governments.

4. Government agencies should treat the various players involved in CED efforts as partners. They should share information with them, consult with them, and avoid preferential treatment for private businesses and the corporate sector, as they have done in the past.

5. There is an urgent need to set reasonable limits in CED work. Better to have modest goals than to have organizations take on projects they cannot possibly accomplish.

FOUNDATIONS

Foundations have played a more modest role in CED in Chicago. After a slow start in the 1970s, many local foundations joined the effort in the 1980s, even though the share of their resource allocation to this field is still very low. More recently, they have moved into other roles such as disseminating information and sponsoring training programs.

Several of the persons we interviewed found many problems with the level of commitment on the part of foundations in the CED work. Funding for CED, they say is extremely limited and risk-aversive. Downtown-type organizations are funded at higher levels, with fewer strings attached, and for a sometimes unlimited number of years. While self-sufficiency and the search for alternative funding sources have been asked of groups doing CED, they are not asked of downtown and established organizations operating in other fields. Some foundations limit operating funds for organizations engaged in CED work to a few years. This is a problem because it often takes years of effort and struggle to bring these organizations to the level where they can start making a difference in their communities. CED groups are forced to continuously come up with new programs because of a tendency in the foundation world to fund "the latest bright idea." Some interviewees indicated that allocations in CED work in minority areas or in minority-controlled groups are small compared to allocations in majority-controlled work or groups.

In spite of recently established programs, empowerment, advocacy, and policy efforts receive little attention and meager funding. Interviewees were dissatisfied with the limited role played by foundations in CED as well as by the way organizations engaged in this work are treated.

Suggestions for improving the input of foundations include:

1) Foundations should treat organizations doing economic development in the communities more fairly and work more closely with them in evaluating successes and failures.

2) Foundations should increase their funding of CED efforts in the

215

inner city and be willing to take more risk. Funding should include pre-development stages and organizational development. Foundations should be more sensitive to the need for community participation and organizing in CED work.

3) Finally, Foundations should include more minorities in their boards and staff.

COALITIONS

Coalitions are the key to community economic development work in Chicago. Their main role is in the areas of policy development, lobbying and advocating for reform, and the development of resources for community economic development. Coalitions have also organized opposition to initiatives with a negative effect on community economic development and have advocated for fairness in government funding and distribution of public employment and resources.

Other less frequently mentioned efforts of coalitions include getting funding for member organizations, promoting and training leadership, helping organizations maintain an adequate equilibrium between backyard and citywide foci, and building capacity for common action. In short, coalitions extend the capacity of single organizations, hence providing a united front with much more leverage for efforts of a more comprehensive nature, or involving more risk, or requiring more muscle.

Our research also identified some problems in the work of coalitions. Bureaucratization or professionalization was perceived as an extreme that takes over coalitions and excludes members from meaningful participation. There has been also a great deal of difficulty with perpetuation of coalitions beyond what they were originally set up to do.

Suggestions to improve the role of coalitions in CED included: (1) Playing a more active role in promoting indigenous leadership, effectively integrating more groups to their work, and providing a forum for the discussion of issues, sharing and the development of ideas; (2) working more in public policy, community education, and evaluation of member organizations; and (3) developing more innovative and flexible structures that better correspond to the nature of their work and the possibilities of their members.

ROLE OF THE PRIVATE SECTOR

The role of the private sector in CED in Chicago is rated by most of our interviewees as well as by most CDC analysts as self-serving, minimal, and often damaging. This sector selectively chooses to intervene when its interests are threatened, when it foresees a unique opportunity to increase its gains, regardless of the effect on the neighborhoods, and when large subsidies are available. Excellent examples of this role are the Chicago 21 Plan and the 1992 World's Fair. In both cases, the private sector developed agendas and plans for communities, without consulting residents' interests and needs, and even coopting some community groups in order to gain their support. It demands large public subsidies to support its interests, without considering the effect of these proposals on surrounding communities. Other examples are the large subsidies received by developers for projects that did not provide promised jobs, that displaced people, or that could have been done without public subsidies. Projects built with UDAG funding (Wright 1987), under urban renewal, or with HUD subsidies such as Presidential Towers and the White Sox Park are good examples.

Linked development and other efforts to steer some resources to the neighborhoods are vehemently opposed by private developers. Meanwhile, many businesses have abandoned the city after receiving multimillion dollar subsidies. Savings and loans located in the neighborhoods have been accused of redlining and using local savings to support development elsewhere.

In the absence of CED efforts by the private sector, CBOs have moved in to fill the void. In some neighborhoods, CDCs organize local businesses and help them cut costs and become more profitable. CDCs try to get some activity going where the private sector fails to provide leadership and economic development. The responses of the private sector have been lukewarm and more often than not hostile.

Suggestions in this area from our research are often controversial, including: (1) making sure that CED efforts to help private business development and retention include direct links to the needs of local or city residents and provide adequate opportunities to them; and (2) reevaluating and advocating for the tax on downtown development to improve funding for CED.

Technical Assistance Providers

The main role of technical assistance (TA) providers in Chicago has been assisting CED efforts with research, information, data, plans, and other general or project-specific technical needs of their work. TA providers have also trained CED players, conducted policy-related research,

217

provided issue consultation, and advocated successful models and technologies appropriate for CED. Questions have been raised whether TA providers, foundations, or coalitions are the most appropriate groups to play these roles. The issue of participatory models for research and TA provision has been also mentioned. Concerns were raised about the need for resident empowerment through skills development and capacity building, the control of information, and the methods of evaluation used by TA providers and others. The quality and appropriateness of TA provision have been often questioned with respect to the predominant business orientation of some TA providers. There is a need for sensitivity to the complexities of community work and the uniqueness of some efforts.

Recommendations in this area include: (1) use of participatory TA models that aim to transfer skills to CED activists and enhance their input into the design and decisions of projects; (2) improving the dissemination of research, policy, and other relevant efforts of technical assistance providers; (3) increasing research, particularly in the area of policy and program development and evaluation in CED work (for this, TA providers should make sure that CED activists are involved in the research from beginning to end); (4) Increasing the availability of free TA assistance with opportunities and efforts that require a prompt decision or action; and (5) developing research agendas closely related to the information needs, current activities, and priorities of CED players.

CBOs

In the absence of traditional institutions and local businesses promoting economic development in their neighborhoods, many CBOs have moved in to fill some of the void. CBOs represent different constituencies (retailers, industrialists, consumers, homeowners, the unemployed, workers) and may often assume controversial positions or support efforts that do not directly help residents. These groups, however, are more often than not formed to bring economic activity to the community or to secure opportunities for residents. In some communities, these organizations have moved to center stage or are the only players leading CED efforts from a local perspective.

These organizations play different roles depending on their focus, the scope of their activities, and their constituencies. Chambers of Commerce work to assist retailers with their needs with the purpose of maintaining viable businesses and sound retail strips in the community. Indirectly, they provide the community with badly needed services and consumer goods and have an influence on real estate in the area. Facing neglect and often hostility from city administrations siding with the downtown service sector, some industrial groups have been organized in the neighborhoods of Chicago to advocate for the interests of manufacturers. The stability and expansion of manufacturing, of course, are crucial to the city, but the link between locally available manufacturing jobs and residents was often so minimal that residents did not share the interests of these organizations. Some organizations were established to protect the rights of minority workers and increase their participation in unions. Others advocated for affordable housing or facilitated the rehabilitation of housing in the area. Each of these efforts implied different roles—from advocacy, organizing, and protest, assistance, and facilitation of economic activity, to development.

Closely related to the variety of local interests and undertakings of these groups are a series of tensions and problems that often hinder the effectiveness of many organizations. One source of contention among many community groups in Chicago is the tension between an organizing and a business development approach. Conflicts between organizations representing different interests and directions are often present in one community. As a result, some groups oppose the actions of others, engage in continuous animosity, or create confusion among residents. Tension between local and outside interests, between contending ideologies of CED, between capacity building and the physical needs of the community, between efficiency and local participation, have been a permanent source of internal divisions within the CED movement. Conflicting directions and roles present in the work of these CED organizations reflect all the conflicting forces present in this society, in general, and in their communities of operation in particular.

Recommendations in this area are also as varied and multi-directional as these tensions. We will include here only those that seem most relevant:

1. The work of community organizations should include a balance between technical undertakings and grass-roots organizing. There are many opinions about the way to achieve this balance. Some interviewees call for control of these organizations by indigenous leaders and persons from the constituency served by the organization. Others recommended separate branches, one doing organizing and the other development. Alternatively, it has been often proposed that CBOs concentrate on organizing and contract out the technical work. At the same time, many insist that organizations should avoid being swallowed up by marginal operations and, instead, look for alternative initiatives that can result in strong community pride and identity. Participants in our interviews were very emphatic about the need for much more organizing at this time in Chicago.

2. Community organizations should define their own agendas and have a strong commitment to them and stop shifting directions on the basis of opportunities. In doing this, however, groups should keep an open mind and avoid parochial and myopic perspectives. Digesting of experiences, dialogue, and coordinated action with their peers is suggested as a way to achieve this. In setting their agendas and goals, groups should be realistic and modest as to the possibility of their achieving them.

3. The need for a citywide agenda-setting process by community organizations is often mentioned as a source of concerted action and inspiration. Community organizations should develop mechanisms to engage in continuous discussion around their work and other events in the city. In particular, they need adequate mechanisms for a proper input in developments such as the recent relocation negotiations with Sears, the third airport, the distribution of CDBG funds, reprogramming of UDAG payback, or the direction of CED in the current Daley administration.

4. Community organizations should pay much more attention to capacity building and continuous development of indigenous leadership. Natural turnover or depletion of local leadership by citywide efforts such as the movement around Harold Washington have proved that communities may be demobilized by a lack of leaders. Likewise, capacity building is necessary to properly manage the organizations and to stay away from the "professionalization" or bureaucratization of community work.

5. Mechanisms should be developed whereby organizations reach out to new organizations or share expertise. These efforts could be coordinated by coalitions for their members or could be the result of mutual agreements between organizations or neighborhoods.

6. Community groups should be encouraged to limit their area of influence to a reasonable size, set reasonable goals for themselves, and be as comprehensive as possible in their work.

7. Community participation should be the sine qua non of CBOs. While there are different opinions about the form, nature, and level of involvement, everybody insists that the less participation, the less effect and meaning of the work. Organizations should be looking for ways to substantially involve residents in the various aspects of their work. This is seen not only as a form of capacity building but also as a form of increasing local ownership in CED efforts. Participation, it has been suggested is the difference between community and noncommunity economic development.

8. Community organizations should make sure to link their efforts to community needs so that a large proportion, if not all, of the benefits of their efforts accrue to the residents of the community.

9. There is a need for collecting the history of community work in Chicago in a way that can be used to educate future leaders and, generally, to help them and the community relate current efforts to the past. This work will help transmit the lessons of the past, keep track of achievements and monitor them, build local pride, build on the past, and give continuity to the struggle.

Conclusion

After examining the effectiveness of alternative approaches to CED work and the roles of the various players, our research suggests two central philosophical orientations: reformism and social change. The first looks at the troubles of inner-city communities as imperfections or limitations in the system that can be improved through marginal adjustments. On this basis, reformism views CED as a series of corrections to make the system run better. The social change orientation perceives the system as inherently flawed and the problems of communities as products of this structure. In this context, CED is approached as a transition to something else, the basis from which new models, indeed a new social order can flow. Many CED practitioners, however, have not realized the importance of taking positions or facing these alternatives. Instead, they have opted for the so-called pragmatic reformist route. In the absence of a decision and a clear direction, CED efforts can often be pulled in contradictory directions.

LIST OF INTERVIEWEES

Bob Brehm, executive director, Bickerdike Redevelopment Corporation, Chicago, July 28, 1989, personal interview.

Doug Gills, community development director, Kenwook-Oakland Community Organization, Chicago, August 2, 1989, telephone interview.

Stan Hallet, co-director, The Chicago Innovations Forum, Center for Urban Affairs and Policy Research, Northwestern University, Evanston, Illinois, August 2, 1989, telephone interview.

David Hunt, executive director, Chicago Rehab Network, Chicago, July 26, 1989, telephone interview.

Sokoni Karanja, executive director, Center for New Horizons, Chicago, July 27, 1989, telephone interview.

Frankie Knibb, former executive director, Chicago 1992 Committee, July 23, 1989, personal interview.

Lewis Kreinberg, Center for Neighborhood Technology, Chicago, July 30, 1989, personal interview.

Robert Mier, former commissioner of the Department of Economic Development of the City of Chicago, currently professor at the School of Urban Planning and Policy of the University of Illinois at Chicago, Chicago, July 25, 1989, personal interview.

Rev. Jorge Morales, executive director, Center for Community Development and Leadership, Chicago, July 26, 1989, personal interview.

Mary Nelson, executive director, Bethel New Life, Chicago, August 2, 1989, telephone interview.

Jean Pogge, president, Woodstock Institute, Chicago, July 25, 1989, telephone interview.

Michael Scott, former vice-president for external affairs of Pyramid West Corporation, Chicago, July 26, 1989, personal interview.

Garland Yates, eastern regional director, Center for Community Change, Washington, D.C., August 8, 1989, telephone interview.

REFERENCE LIST

Betancur, John, Wim Wiewel, and Patricia Wright. 1985. *Organizing and Community Economic Development.* Chicago: University of Illinois at Chicago Center for Urban Economic Development.

Brown-Chappell, Betty, Major Coleman, Matthew Lawrence, and Alec Peters. 1988. *Community Organizations in Chicago: A Report on Community*

Based Economic Development and Job Generation. Chicago: University of Chicago Center for Urban Research and Policy Studies.

Department of Economic Development (DED) of the City of Chicago. 1986. *Business Loss or Balanced Growth: Industrial Displacement in Chicago.* Chicago: Department of Economic Development.

Keating, W. Dennis, and Norman Krumholz. 1988. *Community Development Corporations in the United States: Their Role in Housing and Urban Development.* 1988. Cleveland: Cleveland State University.

Kelly, Rita Mae. 1976. *Community Participation in Directing Community Economic Development.* Cambridge, Mass.: Center for Community Economic Development.

National Congress for Community Economic Development. 1989. *Against All Odds: The Achievements of Community-Based Development Organizations.* Washington, D.C.: National Congress for Community Economic Development.

Peirce, Neal, and Carol Steinbach. 1987. *Corrective Capitalism: The Rise of America's Community Development Corporations.* New York: Ford Foundation.

Perry, Stewart. 1987. *Communities on the Way: Rebuilding Local Economies in the United States and Canada.* Albany: State University of New York Press.

Shiffman, Ronald, and Susan Motley. 1989. *Comprehensive and Integrative Planning for Community Development.* New York: Pratt Institute.

University of Illinois Center for Urban Economic Development. *Community Economic Development Strategies: A Manual for Local Action.* Chicago: University of Illinois at Chicago.

Vidal, Avis C. 1989. *Community Economic Development Assessment: A National Study of Urban Community Development Corporations.* New York: New School of Social Research Community Development Research Center.

Wright, Patricia. 1987. *Urban Development Action Grants, 1979–1986 and the First Round of Illinois Development Action Grants and their Impact on the City of Chicago.* Chicago: Center for Urban Economic Development, University of Illinois at Chicago.

Wright, Patricia, John Betancur, and Wim Wiewel. 1985. "Organizing and Community Economic Development: Planning with People." Paper presented at the Annual Meeting of the Association of Collegiate Schools of Planning.

The authors were all staff members at the University of Illinois at Chicago Center for Urban Economic Development when the chapter was written. This paper is an outgrowth of UICUED's earlier work on the topic: *Community Economic Development Strategies: A Manual for Local Action* (UICUED, 1987). **Deborah Bennett** is an economic development researcher at UICUED and past Public Issues Organizer for the Community Workshop on Economic Development (described earlier). She has background in work related to finance

J. J. Betancur, D. E. Bennett, P. A. Wright

for community-based and minority-owned business. **John Betancur** is Research Assistant Professor at UICUED, has extensive publications on urban economic development, and served as Executive Director of the Institute for Latino Progress in 1981–82. **Patricia Wright,** currently Associate Director of the Voorhees Neighborhood Center at UIC, served as economic development planner for UICUED.

Index